Dear Debra~
Thank i ... ch
for Welcoming y... iston
Barnes + Noble

Love Wants to Find You

Learning to Love Yourself,
Heal Your Heart, and Find the
True Love You Deserve

Warmest Regards~

A True Story of Hope for Divorced,
Broken-Up, or Lonely Singles

Francine Putkowski

dragon
*tree*books

This book is intended to provide advice based on the author's insights on relationships. It reflects the author's present recollections of her own experiences over time and her observations of other relationships. Some names, characteristics and events have been changed, some events have been compressed, and some dialogue has been recreated to provide instructional examples of certain points made by the author in the book.

LOVE WANTS TO FIND YOU may be purchased for educational, business, or sales promotional use. For information, please email: francine@lovewantsto-findyou.com.

ISBN (softcover): 978-1-7337577-3-7
ISBN (ebook): 978-1-7337577-4-4
FIRST EDITION

Cover Design by: Kevin Craig
Interior Design by: Pamela Morrell

Published by

1620 SW 5th Avenue
Pompano Beach, Florida 33060
(954)788-4775
editors@editingforauthors.com
dragontreebooks.com

Dedication

Life always waits for some crisis to occur, before revealing itself at its most brilliant.

—Paulo Coelho

I dedicate this book to all those suffering with a broken heart. When we love, I believe that we become better people, especially if that love encompasses self-love and embraces the person that you are today. It is the possibility of this hope that makes life interesting. May you find solace in the light. May you be restored. May you begin to discover yourself, heal, and be ready for the right love to find you.

Acknowledgments

Writing this book was more difficult than I ever thought it would be, but it was also more rewarding than I ever could have imagined. I wanted to acknowledge the people that I am thankful for in my life. I would like to thank my loving and supportive parents, for always guiding me with a moral compass, helping me, and never judging my mistakes. I thank my wonderful in-laws, who raised the man of my dreams. Both my parents and my in-laws have been married, respectively, for over fifty years each. So, I thank them for their wonderful example of enduring love. I owe credit to my daughter and my son for allowing me to always be my authentic self. My children have always loved me unconditionally, and they provided me with the courage to candidly share my life stories. I love you both, infinitely. I also hold genuine gratitude and love for my wonderful stepdaughters. I hope that your father and I provide a warm example of true love. I have always said that the "wind beneath my wings" was reserved for my sister. My sister is my best friend, and she has been a source of strength throughout my entire life. I would also like to thank my husband's brother (my brother-in-law), who is a well-respected and established best-selling author. He provided me with a sounding board, insight, and great advice, as I wrote my book. I want to thank my closest friends, who showed me that with friendship any obstacle in life can be overcome. I would like to thank my editor, Erica Orloff. She is amazing at what she does, and she helped make my book a reality. I thank Jon VanZile, publisher of Dragon Tree Books, for making my book available to the public. And, a special thanks to Kirk T. Schroder, Esquire, of Schroder Brooks Law Firm, PLC, who provided me with his legal experience and invaluable insight. And this book is in part only possible because of the experiences that I shared with my exes. I learned many valuable lessons about love with each of them. Finally, I could not have written this book without the support of my amazing husband, who is the one true love of my life. Thank you for teaching me that I am indeed worth loving.

Contents

Introduction

Through Failure, Comes Resolve: Don't Deny Your Pain—Learn From It!

It's all about love. We are either in love, dreaming about love, recovery from it, wishing for it, or reflecting on it.

—Michael Bublé

I'm not sure if anyone's life turns out exactly the way they imagined. But if you have ever experienced a painful breakup or divorce, and suddenly lost your direction, there is still hope for a "happily-ever-after." Sometimes you must let go of what you thought your life would be like and learn to first find joy in the life you are actually living.

I am living proof that love can cut both ways. Love is a mysterious word that seems to have many meanings. Love can present itself like a blade's edge. Love can slice through the center of your life, cutting everything in two. You will be left with "the before," and "the after," while the rest of the world seems to fall away on either side. Love is grieved by injustice. It craves fairness, not only for itself, but mostly for others. And with my new understanding of this justice, I was finally able to transform my pain into privilege.

Love wants to find you.

Love wants to be a part of your life and bring you happiness again.

If you feel that you have plunged down to the proverbial "rock-bottom," I want to offer you optimism and hope. Rocks make a strong and sturdy foundation. From here, you can build a beautiful new footing for your life. Ores are rocks that include minerals, with treasured and vital elements, like silver and gold. Many rocks are formed under great heat and pressure, yet they remain. Pressure is also a key part of what turns coal into diamonds. So, look at your "rock-bottom" as a new opportunity. When I hit this lowest point, I was exposed to my greatest transformation. Rocks are constantly changing, in what is called a "rock cycle." There can be beauty found in change, and in honoring the cycles and seasons of your own life. Just because you hit "rock-bottom", does not mean you have to stay there. You *can* turn your life around.

Now it is up to you to alter the course of your lifecycle. There are ebbs and flows in everyone's lives, if you live long enough. Try not to fight against the current. There is something beautiful in the way the ocean refuses to stop reaching out to the shoreline, no matter how many times it relentlessly sends it away. Let any recent trauma in your life drift away, after it has taught you what you needed to know. This is the time to refocus, regroup, and pursue your life with a more reverent heart and refined mind.

I believe that there are defining and undeniable moments in everyone's lives that will suddenly and forever alter you. If you have bought this book during a separation or divorce, you probably never thought that you would find yourself in this position. But here you are. *You are now single.* No one wants the pain of heartache. But you can view this as an opportunity to change and to become a better version of yourself. I spent most of my adult life either chasing love or in romantic relationships that were in between both the forgotten and the foreseen. I longed to be accepted and loved.

I have found that people who are not satisfied with their current path can learn to blaze a new and better trail. Right now, maybe you cannot even see the forest, amid all those trees, because these are the obstacles that have been standing in your way for far too long.

I also believe that the two most important choices that you will make in your lifetime are who to love and how to love them. Life throws difficult choices our way, every day. However, the decision to choose a spouse or partner is one of the most important decisions of your life. This is the decision that will define many other aspects of your life, especially if you have children. How do we know "when and who" we are supposed to settle down with? What I have found is that it is a delicate combination of personalities, compromise, self-love, self-confidence, expectations, and guidance by your own moral compass. These are the foundations of who you are. These are the qualities that must mesh with a partner or spouse. Love is a very complicated and beautiful thing. It can be good, great, exciting, and powerful. But it can also be dangerous, sad, and elusive. However, the more that I began to understand love's complex meanings, the better I could live in its light.

Besides pursuing the pleasure of love, I believe that we sometimes try to avoid the pain of its ending. Are you simply going through the motions of your life to sidestep this? And worse, no matter what you do or what your circumstances are, do you feel that your breakup or divorce labels you as a complete *failure*?

You are not alone. Studies say between 40 to 50 percent of marriages end in divorce. Yes, other people are muddling through your same confusion and pain. You may feel stuck in your life right now. But this is only temporary. You are not doomed to a lifelong sentence of unhappiness just because you have had a failed breakup or marriage. All you must do is accept this simple fact: *Your relationship or marriage failed.* That's it. That does not mean that *you* are a failure.

Most couples get married believing that their marriage will last forever and be full of everything good and blessed. But unfortunately, there is no such thing as a "divorce-proof" marriage. Most people have confidence that their relationship will come in a neat little beautifully-wrapped box that is full of love, happiness, intimacy, companionship, and forgiveness. But the truth is that in some boxes, you may feel suffocated, trapped, and lost. The four walls may seem to be continually caving in on you. You must be very careful to choose your partner wisely (whether it is your first or your last) and to always remember that both people must be ready and willing to fill that "box" with love. Otherwise, it will be empty and void of everything required in a good and lasting relationship.

A good relationship is one of the foundations on which every good and happy life is built. While some people are very happily single, most people are seeking a lifelong match. Without a core, healthy relationship between partners, everything else will eventually unravel into chaos and unhappiness for all involved. How do I know this? My current husband, Wade, and I have both lived through it. Twice.

This book was not written to pass judgment on anyone—not my ex-spouses or ex-boyfriends, not Wade's exes. It is easy to judge someone, but understanding requires compassion, patience, and a willingness to believe that good hearts sometimes make bad decisions. I hope that you will learn from my past mistakes, struggles, and pain so that you do not have to face the same situations that I found myself in.

Before you read on, I have a disclaimer to make: I am in no way telling you to jump into a divorce. In fact, divorce is one of the most difficult and stressful periods of anyone's life. This should be a last resort. Broken-down marriages can still be revived, with great compromise and hard work. I am writing this book for those of you in "unfixable" relationships that have overstayed their proverbial welcome and for those facing a dreaded breakup—as well as those who are still seeking their soul mate. I say to you, don't give up on finding the "One." This book is for the hopeless romantic who is tired of being sad and lonely. It is for those people who are currently suffering through the battlegrounds of divorce. It is for those that feel that there is no hope for happiness and love again. Trust me. Wade and I are living proof that there is hope—even if that love is only for yourself. Wade and I both had to learn to love ourselves before we at last found our "One" in each other.

I am also pouring out my heart to those who have not yet begun a long-term commitment or marriage. Perhaps this book can be a litmus test in determining if your future relationship will stand the test of time.

Within the book, there are real life stories of mine and other people that I have interviewed, encountered, or befriended. I will describe some of my own tell-tale red flags. And, I will share my own private experiences, so that hopefully you can identify with me. Some of the facts have been altered, but there are common instances or issues that come from the facts. I will discuss some of the coping mechanisms that healed my mind, body, and spirit after each of my breakups. I will also briefly discuss some of Wade's personal divorce and breakup stories. I will explain how he felt about and coped with his breakups and two divorces. This will shed some light on relationship breakups from the male perspective.

This book will teach you about self-forgiveness, self-love, and recovery. By the end of the book, I want you to realize that there is a happy life awaiting you, even if you have made the difficult decision to move on. Yes, you will be a humbled member of the "failed-marriage club." So what? It was not until our third marriage that Wade and I "got it right." And we are at peace with our decisions and finally truly happy. We all deserve happiness.

Perhaps the ending of your story will look different from ours, and that is okay too. Maybe your happy ending does not even include another romantic relationship. Perhaps it will be you, on your own, picking up the pieces and starting over. Maybe your contentment will stem from simply moving on, at peace with yourself. No one else sees the world the way you do. And so, the next chapter of your life story is uniquely your own. I want you to love and heal yourself, from your current anguish, so that you are better able to make sound decisions for yourself and your family.

I will provide you with some tools, courage, and hope, as you either take the next step on your life journey, or while you begin to put the pieces of your life back together. I will candidly reveal to you some of my most painful stories, as a measuring stick for your own relationships.

Whether this is it your first marriage, second marriage, or your third marriage, like me, or if you are contemplating committing for the first time, I want to provide hope and insight and enlighten you with my experiences. And, I would like you to understand what real love looks like, sounds like, and feels like. Because when you get this most important decision just right, it will be noticeably different from any other previous relationship that you misinterpreted for love. You will hang onto this love for dear life. My hope is that you will believe in yourself again and the possibilities of giving love another chance.

Most of all, I seek to be honest and share my experiences. Why? Because I think love is out there for each of us. We are all worthy of love, and I believe your love is out there—*waiting to find you.*

We may encounter defeats, but we must not be defeated.

—*Maya Angelou*

CHAPTER 1

Awakened after a Flatlined Life

Each morning we are born again. What we do today is what matters most.

—Buddha

Sometimes we can become so numb to how we are treated and how unhappy we are, that we don't fully realize that a breath of fresh air and hope are within our reach.

There is a common story about frogs and boiling water. If you put a frog in a pot of cold water, and gradually raise the temperature of the water to boiling, the frog will not jump out and will boil to death. But if a frog is dropped in a pot of boiling water, instead, it will leap out.

A wrong relationship is similar to the frog metaphor. Sometimes, we get so used to the misery and unhappiness of our relationship that we don't leap out—even to save ourselves.

My Story

By way of background, I would consider my husband and me to be well-rounded, hard-working, and well-educated. My current husband,

Wade, was commissioned from the United States Military Academy in 1987, and I was accepted into the United States Naval Academy in that same year, where I stayed for a little over two years. I left the USNA on my own accord, and I completed my last year of studies, at Pennsylvania State University, where I graduated early at the top of my class. But even with this quality education, we both failed at choosing the right life-partner, two times each, before meeting one another. Even with the academic backgrounds that we both enjoyed, and the fact that both sets of our parents have been happily married for more than fifty years each, we still felt like individual failures when it came to relationships.

We are *not* taught about how to choose the "right" spouse or partner in school. In fact, there are little-to-no discussions about relationships in school at all, and there were no courses regarding "relationships" in either of our high schools or colleges. Certainly, our faith and our churches taught us how to act, but this still left us with a blank slate, as far as providing us with a framework to build relationship expectations on.

My church sent my first husband, Anthony (not his real name), and me, on a weekend retreat, prior to our marriage. It was called Pre-Cana. Pre-Cana is something that was required before we were married in my church. I was grateful for this spiritual weekend, full of self-examination and practical coursework. However, I found that jamming an entire lifetime of essential relationship topics like spirituality, conflict-resolution skills, careers, finances, intimacy, cohabitation, children, and commitment, into one weekend, was insurmountable for me. So, even though my church was investing in my future happiness, I was still ill-equipped to know the warning signs of a wrong life-partner decision.

My Life Lesson

For many of us, marriage seems effortless for our parents' generation. Think of how many senior citizens and elderly people you know who are in long-term relationships of many years. Or conversely, perhaps we have such troubled role models that we are frightened to trust ourselves with marriage at all.

Wade and I both had wonderful examples of marriage from our parents. Our parents had healthy marriages, with all the ups and downs that life throws at us. But, when things got tough, they stuck together, and they had healthy conflict-resolution techniques. But even having parents with long-term, healthy relationships is not a vaccine against divorce.

So, where do we learn about relationships? I hope this book can be a source of education for you. Through my and Wade's trials and errors, we hope that by the end of this book, you are better informed and more equipped to make the most important single decision of your life: *Who will I spend the rest of my life with?*

Here are a few questions for you to pause and consider:

- Would you say that you are currently in a good and healthy relationship?
- Do you even know what a good relationship looks and feels like?
- Do you know how to find happiness again after a breakup or divorce?
- Do you believe that you deserve happiness in a relationship?
- Do you feel that you are a failure and that no one will want you because you are divorced?

If any of these questions gave you "pause," then this book is meant to help guide and restore you. With four divorces between us, Wade and I certainly know how you feel.

The good news is that you don't have to simply go through the motions of your life. You do not have to put on a fake smile to avoid explaining why you are unhappy. You no longer need to feel alone in your thoughts, thinking that nobody understands you and your silent sadness. I understand, and so does my current husband. I know that some days you may also feel alienated. Some days, when I did not want to explain the complex and gory details of my recent divorces to people, I felt very isolated. This is a very private issue, and it is one that you should only share with the select people that you trust. But you should not hide from the world or feel completely alone.

You should never feel unworthy, simply because a relationship has ended. You are not a failure because you chose a wrong partner, or because you are no longer in love with them. Mistakes do not define who we are, unless we do not pick ourselves back up and learn from them. Don't let your relationship mistakes determine your future. Instead, learn from your flat-lined life—wake up, instead, to joy.

It is my sincere hope that everyone who reads my book will relate to, and learn from, our lives. Some of our choices led to very painful outcomes, especially because children were involved. For too long, Wade and I felt "stuck" in our life situations, whether because of our children, financial reasons, other obstacles, or sheer guilt. For most of our lives, we felt that maybe we were not supposed to be happy. We both wondered if we would ever have the emotional strength to cut the ties with our respective spouses. At some point, we made the decision to "turn it all off." The system was already too stressed. Our relationships were like a chaffed rope that had worn too thin over time. In at least two of our marriages, we shut it down before it completely imploded.

Wade and I came to understand that our unhappy marriages were setting an even worse example for our children. We wanted to show them what a good relationship could look like. Children should see their parents holding hands, laughing together—and having healthy disagreements. They should see a healthy love that they can hopefully emulate—not two people in a stalemate, or an emotionally dead marriage. If you are in a marriage in which there is emotional or physical abuse, first, I would urge you to reach out for help, but if you have children, consider what the abuse shows them about marriage. If you have left an unhealthy marriage, talk about your perceived failures with your kids.

Wade and I have talked to our kids about our mistakes. And we have talked with them about our happiness. Our children would often say to us, "You have four divorces between the two of you, so you are probably not the best people to be giving marital advice to us." But we are absolutely the ones who should be talking about relationships. We failed multiple times. And consequently, we learned. We do not want our children to suffer the same relationship outcomes that we both endured.

Did you know that we are teetering on the edge of some significant life-expectancy increases? Some forecast that to live to be one hundred years old will become the "new normal." If you are middle aged, you are now potentially only halfway through your life. So, even if you are fifty years old, like me, shouldn't you reevaluate how you spend the second half of your life? You should spend as many years as you can, at peace with yourself, your life, and your love.

Later in the book, I will describe our four combined failed marriages. All four dissolutions were a little different, although many of the underlying feelings and fears that we experienced were the same. And, many of the reasons for our respective breakups were similar. I believe that sadness, loneliness, regret, and fear are all basically universal emotions. And we know the feelings that those emotions elicit in us. If you close your eyes, you can probably pinpoint the lowest times of your life. You can almost smell, hear, and feel—that time and place. Wade and I chose the wrong partners in our first marriages, and then attempted to "counter" those first unsuccessful decisions in our second marriage attempts. But instead, we rebounded into altogether different, but wrong, marriages for the second time. Until at last we found each other.

When you awaken love and laughter into your daily life, your spirit will become a healing ointment that will transform every aspect of your human experience into peace and joy.

I had a friend who worked as a hospice nurse. She said that in people's final moments of life, they did not discuss their awards, successes, money, fame, or other worldly accomplishments. They only spoke about their loved ones and their regrets. I think this is very telling. So, our hope is that you each discover a true love to cherish all the days of your life.

Never love anybody who treats you like you're ordinary.

—*Oscar Wilde*

You are not alone. When you go through deep waters, I will be with you. When you go through rivers of difficulty, you will not drown.

—*Isaiah 43:2*

CHAPTER 2

The Death of a Dream: Marriage Doesn't Change People—It Unmasks Them

It takes courage to grow up and be who you really are.

—E.E. Cummings

Oftentimes, we think if we just love a person enough, they will change, and we'll at last be happy. If only the depth of our love, or the efforts we make, would be enough to change another person. But part of my path has been learning that simply is not so. Change comes from within, and the other person has to want, truly want, to change—and be willing to do the hard work change requires.

In a healthy relationship, you do not want to change your partner. You love them, and they love you for who you really are. In fact, in a healthy relationship, the partners really know and see each other for who they are precisely because the trust is there to reveal their true— and healthy—selves.

My Story

Rock bottom was my decision to change.

My current husband, Wade, and I were both in our second failed marriages, with innocent children involved, and nothing seemed to be working. Heartache hit us like a recurring hurricane. We sometimes wondered why God didn't love us, as he loved others. But he did love us all along. I believe that God created us for one reason—to love and be loved in return. God helped us understand that we were more than the sum of our past mistakes.

After we were healed, Wade and I found real and true love, in one another. For me, in my faith, God is amazing. He was able to know exactly what was in each of our hearts, and he knew exactly what we each needed as individuals and as a couple. The relationship that we now share cannot be properly described with mere words. It is incomprehensible.

But this is not where we started. We started with two failed marriages each and a sense of complete failure. This failure was laid at our feet every time we looked at our children. This failure was overpowering. It had a death grip on both of us. Before you can ever move on to a new relationship, you have to grieve the failure or loss. So, let it all out. Expressing emotion, when you have gone through extreme pain, is not weakness. It is human.

During the last few years of my second marriage, I had scars on my soul that I was afraid to reveal to anyone. Therefore, not very many people knew that I was unhappy. I did not want to experience those uncomfortable break-up conversations with anyone *again*, even though those are the very conversations I needed to have. So, I would force a fake smile to hide my injured soul. I had trapped myself in this world that had little to do with my own reality. And I had meticulously curated this false storyline for years. Also, my second husband was a nice person, so I did not want to cause him any pain either. So, I lived for years suppressing what my heart was telling me. I was afraid. I was lost, and I was broken. I held onto my shame and embarrassment like a lifeline. I had the picture-perfect life on the outside, yet on the inside, it was a different story.

My "ah-ha" moment came when I was sitting alone in my bedroom crying. I had become far too talented at silent weeping. I am talking about the kind of crying where you can taste the sting of the salt from your own tears. I remember feeling like there was a thousand-pound weight pushing down on my chest, threatening to suffocate me. Physically speaking, it felt as though there was this gaping hole in my chest, and there was this invisible hand that relentlessly kept wringing my heart and ripping my lungs to shreds. It was awful. Emotionally speaking, it wasn't any better. It was an unrelenting and constant scene of darkness, grim introspection, self-questioning, and reflection—all of which tipped me into depression and many other things, from a darker version of me that I never thought existed. I used to wonder how I could be in so much emotional and physical pain and continue to breathe.

I thought I was home alone. But my then fourteen-year-old daughter, Gabriella, knocked and entered my room. She immediately grabbed my hand to console me. My daughter is an extremely spiritual young lady. She always has been, from the time she could formulate a sentence. My young daughter very softly told me that God wanted me to be happy. I responded that I thought God did not believe in divorce. She said, "God is a loving and kind God, and your happiness is of the utmost importance to him." She went on to tell me that God would forgive me if I left my then-second-husband. She explained that God wanted me to be happy, and by extension, he wanted my two children to be happy too. I also have a son, Savino, who was ten years old at the time.

I took my daughter's words to heart. And that was the moment that I vowed to change my life. I knew that I was not powerless over my destiny. That was the moment that I set myself free. I was finally brave enough to seek the life that I wanted, and I was brave enough to pursue it.

Before the decision to permanently part ways from our spouses, and before we started dating each other, my current husband and

I both put in tough times, attempting to reconcile our respective marriages. We attempted to get ourselves back on a road of redemption with our spouses, if for no other reason than for the sake of our children. We both spent many nights alone, contemplating our future, and worrying about our children's well-being. To say that we were lonely is an understatement. And we are quite certain that our spouses felt the same.

My Life Lesson

Marriage is something most of us hold sacred. As an institution held in such high regard, I don't feel anyone should take divorce lightly— and certainly not without doing all you can to save your marriage. That said, sometimes we hold onto a very bad situation for far longer than we should. The innocence and authenticity of my daughter's comforting words helped me see that.

Sometimes, we are holding on to our marriage, even if it is not the right decision for us. We are holding on because we are not yet willing to give into the "death of our dream"—the dream of a perfect marriage. Leaving a toxic marriage is sometimes the healthiest and best choice we can make. I had to find the courage to let go of what I could not change. But only *you* can decide when you have stayed too long.

Ending a relationship can be incredibly difficult, no matter how incompatible it is. Part of this is obviously emotional. But there are some biological reasons for this too. Some scientific studies have shown that being in love activates the same areas of the brain as being high on cocaine.

Brain scans of lovers and people experiencing cocaine addiction both display increased activity in the pleasure centers of the brain (most notably the dopamine centers) and decreased activity in the frontal lobe, which is the area responsible for cognition. This means that while falling in love can make us feel good, it can also profoundly affect our judgment on the actual state of our relationships.

All relationships, even the wrong ones, help mold us into who we are today. And we all have regrets in life. "If only I had done this," or "If only I didn't say that," plague our wandering thoughts, as we think back to the pivotal moments in our lives. But you will not leave any relationship empty-handed. You will have an arsenal of knowledge, to make better relationship decisions in the future. Every person who comes into our lives can teach us something. Rather than looking at your relationship as wasted time, try to find the lesson in it. What did this person teach you? How have you changed as a person, and how might you do things differently next time? In life, lessons may often be repeated—until they are learned. Look for the lesson from this relationship, and you may be less likely to carry the same lesson over into your next relationship. Some people say that the definition of insanity is doing the same thing over-and-over again—but expecting a different result. Think about it.

There is even a song entitled, "Thank U, Next", by Ariana Grande. This song aptly describes some of the lessons that she learned, from her own lost-love experiences. She talks about her own introspection, after each of her past relationships ended. The lyrics are simple, yet important. Ariana describes how thankful she is now for all the lessons that were taught to her, through and by, her exes.

Do not ever take divorce lightly. Conversely, if there is no saving the marriage, it is acceptable for you to make changes to better your life—and the lives of your children.

Some people believe, holding on and hanging in there, are signs of great strength. However, there are times when it takes much more strength to know when to let go and then do it.

—Ann Landers

3

I Needed but Questioned God: God Has Not Forsaken You

Part of my story is my faith. I realize that my readers will be from all faith traditions—or no faith traditions. For those reading this who have a faith in a God, or Higher Power, you have no doubt tried to rely on your faith, as you have walked or are walking, a lonely path or are trying to recover from the pain of a failed marriage or relationship. One of the most essential parts of many faiths is the comforting concept that God is always there for you.

What about those who don't believe in a God? I have many spiritual friends who don't espouse to a religion, or who are agnostic. But even they will say if you look for signs that the Universe wants things to go well for you, you will find those signs.

For me, I am grateful for my faith, because it got me through many challenges.

My Story

It is important to know that *before* Wade and I walked down the proverbial aisle with our exes, we each had gnawing doubts. For us, this was more than nervousness or "cold feet" on our wedding days. This was a rasping, sinking feeling. Every clue was there from the beginning, but because we desperately wanted things to work out, we ignored the signs. Speaking for myself, I wish I had married for love—but I didn't.

Although I am not a perfect Christian, I strongly believe in God. I must admit though, when pain and trauma had a grip over my heart, I began to question his love and empathy. Over the years, and many times during the most tumultuous episodes of my marriages, I sought out solace from God. I begged God to lead me. I needed direction, and no other earthly alternatives seemed plausible. And God always "spoke" back. I just had to be still and listen. Sometimes it is hard to accept the answer, "Be patient." God's delay is not his denial. Time doesn't mean that God is denying you; it means that God is preparing you for something better, and with more substantive meaning.

As we faced our second divorce each, my current husband, Wade, and I each thought divinity had given up on us. People often ask me what I did in my deepest hour of need. I leaned on my family and closest friends. I tried my best to keep the lines of communication open with my then-spouse, in the hopes that our love would be restored. I spent a lot of time with my children, my parents, my sister, my brother-in-law, and my nephews. And I prayed to God for direction. I prayed to God for peace and forgiveness. And I prayed for patience and a forgiving spirit for all involved.

Often, I found myself crying out, "Why is God doing this to me?" But it was just a cry of pain. There should have been an exclamation point after those words, not a question mark. I was not looking for a tutorial in theology; rather, I was looking for sympathy. I was looking for reassurance that I was still a good person, and this breakup was terribly unfair. I did not want anyone to minimize my pain. I wanted affirmation that my agony was indeed warranted. I was desperately trying to hold onto any self-worth and self-respect that I had left.

My Life Lesson

I was taught that one of the highest representations of the image of God is a husband and wife serving each other. Wade and I were both living separate lives from our spouses, for an extremely long time, before we made the decision to permanently part ways with our spouses. We won't lie to you. These breakups did not come easy, and I have never heard any of my divorced friends describe their separations or divorces as "simple or pleasurable." Even in the rare "amicable" divorce, each spouse will feel the pain and grief of loss. Who you marry is probably the most important decision of your life. But terminating a marriage is the most difficult decision that you will ever make. I can tell you that Wade and I are finally at peace with ourselves and our pasts. We are finally complete, in and with, one another.

Hope. It's a funny thing. Most people cannot live without it. And I believe that hope begins when you stand in the dark and look out into the light.

Yes. I believe that God wants you to be happy. And yes, God's plan for you in marriage is a lifelong union. And this is the best design. Marriage is the first institution created by God. When God first created man, he declared that he did not want Adam to be alone. My view is that God was saying that Adam was incomplete. So, God created Eve, for Adam, and he blessed their union.

Looking at it from a spiritual perspective, marriage provides a partner. Life can be very hard. We all face crises, from job loss to loss of loved ones, from illness to personal challenges. Who wouldn't want a hand in theirs, and someone to walk beside them? Who wouldn't want to know that there is one person who always has their back?

Marriage provides that person who is there for you. But in my more religious background—and Wade's background too—marriage goes beyond companionship and support. Marriage is sacred. Jesus revealed the importance and sacredness of a lifelong marriage through his teachings. So, we firmly believe that all steps should be taken to preserve this rightful union of marriage. We believe that divorce should be a last resort, after all measures are taken to avoid such an outcome, unless you are in a situation that is unsafe for you or your children. In other words, it should never be right or just to divorce nonchalantly. But conversely, we believe that God desires each one of us to be happy and whole as we live our lives. We believe that he has a spouse chosen for you. And we believe that you will be forgiven if you have made mistakes in your choices, so long as you are not setting out to intentionally hurt anyone, and you endeavor to make things work before ever deciding to separate.

In my view, the Bible does not clearly state if there are reasons that God receives as "acceptable" for divorce. However, in my silent talks with God, he answered me in many ways. My interpretation of his response was that once we had tried all remedies, without success, he would indeed still love us, even with our sins. He would love us even if we were to divorce. I can believe that, because the Bible clearly states God's love "surpasses all understanding." A love that is unconditional will, by definition, forgive and treasure us.

Some believe that God may even reveal in the Scriptures that divorce is acceptable in certain circumstances, such as if your spouse has committed adultery or if your spouse willfully and permanently deserts you. Although it is not clear, it is my belief that if your spouse has abandoned you, giving you no option or alternative, God will forgive you if you move forward with your life. Personally, I also believe that if a spouse is physically or emotionally abusive to either you, or your children, that God loves you enough to want you to take measures to be safe and happy. God does not want you to remain in the lowest place of your life, where you are too sad and miserable to enjoy his blessings.

I do not think that God wants any of us to be deeply hurt. And, initially, divorce will paralyze you emotionally, spiritually, physically, and even financially. It will initially shred your heart and soul into minuscule pieces. Most importantly, nobody in your life will be happy—unless and until you are happy with yourself. I also believe that there is no way to be happy with yourself if you are suffering in the wrong marriage. I purposely said "wrong" marriage versus "bad" marriage, because sometimes marriages fail, and no one is the "bad guy." It is true that you can have two good and decent people, as individuals, but together they are wrong. Sometimes two people are just not meant to cohabitate together. And yes, sometimes people "fall out of love." End of story.

While praying one night, these words came to me: "God helps those who stop hurting themselves." There it was, flashing in neon lights, in my mind's eye. I could not be happy if I did not first see an issue with the way that I was living and coping, in my unhappy marriage...and its aftermath. I needed to take personal responsibility for my life. I realized that God gave us all free will. I could use that freedom to rebuild, or I could stay chained in the castle dungeon that had crumbled around my vision of a fairy-tale marriage. I began by praying.

I strongly believe that God intervened on my behalf, while there was still time left for my emotional survival and the emotional well-being of my two precious children. I cannot help but believe that God hates divorce but still loves divorcees. God loves all his children. And God forgives all his children, so long as you have a truly repentant heart. It is my belief that God may not agree with all our reasons for divorce, but he still loves you. This was an important concept for me to remember, as I began to forgive myself and move forward into the light of my new life.

God has not abandoned you, just because you are going through a break-up or divorce. I fully believe that God loves you, and he will forgive you. I believe that God wants you to lead a full and happy life, full of healthy and reciprocating love.

Never will I leave you: Never will I forsake you.

—Hebrews 13:5

CHAPTER 4

Is He or She Right for Me?
No More Doubting Thomas

In one kiss, you'll know all I haven't said.

—Pablo Neruda

It is one of life's constant questions. *How do I know when I am in love?* Teens ask that question. Adults ask that question. Deeper still, as we get older, we will ask, *How do I know this person is the One?*

"You'll just know." That's often the answer, but I suppose that is not very satisfying for those grappling with these issues. Now, with the wisdom of our painful life experiences, Wade and I both know what love isn't.

Love isn't hiding who you really are. Love isn't being belittled. Love isn't crying all the time because nothing is quite right. Love isn't being unable to talk with complete openness and trust. Love isn't fear. Love isn't doubt.

Here's a little of my story, along with a list of questions to contemplate, before becoming serious with someone or contemplating marriage.

My Story

When Wade and I married each other, it was our third marriage each. But we had no doubts whatsoever. We had pure excitement and joy leading up to our vows. When we married one another, it was the first time that either of us felt no hesitations and no reservations.

People have asked us, "How did you know he or she was the one for you?" You will absolutely know, especially if you have been in any other long-term relationships that were not the right match, were emotionally abusive or toxic, or even indifferent. Our relationship is nothing like what we had experienced previously. It is completely and totally different. It is absolutely polarized from all other relationships. It is so different that it is hard to describe with mere words. But once we both took the reins of our own destiny, the answers to our prayers came suddenly, in the form of one another.

Approximately six months before I got married the first time, I distinctly recall when Anthony and I attended our Pre-Cana class, a requirement to get married in my church. We were asked to make a list of all the great and wonderful qualities that our respective fiancés possessed. Additionally, we were asked to candidly list any current, or potential problems or issues, that we had in our relationship. I recollect sitting in an empty room, at the lodge where the class took place, staring emotionlessly at the stark white walls. I felt detached from the world. I felt detached from myself. I remember thinking that it should not be *this* difficult to come up with some good qualities of the man that I would be spending the rest of my life with. Conversely, it should not have been that easy to come up with the litany of issues that we had, and that I could forecast to be problematic in the future.

In fairness, I am certain that Anthony had the same difficulties regarding me, my nature, and the gnawing truth that our personalities were not in sync and probably never would be.

When I got married the first two times, I was almost ready to call off the wedding, the day of the ceremony—both times. I chalked it up to nerves, but I should have listened to my gut. I also knew that my father had put down a very sizeable monetary deposit for my first wedding reception. I knew that he would have lost his money had I called off my wedding. Looking back now, my father would have paid ten times that amount to avoid the heartache and pain that I endured during my first marriage.

My Life Lesson

You can ignore reality, but you cannot ignore the consequences of ignoring reality. After two failed marriages, I finally learned that lesson. And you will too, if you want to successfully enter any long-term relationship or marriage.

Pay attention to your intuition. Pay attention to your heart. And, pay attention to your mind.

The questions I offer here are ones that I wished I would have asked myself before getting married. Had I been completely honest with myself, my answers would have prevented me from getting married to either of my first two husbands.

So, listen to your heart. But, before you walk down the aisle, really look yourself in the mirror and have a candid conversation. The questions below are there to help guide you. Think long and hard about your answers.

- Can I live with this other person for the rest of my life?
- Do I *want* to spend the rest of my life with this person?
- Do I have any reservations about my impending marriage?
- Do I feel any outside pressures to get married?
- Do I trust this person completely, with no reservations?
- Is this person financially responsible?
- Does this person work too much or conversely, not enough?
- Is my relationship serving my highest good?
- Is my relationship negatively impacting other areas of my life?

- Is my relationship detrimental to my self-esteem?
- Do I have the utmost respect for this person?
- Do we both feel the same about beginning a family?
- Would I want my children to have this person as their role model?
- Does this person exhibit any signs that they could be emotionally or physically abusive?
- Does this person exhibit any signs of addictive behaviors? (drugs, alcohol, gambling, strip clubs/sexual deviancy, partying, vaping, etc.)
- Do we have the same intelligence level?
- Does this person have the same moral, political, and spiritual views as my own?
- Does this other person support me in my dreams and goals?
- Can I envision my life without this person?
- Does this person make me laugh?
- Am I only getting married because I am afraid to be alone?
- Am I only marrying this person because I am getting older, and I want children?
- Does this person make me feel treasured and valuable or are they controlling?
- Does this person demonstrate love in healthy ways?
- How does my partner treat his or her own family members?
- Do we have a healthy sexual relationship?
- Do my partner and I handle conflicts in a healthy way?

What if you are just reading this and realize that you made the wrong decision? Then what? Should you soldier on in an unhealthy relationship? Will the children be better off if you somehow manage to go through the motions of your marriage? Will people judge you? Worse, will you spend the rest of your life sad and alone? I don't think so, and I will explain this throughout my book.

Remember this important fact: Most people do not change their behavior. So, if you think marriage will "change" someone, or that you will suddenly get along better or fall in love just because you are married, you need to think again.

Sometimes when I talk to my children about my failures, I say that just because a marriage has failed, does not mean that the two people involved are failures. You only fail if you have not learned from your mistakes. Sometimes what one person is looking for cannot be given by the other person, emotionally. And just because you are an adult does not mean that you don't make mistakes. We all make mistakes and errors in judgment. For to be human is to err.

Love is many things. But it is never deceitful, cruel, or toxic. Nothing toxic comes from genuine love. Always remember that. Prior to our current marriage, Wade and I had always lived in a terribly false world, which is also why we were in perpetual pain. Two people must love one another, exactly as they are. There cannot be any false pretenses. When you love unconditionally, there is a transformation in your relationship. You each become the truest and greatest versions of yourselves. And when that occurs, you will find true happiness.

We are often told not to listen to what people say, but rather watch what they do. Someone's actions will tell you all you need to know about them. So, watch them closely, in all different situations, good and bad. Remember that at your absolute best, you will still not be good enough for some people. And at your worst, you will still be worth it to the right person.

The great Maya Angelou summed this up with a quote: "I've learned that people will forget what you said, people will forget what you did, but people will never forget how you made them feel." I think it is the perfect quote for what a true and healthy love reflects.

Realizing that real love is about being loved as you are, and accepting this deep down in our hearts, was a fundamental turning point for both Wade and me. I have found that most successful people have experienced this "defining moment," where they had to make a specific unequivocal decision that they were going to change their lives.

It is that point where you draw that proverbial "line in the sand" that you will not cross. Some people are fortunate enough to make this "stand" regarding the meaning of real love and self-love when they are teenagers, and some do not take this stand until they are midway through their lives, like us. Unfortunately, some people never experience this at all. Don't be that person.

Sadly, the Universe does not always protect those with honest and good hearts. And some people are incapable of seeing your genuine soul. It is not your fault that your real essence goes unseen by some—even the person you have committed to or married. Some people may not possess the ability to respond as you would. Maybe they did not have loving parents raise them. Maybe they have an entirely different faith, education, or socio-economic background that makes relating to you very hard for them. Maybe they do not have the same moral standards you do. We are all different people, of course. Or maybe, sadly, they are just not decent human beings. For these reasons, your partner's actions may not make sense to you, so you may continue your attempts at transforming that person. You may feel indifference for them. But, whatever the cause, that person is undeniably not the right match for you. It is also important to remember that your value does not decrease based on someone's inability to see your worth.

And, I would like to briefly discuss an important side-note. If you are currently in an emotionless, loveless, or volatile marriage, then I would strongly urge you to hold off on bringing children into your family, unless you have both undergone therapy and reached a good resolution. This dynamic is a very common mistake. People think that if they bring children into their lives, the baby or child will cement a couple together. Children take a lot of work, time, sweat, and tears. Yes, they are certainly adorable, and they are a true blessing. But the birth of a baby can be both thrilling and overwhelming for a couple. As new parents, you may be surprised to find that most of your time and energy will be used to care for your newborn. Lack of sleep, along with emotional changes can put a strain on even the best relationship. And, if you are in a wrong marriage, the responsibility of children will only add more stress to the already-strained situation. They will inadvertently be the match to the powder keg. This is not their fault, and they should not suffer because of it.

However, if you have a great marriage, children will make things even more restorative and special. The joy multiplies when a solid partnership is the base of your love story.

On the other hand, if you have the kind of marriage where one of you (or both) carries around a proverbial "measuring stick," (something that I used to do) to compare who is doing what chores in your relationship, then you need to really examine the idea of bringing children into that dynamic. If you argue over who is going to do the dishes, who lets the cat or dog out, who goes to the grocery store, or who cooks or cleans up, then you should reconsider bringing children into your family. Because once your little bundle of joy is born, they will require full attention and work most of the time, unless they are asleep. I will delve into this phenomenon a little later in the book.

In conclusion, sometimes we can't "see" how much we are pounding a square peg (representing our mismatched relationship) into the proverbial round hole, of a heathy marriage, until we leave that harmful person. But I can promise you, when you have done your healing work and the timing is right for a healthy relationship, the difference will be profound. Marriage is work—and Wade and I work very hard to keep ours healthy. We face the same trials and tribulations as all couples. We need to work hard for our family, and we both have children from our previous marriages—and the teen years can be tricky. But there is a true *ease* to how we work together. We are not also fighting our relationship, as we traverse the ups and downs of life.

When we said our vows, we had no doubts.

We were home.

Have enough courage to trust love one more time and always one more time.

—Maya Angelou

Lost Innocence: Stay Away from People Who Make You Feel That You Are Hard to Love

It is difficult to convey to my children what life was like when I was younger, in terms of technology. No cellphones, no Internet. Can you imagine? But then again, there was an innocence in days gone by. That probably had both good and bad implications in my story, as you'll see in this chapter.

Even today, with dating apps and technological advancements, there are simply some of us who are trusting, innocent, kind-hearted, and naïve—and those who are much savvier, or who are calculating, which may cross over into manipulation . . . and much worse.

My Story

I would like to be able to tell you that I had no idea what I had gotten myself into when I married my first ex-husband, Anthony. But, deep down inside of me, I did. I also did not yet understand that, for the most part, people do not change. People reveal who they really are with the passage of time. If you think *you* will change your partner, think again. The only person that you can change is yourself.

Even though I knew my relationship was not happy or healthy, I would convince myself that this is what all relationships looked like. I knew that I did not feel like myself around Anthony. Not anymore. Everything that I had previously liked about myself, and that I was proud about myself, vanished into thin air. I was a watered-down version of my former self. But this happened so gradually that it was hard for me to measure how bad things had gotten. I also felt like it was too late to start over.

I remember often being told by my first husband, Anthony, that I was overreacting, being dramatic, blowing things out of proportion, lazy, ugly, overweight, etc., and I was constantly trying to prove my worth to him. If you must do this in your supposed closest relationship, then you need to rethink your situation. Most of my ideas (on anything) were shot down immediately. Now that I think back, the conversation rarely even involved me or my extended family. I felt invisible. At some point, I completely faded into the background, and I ended the relationship that I had with myself. Essentially, I gave up on me.

I was in love with the concept of love and marriage, as if relationships were all just how I imagined them to be. Unfortunately, life doesn't work on desires and wishes. So, reality came crashing in all around me, like a tidal wave striking land. I was underwater quickly. And I was in too deep.

I was also getting older. Part of the reason I got married was I felt pressure to do so. Some of this pressure came from society in general. Whereas today, it is not uncommon to see young people living together or having many partners over time. When I first got married, it was still an era when marriage seemed to be the ultimate goal—especially for young women. I felt an unspoken pressure to settle down and have children. And subconsciously, I was getting tired of always being the bridesmaid but never the bride. The lesson that I learned from this decision is that it is never too late to change your mind, and you are never too old to start a new relationship. Moreover, you cannot live your life for other people. You have got to do what is right for you, even if it hurts or disappoints some of the people that you love.

Midway through my first marriage, I began to cut myself off from my family and friends, in a pitiful attempt to cover up my deteriorating marriage. It also felt like Anthony was purposefully isolating me. It was a "one-two punch."

I also remember the enormous elephant in the room. Guilt. I felt so guilty every time I thought about leaving, because I had a daughter with this man, and I was pregnant with a son. They were the innocent and silent victims. This pain of thinking of them growing up in a divided home seared my heart. Like most women who are mothers, my children are my breath and my life, and so if they are unhappy, I cannot be happy. I assumed my children needed an intact parental marriage in order to be happy. But this was not so.

Which brings me back to the question of what I was deriving out of the mismatched relationship. First, I was holding on to my misinterpretation of what love looked like. As a little girl, I had always dreamed of getting married. I thought about the "princess gown" that I would don, with the white doves flying overhead after we had said, "I do." I dreamed of my "knight in shining armor" swooping in to rescue me from all of life's difficult circumstances. And, I dreamed that I would return this favor back to him.

In my first marriage, I knew that I was not living in "that" fairytale. It wasn't even close. Even though that was never my reality, I would "will" myself to believe that everything was "in the range of normal," for my marriage. I clung onto the few memorable and positive times that we shared, to overcome my growing disappointments, times of sadness, and pain. Because for me, the worst feeling in the world is knowing that you are trying your best, but it still isn't quite good enough.

Frankly, I was also staying in my marriage, because I was afraid to leave. The most pressing and imminent fear was that I would fall short on paying my monthly bills for me and my two children. I knew I could pay all our bills before, so this may have been an unrealized fear, but it was still an overwhelming fear of mine. I also knew that as the children got older, their expenses would also increase. I was fortunate; because of my education, and the support I always had from my family, I *did* have the option of supporting my kids financially, as a single mom. I am well-aware there are millions of women—and men—who struggle from paycheck to paycheck with *two* incomes, and separation or divorce is even more terrifying because of it.

I was also anxious that no one else would ever want me because I felt that I was damaged goods. I would be entering the dating pool with one very big strike against me—or so I thought.

My Life Lesson

It is easy for outsiders to say, "Well, I would never put up with that sort of manipulation like she did." But research proves that anyone can end up mistreated. And blaming the victims in this way is a huge part of the problem. My impression of what I thought I was supposed to endure, skewed my view on marriage. And once I was in a weakened state, I became more susceptible to accepting behaviors I now see were not healthy for me. Like a hamster on a wheel, I felt like I was powerless to stop the revolving torment. Losing this control also reinforced my shame.

Realize that you are good enough, just as you are, for the right person. You are not hard to love, just because you want to be treated well and want a healthy and loving relationship.

Pain doesn't just show up in our lives for no reason. I am a firm believer that it is a sign that something in our lives needs to change. Always remember that a marriage involves two people; so, it won't matter at all what your intentions are if your partner doesn't feel the same way you do about staying together. I learned the hard way that marriage is a breakable contract, and promises are not legally binding…just because we wish that they were.

After a dissolution of a marriage or long-term relationship, sadness doesn't have to last a lifetime. Yes, you will probably be sad for a period. You may even experience physical pain as you begin to heal. You may cry randomly, as you remember the good times together. You may even find temporary comfort in reading old text messages, cards, and letters. Even if you were in a hurtful or "wrong" marriage, you will be sad over what divorce symbolizes. This sadness is normal. You will feel as if no one else understands *your* pain and that your world is closing in on you. But, the day *will* come when you no longer give credence to your past mistakes, because you will feel the relief of knowing that you were not in the right marriage, and you can now begin a new life that you deserve.

We accept the love we think we deserve.

—*Stephen Chbosky*

My First Marriage: Shattered Lives, Refracted Light—An Accumulation of Issues

My Story

I do not think that my first marriage ever really got off the ground. First, we were raised completely differently, by two different moral standards. It was quickly obvious that we did not have many mutually agreeable foundations, to share or grasp onto, in difficult times. On the exterior, we seemed a good match. We were both Italian. We were both driven in our career paths, and we "looked" like the typical all-American couple. But I soon discovered that was a façade that would implode, really before the marriage ever began.

I met my first husband, Anthony, through a blind date. A close friend of mine knew him, from the apartment complex that they both resided in. Our first encounter was in a quaint upscale town in Eastern Pennsylvania. This swanky town had many local eateries and pubs along the main street. I recall going to a dark nightclub at some point during the evening. We had all consumed too much alcohol, and judgment was impaired. This is not a good idea on a first date. I strongly recommend coffee and biscuits, as opposed to nightclubs and beer. But I was young and full of energy and "on the hunt" for a good man. I was getting older and was still single at twenty-six years old. Interestingly, the age for first getting married has risen by years since 1960. Getting married later is common—and is a good thing because it allows young adults to know themselves deeply before they commit to another person. At the time, though, I thought I had struck gold! This guy seemed "too good to be true." I later found out that—for me—he was.

Before we were married, my first inclination that Anthony and I may have been raised differently, occurred at a dinner with a few of our neighborhood acquaintances. A conversation was broached about domestic violence. Someone regurgitated the headline news, explaining that a famous popstar was making allegations of domestic abuse. Someone at the table made a disparaging comment, saying the popstar's husband "should have punched her, because she deserved it." I remember being stunned—and incensed. I was still strong enough at this point to muster up the courage to disagree with the speaker. At this point, I still wasn't afraid to speak my mind. I remember gathering up all my courage to dispute this statement. I said, "I do not think there should ever be provocation for a man to strike a woman, or a woman to strike a man." That went over like a lead balloon with the person that proudly proclaimed that this black-and-blue woman somehow "deserved" to be abused. The table grew awkwardly silent. I thought Anthony would have supported my position on this, but he remained silent. So, I never knew his feelings on this subject. I should have asked him.

Now married, another small telltale sign of possible problems down the road, should have been when I would start my laundry, or the laundry for our children. If Anthony had something that he needed washed—his clean clothing always took precedence in our household. So, he would stop the washing machine and literally remove my (or our children's) clothing from the washing machine, no matter what cycle it was on. He would then proceed to deposit our clothing onto the floor. Our washer and dryer were in the unfinished part of our basement, so our clothes were dumped on a damp and dusty cement floor. The clothes would stay on the floor, until I would discover them there. In the summer, if it had been a hot and muggy day, our items smelled like dungy mold. So, I would have to begin the wash cycle again, from the beginning.

I wish I would have said something about these issues then, instead of letting them fester, multiply, and create hostility between us. But, I didn't. These smaller incidents were desperately trying to foreshadow things to come. And, there were many other relatively negligible issues, like the ones I just described. But, it was the accumulation of *these* situations, without relief or resolution, that made these problems become worse with time. Unbeknown to me, it was causing increasing stress on our relationship. Because our problems were cumulative, and they were never properly addressed; things got exponentially worse with time—especially when I became pregnant. For example, there was now a whole new litany of insults being spewed at me daily, by my first ex-husband. He berated my weight and appearance, too many times to count.

My Life Lesson

I am sharing some of my seemingly innocuous stories now, to provide you with insight as to how my self-worth began to incrementally fade and wither away altogether. I learned years later that these continual words and actions had a tremendous negative impact, on both me and my self-esteem. So, do not discount the subtle harmful things that may be occurring daily. Over time, these seemingly small issues can accumulate, presenting a much larger problem further down the road. For me, because my situation was persistent, chronic, and long-term, I ended up with an overall feeling of inadequacy. Sadly, I cannot even pinpoint exactly when I lost my self-respect, dignity, self-esteem and voice. I don't want this to happen to you. So, detect any negative interactions or patterns early, and take steps to correct each behavior or situation, *as they occur.* If the first minor issues are resolved immediately, then it will help your overall issues from accruing and becoming compounded. Sometimes, it is when all the little problems are left unresolved—that the bigger issues begin to mount.

> *Never be bullied into silence. Never allow yourself to be made a victim. Accept no one's definition of your life but define yourself.*
>
> **—Harvey Fierstein**

My First Pregnancy

I was diagnosed with pre-eclampsia with my firstborn. I was so severely swollen that I could not fit a man's size-twelve flip-flops, over my puffy feet. I was gaining anywhere from one to five pounds a day, in water weight, in the last month of my pregnancy. (Yes. I was big!) I was also told by my mid-wives that I needed to quit working for my own safety. However, during this time, Anthony was trying to make a go of a new business, but it was still "in the red," and we needed my income. Any mention of me taking a leave from work, was met with resistance, and this made me feel lazy. My ex frequently insulted me, in particular about my weight or appearance—and if I reacted with tears, I was called "oversensitive."

So, I soldiered on, trying to earn his approval. I continued to work every single day. I was basically the sole breadwinner during this time. I was repeatedly warned to stop working, but I couldn't. I also carried the health insurance, and soon, I would have three mouths (and later four) to feed. I forged on, in extreme pain and in the dead of summer, to sustain my family. The company that I worked for was kind enough to set up a home office for me, where I continued to tap the keys, with my engorged fingers. I would see "eye-floaters" (spots in my vision) all day long because my blood pressure was so dangerously and life-threateningly high.

My Life Lesson

Do not ignore warning signs, especially if you are seeing them before you get married. It is never too late to cancel a wedding. Trust me. Your family and friends would rather see you happy, than have false nuptials and a transparent after-party. In due time, you will recover from any embarrassment and pain that you perceive will mar your life forever.

Do not excuse his or her behavior, just because you do not want to be lonely. There is no lonelier feeling than being in a relationship yet being all alone and misunderstood or mistreated. Your relationship may be exciting now, but you do not want a romantic interest to move towards marriage too quickly or naively. It usually takes some time to identify someone's weaknesses or the ways in which you may be incompatible. If any of your partner's traits leave you scratching your head, especially more than once...you may want to reexamine your situation. Don't force the relationship forward, just because you are getting older and/or you don't want to end up alone. Sure, we all want romance. Just make sure that you are getting what you deserve, and you are not settling for other reasons.

In addition, it's important to note that sometimes the other person is *terrific.* Just not for you. I have a friend, for example, who lived with a wonderful man. He spoke seven languages, was incredibly intelligent, and they had a passionate sex life. But he did not want children—and she did. She kept ignoring this fact and fell deeper and deeper in love, until it was truly time to either accept her life without children or make a painful break. She chose the latter and is now a mother of four. But the "warning" signs that this was not going to be her lifetime love were there. We need to be honest with ourselves.

A mistake repeated more than once...is a decision.

—Paulo Coelho

A Note on Faith

I was raised in a Christian home, as a child and young adult. These trying times were the first time that I ever lost faith. I had tumultuous times in my past, like everyone. But when I prayed reverently, my prayers always seemed to be answered.

One example of this was in the nineties. I was engaged to a man who lived in a state almost thirty-seven hundred miles from me. We were both extremely close to our families. He was raised by a single mother and was close with her and his siblings—who all lived within a few miles of each other. Obviously, if we were to be married, one of us would have to make the long cross-country move to be with the other one. He offered to move east. He never let on to me that he was troubled about this decision. I knew it was an agonizing choice, but I had no idea the extent to which he was conflicted. In the end, we broke our engagement because he just could not leave them, and I could not leave my family.

Painful though it was, I understood. However, he later tried to take his own life. Because we were split up, his family did not relay to me his condition, and I had to rely on secondhand information from his friend.

Ken's medical condition was grave. His best friend told me that they were keeping him alive on machines, to meet his organ-donor wishes.

My parents were with me during this entire week. On the fourth day, my parents took a difficult call, in which they were told my former fiancé was given only hours to live, before the painstaking task of removing him from life-support. Knowing that I would be devastated, my father offered to take me for a drive. I had no idea of the impending devastation, but I was still a hysterical mess. I had not been able to work, eat, sleep, or do much of anything. I remember looking at my father, and he looked so helpless, that I said yes. I felt terrible for what I was putting my parents through. While we were driving, I saw an outside marble cross, with stairs leading up to it. The cross was white, which was a stark contrast against the very blue sky. I asked my father to pull the car over. He let me out, and I prayed there for approximately two hours. I was pleading with God to save Ken's life.

When we got back to my apartment, the phone rang. My father quickly answered it, knowing that it would be the grim news of my former fiancé's demise. It *was* news. But it was a miracle! He had emerged from his deep coma, had sat up, asked for a drink of water, and made a full recovery during the time that I was praying. He had no long-term medical issues. The doctors and nurses were baffled. But I wasn't. I knew that God had intervened. I was in my early twenties, and this was one of the most traumatic events in my life to that point. But then, I knew for certain that God existed. And I knew that God answered prayers. Specifically, he had answered *my* prayer.

I was thirty-two years old the next time I prayed like that—the next time I needed God to answer my prayers. Only this time, I prayed for my first husband to return to our family. That prayer went unanswered. So, my faith was tested. I failed this test. I found myself living a life far from God. Yet, although I was keeping God at a distance, he continued to seek ways to close the ever-widening gap between us. After Anthony left, I tried to fix myself. My methods were not working. So, I fell back to what I was taught my entire life. I fell back to God. I began reading my Bible again, and I started praying and going to church, regularly. I was crying out to the Lord once again for help. I begged him to heal me, and fortify me with his strength, as I knew only he could. God was right there waiting for me. He forgave my sins of doubting him, and he fortified me with an overwhelming joy and peace. I didn't even know this feeling was possible. But, by studying his word and walking closely with him, God changed my life completely. He restored me as a person. The gospel began to fill the emptiness inside of me. He made me whole. He renewed my heart and my spirit. He has given me more blessings than I can count.

I now understand that no matter how much distance I thought was between us, God was right beside me all the time. And I now understand that in God's infinite wisdom, he answered some of my prayers and did *not* answer others. In both situations, he did so out of abiding love for me. He did not forsake me. I certainly did not understand this at the time, as God sometimes works in mysterious ways, but he always does so out of his enduring love for each of us. Unfortunately for some people, they may not know "why" some of their prayers have gone unanswered, until they reach Heaven.

> *Sometimes I thank God for unanswered prayers. Remember when you're talking to the man upstairs; that just because he doesn't answer doesn't mean he don't care. Some of God's greatest gifts are unanswered prayers.*
>
> *—Garth Brooks*

My Life Lesson

God loves the broken, and he loves the lost. He doesn't give up on anyone. When I was lonely and scared, I saw his arms wide open, upon the cross. It was his arms that I ran to in my darkest hours. With his grace, I learned to train my mind to be stronger than my emotions. He helped heal me, and if he can save me, he can save you too.

People have weaknesses, but God doesn't. People may betray you, but God won't. He is forever faithful, and he won't leave you alone. He is your Father, and he will hold you in his arms for the rest of your life. This is true, even when you feel that your own healing is not progressing as quickly as you hoped it would. It is true, even if you feel your dreams have come completely unraveled.

I have found that you can make plans, but the Lord's purpose will always prevail. It was not until years later that I understood that God answers prayers when it is the best timing for your life. God's timing is rarely the same as our timing, but his timing is always perfect, so trust him. I still do not understand this mystery of my faith, but I now know that keeping my first ex-husband from returning was a blessing in disguise, for both of us, and our two beautiful children.

He heals the brokenhearted and bandages their wounds. He counts the stars and assigns each a name. Our Lord is great, with limitless strength. We'll never comprehend what he knows and does. God puts the fallen on their feet again.

—Psalm 147:2-6

The Lord himself goes before you and will be with you; he will never leave you nor forsake you. Do not be afraid; do not be discouraged.

—Deuteronomy 31:8

My Very Short-Lived Counseling: My Denial

My Story

Approximately six months before Anthony left me, I was finally comprehending that we were grossly mismatched. I also knew that I could never really look at him, or our relationship, the same again. I remember feeling pity for him sometimes, because I felt like there was so much beauty in our children, and in the world, that he simply was unable to see. And, I know that he thought I was a weak and pitiful person—because I was, at that time.

Towards the bitter end, we attempted marriage counseling. We only had two visits. During the second session, the therapist asked to speak to each of us, individually. My ex-husband was asked to go first. When they were done, my ex-husband exited the therapist's room, and he was in tears. My heart sank. What had he revealed to the therapist? I already suspected infidelity, so I thought maybe that was what he had unloaded on this counselor.

When I went into the therapist's room, the counselor looked me square in the eyes, and he said, "You seem like a smart young lady. What are you doing with this man?" Of course, I was appalled. Anxiety was lurking all around me. It knew all my insecurities, and it was using them against me. I just wanted to push these feelings away from me. Still, I found my voice, and I began to beg and plead for him, to share exactly what my ex-husband had just exposed to him. He said that confidentiality rules prevented him from telling me. However, he then looked at me, speaking more with his eyes, than his mouth; he said again, "What exactly are you doing with this man?" My mind was finally willing to decipher his "code." Enough said. Yet still, I did not leave.

My Life Lesson

Denying what you feel, or what is going on around you, will not make it go away. But it will ensure that it never gets resolved.

Sometimes your heart needs more time—to accept what your mind already knows. Be careful that you are not in denial about the state of your union. Most of us have a variety of self-sabotaging behaviors that prevent us from manifesting the life that we truly desire.

The first step in changing any behavior is to first recognize it as a problem. One of the most powerful self-sabotaging behaviors is denial, and this was no different for me. Denial is a defense mechanism against emotional discomfort. By denying there's a problem, we don't have to feel bad about the fact that there actually *is* a problem. Unfortunately, this doesn't solve anything or make our lives better. It just sweeps our problems under the rug. They're still there…gnawing at us, and still getting in our way.

If your denial is a result of self-hatred, shame, guilt, or the avoidance of personal change, then the only way to end this self-sabotaging denial is to love yourself and forgive yourself.

Helping yourself means also ending those "negative tapes" we have on a loop, of self-criticism. We're too fat, too thin, too old, too young, we're not a good enough mother because we don't feed our kids organic, we're a terrible mother or father because we have gotten divorced, etc.... Those tapes are unique to each of us, but they love to play on repeat.

Positive people also have negative thoughts. They just don't allow those thoughts to control them. You must learn to control your emotions and your thoughts, or they will control you. Soon, you will begin to truly understand that you are a good and loving person, who deserves happiness. So, stop whispering the negative messages to yourself. Do not encourage this self-destruction for even one minute longer.

Once you replace negative thoughts, with positive ones, you will start having positive results.

—Willie Nelson

Forgiveness is the most effective way of dealing with arguments; altruism and forgiveness bring humanity together so that no conflict, however serious, will go beyond the bounds of what is truly human.

—Dalai Lama

Finding Courage and Looking Fear in the Face: "Her Last Night... Save Me, Save We"

Courage is the most important of all the virtues because without courage, you can't practice any other virtue consistently.

—*Maya Angelou*

One of the reasons I believe I have a great deal of compassion for other people is I have hit rock bottom in my life. I know what it is like to truly feel there is no deeper part of the pit to fall into.

One of those rock-bottom nights was the "final straw." We all have a breaking point. Marriages have a breaking point too, which is why it takes two people treasuring a marriage to keep it healthy.

My Story

On the last day of my own marriage, I remember my body turning numb. Even though I knew, deep down in the pit of my soul, that I was not being treated well, I believed in the institution of the family. Letting go of that ideal took me some time.

I was inspired in my strength, by knowing I was not alone. I eventually joined a support group, and women there would share their "last straws." It helped me develop a spine of steel. I learned from my own experiences—and those of others.

One woman in the group shared her rock bottom. She had recently moved from New York to Pennsylvania. She began by describing one pivotal evening in her marriage. She explained that it was very late, and it was a particularly dark and chilly evening, in February. She and her now-ex-husband had just had another fight. She reasonably wanted him to stay home this night—she had an infant and a toddler. After her newborn's birth, she had slipped and fell outside of the hospital, breaking her hip. Here's a warning flag: if someone treats you badly when you are down and out, that is the lowest of the low. It is bad enough when someone fights with their spouse when both are feeling OK—but to escalate an argument when a spouse is sick, under the weather, depressed…these are some warning signs. That is when your partner should be supporting you most.

In any case, he told her that he was "going out for the night." She had already suspected that there was infidelity, and she was worn out from her hip replacement surgery.

She said it played out like a muted, slow-motion dream. Although she said that the memories were a little disjointed, she recalls begging him not to leave the house. One of her fingernails snapped as she tried to grab for his leg, as he was attempting to exit through the back door. She vehemently pleaded with him not to leave and grabbed at his legs and feet. Her ex was six-feet four-inches tall, and she was five-feet three-inches tall. This is where things got physical. She said that his dark brown eyes, "looked crazed, and things escalated quickly." She found courage from who knows where and stood up. But he put his hands around her throat and began to squeeze. For the first time in their unhealthy relationship, she was afraid for her life, because this time felt different. She said her only thought was that this monster would be raising her children if something ever happened to her. So, she fought, and she fought valiantly. (And please know this is *not* a criticism of victims of domestic violence who choose not to physically fight back.) At one point, she almost passed out, and maybe the beast got scared too, because he let go. As she gasped for air, and she began to focus her eyes, she saw her two little girls standing there. They had witnessed this entire scene unfold.

In many prior fights, involving abuse, she never had the courage to dial 911 for help. Deep down, she knew that if she did this, her relationship would be over *for good*. How many people accept "bad love" because they think it is better than "no love"?

She was also rightfully afraid of his retaliation against her and her children. This is such a horrific way of controlling people. Sadly, it's a headline every single day somewhere—that a woman (often pregnant) tried to leave a man, and now she has "disappeared" or turned up dead. Still, this woman shared that looking back now, she wishes she would have had the nerve to call the police earlier, before it escalated to this terrible night. However, we all know this is very common in domestic violence situations. Victims can feel powerless—and paralyzed. (This type of situation can also happen to men.)

She explained that this time, it was different for her. Maybe it was those large eyes of her children, staring at the scene. She managed to pick herself up off the floor, and she noticed that her shirt was ripped from the altercation. She felt a larger power moving her towards the landline telephone, that was mounted on the wall. She described that there was some force, that pushed her forward with purpose, towards that telephone. She picked it up and dialed 9-1-1. She immediately asked for police assistance for an escalated domestic abuse situation.

Two very large officers entered this couple's home, with weapons at their ready. She had obvious scratch-marks on her arms and face, and her neck was bright red. One of the officers asked her now-ex-husband if he struck her. Apparently, he smirked, "Yes, I did hit my wife, and she deserved it." She said that one of the officers repeatedly asked him, "And you think this is funny?" Then, the officers told him, "You have five minutes to get whatever personal belongings you want from this home and depart the premises."

The abuser ran upstairs and was carrying large bundles of his clothing out to his pickup truck. He threw his belongings into the bed of the truck. It then began to rain. The rain was a deluge, just pummeling the earth, and dumping sheets of rain all over his clothes. All this woman could think was...*poetic justice*. When she shared the story, she could not help chuckling at that part.

The police explained the procedure to her, for obtaining a PFA, which is a Protection from Abuse order. They both told her that it was imperative that she do this immediately, or at least, the very next morning. But she explained to us that she never took that trip downtown to file that paperwork. You see, she was a broken woman. And she was afraid. She was ashamed that she had allowed this to happen to her, and she was afraid that he would seek revenge if she filed the PFA.

Even amid her anguish, she said that she recalled being embarrassed over what her neighbors would think. Surely, she said, they had heard the sirens and seen the flashing lights. Afterwards she realized that many of her neighbors had suspected that their marriage was not as stable as she wanted everyone to believe, and to her surprise they were very sympathetic and helpful.

One of the lessons that she learned was that when it comes to unrequited or wrong love—the sooner you stop it the better.

When my own ex-husband departed our home, reality sunk in for me, much like the woman from my support group. I was pretty sure that I was now a single mom. It felt like I was sinking into quicksand, and I weighed a thousand pounds. But even after our own "last straw," I had delusions that we would "work things out in the morning." I vividly remember begging him to come back, even though I knew I was not in love with him, and he certainly did not love me.

At the end of most relationships, most everyone has their own "last straw" moment. The one thing I would *urge* each and every reader of this book is—be careful. If your last straw is true danger—you have waited too long.

My Life Lesson

Though my rock-bottom moment of shame, fear, and acute loneliness was different from my friend's experience, I still had lessons to learn in my first marriage. I needed to really see how I was being treated—I still had a long way to go toward loving myself.

In the aftermath of our last night together, I tried to hold on to hope that my marriage could be healed. I see now that there was no way that was going to happen. But at the time, it required several more incidents of what I perceived as cruelty to occur, before I could accept it. In one case, there was a financial disagreement over a large household purchase that ended up needing to be settled by lawyers.

Some people go through a breakup or a traumatic experience, of being abused in a marriage, or being cheated on, or discovering a deceitful secret, and their self-esteem or their nature allows them to bounce back relatively quickly. Others need a very long time to heal and to learn their worth.

Letting go is the hardest part of a breakup or divorce—but it is also the most liberating. If you are not yet ready to let go...that is very normal. It can be painful to end a relationship, even if it was not serving your highest good. Honor any feelings of grief that you may have, and allow yourself to feel those emotions, rather than attempting to suppress them. Accept grief as a part of the experience and allow yourself time to heal.

You survived what you thought may destroy you. Now straighten out your crown—move forward like the king or queen that you are. I knew that I would have to rely on my mind, and not my heart, to move forward. And so, as I began to really think about all the moments when I was truly unhappy, or the way we interacted and behaved towards one another—my mind began to accept that living without him was my new normal.

We cannot solve our problems with the same thinking we used when we created them.

—*Albert Einstein*

Grow in self-esteem rooted in being God's workmanship.

—*Ephesians 2:10*

Unwrapped Christmas Box: I Love You, I Love You Not

Nothing hurts more than being disappointed by the person you thought would never betray you. I always thought that my marriage would get better. I had this perfect picture in my mind, of how my marriage was going to be, which is why I kept setting myself up for disappointment. Sadly, I had been let down so many times in the past, that I should have been more realistic in my expectations. Yet, there was always a part of me that dreamed of something different...something better. Because of this naïve part of me, I was always ready to trust, which continuously placed me in the direct path of hurt and pain. Things are as they are, and we suffer because we imagine they will be different.

My Story

Directly after he moved out, I discovered a deceitful "trick" that Anthony played on me. Every Christmas, for the six years that I was married to my ex-husband, he would get a large gift that "we" both wanted. The real "kicker" came, when in December 2002, a short few months before he left our home, he asked me what I wanted for

Christmas. I remember calling my mom, and I was very excited at the prospect of getting to choose our "new" household item that year. My ex-husband told me, "You deserve a special gift this year, because you delivered my son and just had surgery." I asked him if we could get a new sofa and loveseat. He readily agreed to this. I thought, "Wow, my luck is changing!" I was quite frugal, so I suggested that we look at one of the discount furniture warehouses. Shockingly, he suggested that I should go to Ethan Allen Furniture Gallery, which is a very high-end furniture chain, with stylish, yet traditional pieces. So, off I went to the store. I took my mother with me, because my ex-husband said that he had a work function that weekend.

I found a functional, yet lavish sofa and matching loveseat that someone had special-ordered, but never picked up. So, the price was right. I was thrilled, and I called my then-husband to tell him about my "find." He instructed me to get the special-order decorative pillows and a matching ottoman too, which I eagerly ordered.

When I left that store, I felt like a million dollars. I was very excited to get our new furniture pieces, and I even changed the paint color in our living room, in preparation for the new furnishings. The store told me that it would take approximately eight weeks for the special-order ottoman and pillows, and that I should have all the pieces delivered at once, to save money.

After eight weeks, I began to excitedly call the store, to see if our furniture had arrived. In the meantime, my husband had left me. On a hunch, I called Ethan Allen the day after my husband departed. I will never forget this telephone call. The saleslady told me that, "Why, that furniture was already delivered a few days ago." I assured them that I was standing in my family room, and the items were not there. I asked what address they were delivered to, and guess what she told me? She could not provide me with a specific address, because of a confidentiality clause, but she had slipped and told me that, "The items were successfully delivered to your husband, at an apartment building." Ouch! You guessed it. My ex-husband had "my" Christmas gifts delivered to *his* new bachelor's pad. (But, don't worry. My lawyer made this a line-item in our property settlement agreement, and he had to return "my" Christmas gifts to me, within ten days of the documents being properly executed and filed with the court.)

My Life Lesson

Selfish is as selfish does. And, I am a firm believer in that thing called karma. Happiness will never come through selfishness, but rather it comes through selflessness. Pleasure and pain come from our own past actions. Everything you do comes back around. I remember playing Justin Timberlake's song, "What Goes Around…Comes Around," repeatedly during this time. This song embodied everything that I was feeling at the time. That song was part of my therapy. The words spoke to me. I felt like Justin wrote that song for me. And if Justin Timberlake once felt that way, maybe I was not such a freak to feel that way myself. It was my redemption song. It was one of the first times that I remember valuing myself and deciding to fight for my own happiness.

> *How people treat you is their karma. How you react is yours.*
>
> —*Wayne Dyer*

> *You are what you settle for.*
>
> —*Janis Joplin*

Iceman in an Ice Storm

My Story

About four months after I separated, a friend took me out for coffee. She wanted me to know that I was not alone. I was spending a lot of my time wondering *why?* Why was Anthony the way he was? And *how?* How could he leave our little family? But I realized this was wasted energy after my friend's story.

Shortly after her own separation, in our area of Pennsylvania, which can have some severe winter weather, a terrible stormy afternoon occurred and most of the roads were closed due to blizzard conditions. She was almost out of baby formula for her then three-month-old son. Desperate, she called her ex to see if he might venture out to purchase some for him. He bragged to her, "I am out in the snow, with my new four-by-four truck, doing 'donuts' on the ice." She asked him very politely if he would please go to the store to pick up formula for their son, since he was already out-and-about, and her car was completely buried beneath the heavy snow—not to mention it did not have four-wheel drive, and she certainly did not feel safe bringing the baby out in the blizzard. He laughed at her, and before he hung up the phone, he proudly declared with a disturbing chuckle, "No, I will not get you baby formula. I am Iceman." He apparently always proudly referred to himself with that self-imposed nickname. So, she ended up rationing the formula to get through that entire day and evening, with what should have been one-feeding worth of formula. Towards the morning, she was basically feeding her son water through his bottle.

She once asked her ex what he meant when he called himself "Iceman." He told her, "I can turn my emotions off in a split second." He went into further detail by explaining that he could shut off his conscience, as if he had no feelings of guilt or remorse.

Hearing her story helped a little. I stopped wondering. Maybe I had been married to my own version of an Iceman. After all, I wondered how Anthony could just leave me, like I never even mattered. A normal person cannot just turn off love. But I realized something very important. I could *not* just turn off my feelings. And as my friend asked me over coffee, "Would you want to be able to do that?" No. The capacity I have for love is part of what makes me special.

My Life Lesson

If someone tells you that they are a bad person, believe them. If someone repeatedly tells you, "It's not you, it's me," believe them. If someone tells you from the get-go, they have difficulty with monogamy, or they don't want to have children (and you do), or any of countless "warning signs" they might not be the person for you, *believe them.*

> *Just because you are available for a relationship, doesn't mean you are ready for one.*
>
> **—Dr. Steve Maraboli**

"My Son Is Not Handicapped": Standing Up for Our Children

If it looks right, but it feels wrong—it's fear. If it looks wrong, but it feels right—it's intuition.

Little by little, I started to listen to my internal voice. I had to train myself to trust the small voice inside of me. I learned to document my ex's behavior to protect my children. I learned to stand on my own two feet—even if at times, I felt wobbly.

My Story

In my case, nothing was easy about co-parenting. Things that to me seemed obvious and simple—just weren't. This was likely a good sign that our marriage was not compatible to begin with. I am sure in your life, you have known divorced couples who argue over crazy things. I know one friend whose ex-husband sent her a bill for $1.21 for her "share" of ball point pens.

Sometimes, even children's *health* is not enough to pave the way to peaceful co-parenting. A friend of mine's son Henry was diagnosed with a severe left eye astigmatism. It was discovered when Henry complained about experiencing eyestrain and headaches at school. He told his mom that he had to squint to see the blackboard. My friend contacted her ex to see if he wanted to join them for the eye appointment. He declined. So off she went to a respected local ophthalmologist who diagnosed Henry with a very severe astigmatism in his left eye. He was given eyeglasses to correct this astigmatism, and my friend was told that he categorically *must* wear the glasses, or he would run the risk of going blind in that eye—that's how severe it was.

She promptly contacted his father to explain this diagnosis to him. The man's response was, "My son is not handicapped!" When my friend thought she mis-heard, he repeated himself saying, "My son does not have a handicap, and he will not be wearing glasses on my weekends."

She argued. She explained. She offered to go to the doctor with him so he could hear this important information for himself, to no avail. She sent Henry off for his dad's custodial weekend wearing the glasses to save his sight.

When the boy returned home, after the weekend with his father, he was not wearing his glasses. His father sloughed off the loss. "He must have forgot them somewhere." Because my friend knew the real consequences of Henry not wearing his prescription glasses, she was forced to order and purchase another pair of prescription glasses. She suspected that her ex had just "kept" the glasses from her son, because in his mind, donning glasses was somehow showing weakness.

When the next pair of glasses did not return home with Henry, she was told again that the glasses were "lost." Like any good parent, she ordered a third pair—but after that stopped sending them on Henry's weekends with his dad. Even though she said that she was afraid of taking legal action, she mustered the courage and strength, with the help of her lawyer, to request (and be granted) the Court's intervention.

There is a medical duty owed to your child to receive proper medical treatment, especially in serious medical situations. Of course, the courts *do* provide remedies for situations like this—but it's a horrible shame that some parents need to go through scenarios like this, just for the other parent to agree to do the right thing for their children. Unfortunately, this may be a reality that you might find yourself in. My point is, there may come a time where you will need to gather all your strength, and regain your backbone, to do what is in the best interest of your child.

Co-Parenting Pains

One of the hardest elements of my divorce was co-parenting with my ex. It is very difficult to co-parent if both parents are not on the same page. I have seen it over and over, not just with my own life but in the lives of friends and loved ones.

I have known people who, for example, provided structure for their children—only to watch the rules and behaviors they set and instilled in their kids, be thrown out the window when it is the other parent's turn to have the children. I have also seen people use their children as nothing more than pawns to hurt their ex—when really, the ones who are hurt are the *children*.

Unfortunately, you may need to legally document aspects of co-parenting with your ex. Nothing was easy for me, and things that should have been straightforward…were not. But, like all "Mama Bears," I was willing to do anything and everything in my power to ensure my kids were safe and were being well-cared for. I discuss these issues in greater detail, later in the book.

My Life Lesson

If you know your co-parent is doing something, or conversely, not doing something that will affect the well-being of your child, document everything. You can have the court mandate the medical treatment be adhered to, if it is medically necessary for the well-being of your child. Parents may not be strong enough to fight for their own rights, but most will fight for their children's safety, health, and well-being, until the bitter end.

When I am afraid, I put my trust in you.

—Psalm 56:3

In the depth of winter, I finally learned that within me there lay an invincible summer.

—Albert Camus

CHAPTER 7

Learning to See the Red Flags: Green Light—Yellow Light—Red Light...Stop!

Nice people don't necessarily fall in love with nice people.

—*Jonathan Franzen*

Sometimes, we do not see the red flags in front of us about our partners, until it is too late, and we are deeply enmeshed. When we have children with someone, we are often so intent on not splitting up our "family"—no matter how unhealthy that might be—that we are even more in denial. But there are some telltale red flags, that some people will reveal, as part of their natural behavioral repertoire.

Some common red flags include:

- Temper issues
- Belittling comments
- Alcohol or drug abuse
- Emotional cruelty toward a partner or the children

- Narcissism
- Extreme coldness or "icing out" behaviors
- Unfaithfulness
- Frequent lying (about matters big and small)

Addiction, for example, is a complex problem and disease. Oftentimes, a partner is ill-equipped to understand it. They may try to "fix" the person without understanding that only the addict can fix themselves. Another tough issue is extreme self-absorption. Merriam-Webster's defines a narcissist as an extremely self-centered person with an exaggerated sense of self-importance. I think probably every single person has dated or been involved with a narcissist at some point or another—or perhaps you've worked for one or have someone like that in your office or book group or neighborhood association.

Unfortunately, because narcissists rarely ever admit when they are wrong, if you are intimately involved with a narcissist, you can start to feel like *you* are the one in the wrong all the time. You may find yourself in their twisted logic. Narcissists don't just break your heart; if you are not careful, they can also break your spirit.

I also would like to offer a disclaimer that I am not a psychologist or psychiatrist. I base this chapter on my experiences and observations. People's ability to "get along" depends on their specific personality traits. For example, egotistical people can successfully get along with others, but I believe that they only achieve harmony if they are the completely dominant partner. I was not willing to be controlled in my life, and I was not willing to have my opinions silenced. This created friction in some of my past relationships.

Wade and I were always craving love. We entered each of our relationships to love and be loved in return. We wanted the connection and bond that comes from a loving partnership. Sometimes that made us vulnerable because we were so over-willing to please. Remember, other people enter relationships for their own personal reasons. And sometimes those reasons will be suspect or not based on kindness or love. Especially in newer relationships, it is good to keep an eye out for those red flags.

My Story

Obviously, if Wade and I were matches for our past partners in life, we would still be together with them. Unfortunately, while I now have a list of red flags stored in my heart and brain, back then, I didn't until it was too late. For example, my ex Anthony exuded confidence. That was a trait I found attractive. However, other traits were not a match for me, in terms of my values and beliefs (and vice versa), and I just did not see them until I was in so much emotional pain that I was collapsing under the weight of it all.

In addition, I was frequently belittled and put down for my faults—both real and imagined. After a while, I did not recognize myself. I had become a shell of my former self. I did everything possible to try to appease and make things better. But no matter how much I tried, in the end we utterly incompatible, and the relationship was unhealthy.

My Life Lesson

I believe that there are narcissistic personality traits or tendencies in most of us. However, I also believe that some people are so self-absorbed that they become emotional manipulators. I do not think that narcissists by nature have genuine relationships. They often reinvent themselves, depending on who they are trying to impress. For some of these people, they never knew love. They never wanted love. Rather, they just loved to be wanted.

If someone is an addict—or has an explosive temper, or frequently lies, or is ice cold—any of these red flags should stop you in your tracks. We need to remain detached enough from our own emotions in order to make clear-headed decisions. If we allow ourselves to spiral down into the other person's "mess," and we ignore red flags, it will be that much harder to pull ourselves out. You need to "see" like a friend would see. For example, I am sure everyone reading this book has had a friend fall in love with an unhealthy person, or with a person who treats them terribly. We can see it plainly, and we worry for them. We may even *tell* them they deserve better and that this person is toxic. But when it comes to *ourselves,* we cannot see. Perhaps, though, reading this, you may have some nagging doubt, some tugging from the corners of your heart or mind. Listen to that voice. It might be a whisper right now—but listen. That voice knows the truth.

The reason that I would never judge someone else's weaknesses is because they act and behave in the ways they do, because of the large void that fills them. Wade and I can relate to this in a different way. We lived with our own version of that "black hole of emptiness" all our former lives, until we met one another. But ours stemmed from a deficit of self-esteem. Other people may have different voids. Perhaps they tie their entire self-worth on the acceptance and admiration of others.

You may get hurt by these toxic people, because they are oblivious to your pain. Some people enter relationships to fill their empty heart or for their own twisted reasons. If you are in a weakened state, you will be taken advantage of, until you are totally exhausted.

The word toxic comes from the Latin word, *toxikon,* that means "arrow poison." Toxic people are not good for you. They may spread untruths about you. They may begin rumors about you, so that you never know what falsehoods are being spread about your neighborhood and community, or who is operating under those false pretenses. This makes you very unsure and unsteady in the world around you. This is done by design. Remember that love does not rejoice at injustice and unrighteousness.

I personally do not feel that *all* narcissistic people are cruel or uncaring. Many of them have good intentions, but they are misguided because of their overwhelming needs, and their tainted historic relationships and ways of existing, prior to entering a new relationship. Because of their intense needs, they sometimes force us to compromise ourselves and our own happiness. Sometimes they are not inherently bad people; they just aren't the right people *for us*. And as hard as it sometimes is, we must let them go, to free ourselves. Life is difficult enough without being around people who bring you down. You should never have to destroy yourself for anyone else to feel better.

And remember that when you disagree with a rational man or woman, you let reality be the final arbitrator. If you are right, then they will learn, and if you are wrong, then you will learn. One of you will "win," but both of you will profit. However, if you disagree with an irrational man or woman, any alleged "right" of theirs, will most likely necessitate the violation of your own rights. And that is not healthy.

Sometimes you want to be loved so badly that you cannot tell when you are in a bad relationship. When this happens, you will no longer be able to decipher when it is love—and when it isn't love. This is the point that Wade and I were at, prior to entering our previous marriages. What we failed to realize was that we were not problems to be solved. We had value and worth, and we were capable of being loved as we were. And so are you.

If you find yourself constantly trying to prove your worth to someone, you have already forgotten your value.

I know that some of the darkest times are followed by the lightest.

—Michael Bublé

Unmasked: Lost Identity

My Story

One common thread that both Wade and I shared was that we felt we were "not allowed" to be angry in most of our previous relationships. This is a basic human right and emotion. It is okay to be angry, but it is never okay to allow your anger to rise to the level of physical or emotional abuse. It is never okay to be cruel. But, no matter how poorly or badly we were treated, our voices were to be silent. And if we did show any signs of universal anger, after being put down time and time again, some of our former partners used this anger against us, proving that we were "irrational" or "overly emotional," or "hypersensitive."

Another element to my story is that my priorities were always my children. I vacationed with them, and I viewed any and all time with them as a gift. I always tried to make decisions with *them* in mind. While I can never be sure of what went on in my ex's head, I did not think he viewed our kids and parenthood in the same way. Maybe it was just a difference in values or simply in my perception of his parenting. But I knew when I met Wade that I was seeking a man who would put his—and my children—as sacred.

There was clear evidence, from the very beginning of my relationship with my first ex-husband, that it would not be a marriage formed from mutual love and respect. I ignored the warning signs. I wanted love so desperately that I lied to myself about my choices. And, desperate people do desperate things.

My life has been difficult, only because of the poor decisions that I have made. I am not placing blame at anyone else's feet. Rather, I want you to learn from my mistakes. Some people will not love you, no matter what you do, and how hard you try. And some people won't stop loving you, no matter what you do, and they will always have your back. Please go where the love is.

My Life Lesson

I am not equipped to say whether *any* of my exes were narcissistic. But, from what I have read, there are certain tell-tale symptoms that some narcissistic people exhibit. First, because they feel that they are much more important than others, they will often interrupt conversations. On this same line, they also love to hoard the conversation, giving others little to no time to express their thoughts or views. These people act differently in the public eye than in private. They will lie and distort the facts to suit their own agenda. (And I think they begin to believe their lies.) They become emotionally distant and unavailable, unless they want something from you. They lack sympathy for others but crave empathy for themselves. They arrogantly believe that they are "above the law," in that they enjoy getting away with breaking rules, such as butting in line, disobeying traffic laws, parking in non-parking spaces, and rescheduling appointments with others, multiple times, without regard to the other person's schedule.

I want to say a few words about boundaries. We often hear the term. But what do "healthy" boundaries mean? Healthy boundaries mean you know your worth—and if your partner does not respect that worth, you must clearly spell out what you will and will not accept. This leads into what I believe is one of the worst offenses of someone who is a narcissist. They do not respect boundaries set by others. They show very wanton disregard for how another person is feeling. They do not want others to express emotions like anger and disappointment, and they certainly do not tolerate people questioning them, or their authority. They show very little remorse, and they are professionals at placing the blame at another's feet. Another trait that these manipulators tend to have is the ability to shine in public. They do things to outwardly impress others, while making themselves look good. They seldom do anything good, without getting something that they deem more valuable, in return. For example, all charitable donations are done in the public eye, or for a needed tax write-off.

All these tendencies lead to the fact that most narcissists have a sense of entitlement. They expect to be treated better and for others to cater to their needs and wants. In other words, they feel that the world revolves around them, and they give no merit or credence to how they treat others in return (unless, again, they have an audience). These people are true "charmers" to those that know them superficially. Their armor only cracks when you know the person intimately, and they are not getting what they want. These people also like to elicit negative emotions, to keep others down, off-balance, and inse-cure. They are extremely sensitive to criticism. And the final trait that these narcissists have is that they will think nothing of manipulating people, even their spouse and children. They make all decisions based upon their own selfish needs.

Surround yourself with people who see your value and remind you of it. In my life now, I can see my personal growth, simply by looking at the people in my inner-circle. But I also measure my growth by the people that I avoid. One of the side effects of learning how to set boundaries and love yourself is that you won't have to remove all the bad people from your life. Sometimes, they will remove themselves, as you heal and grow.

Stop trying to change someone who doesn't want to change. If someone shows you their true colors—stop trying to repaint them. Stop giving chances to someone who abuses your forgiveness. Stop walking back into the place where your heart ran from. Stop trusting their words and ignoring their actions. Stop giving your all to a per-son who gives you nothing in return. Stop fighting for a relationship, when you are standing in the ring alone. Stop breaking your own heart. Whatever you do, never run back to what broke you.

General Traits of a Narcissist

Here is a little checklist of some signs and symptoms of a narcissist. If you are seeing any red flags here about your partner or potential partner, take them seriously.

- They namedrop.
- They never admit when they are wrong.
- Nothing will ever be their fault. They have an excuse for every mistake they make.
- They blame others for anything that goes wrong in their lives.

- They have a sense of entitlement.
- They are excessively self-absorbed.
- They always portray themselves as the victim.
- Appearances are everything to them.
- They like to show off their wealth, possessions, and accomplishments.
- They dominate or hijack conversations.
- They never ask questions of others in conversations and are uninterested in others' stories.
- They cannot handle criticism; however, they frequently criticize others and exploit their weaknesses.
- They like their life to look perfect on social media.
- They take everything personally.
- They frequently lie.
- They will invent stories, distort facts, and change events to suit their own agenda.
- They are arrogant. The world always revolves around them.
- They blame their lack of success and failures on others.
- They exaggerate their positives and minimize their negatives.
- They are emotionally distant and unavailable...unless they want something.
- They lack reflective-thinking ability.
- They do not delve deeply into other people's emotions...because they really do not care.
- They are very controlling.
- They are angry, for at least a period, almost every day. (This can present as passive-aggressive.)
- They need constant attention and admiration.
- They have unreasonable expectations of favorable treatment.

- They do not manage conflicts successfully. It always turns into a contest—who is right, and who is wrong.
- They have no spirit of teamwork.
- They are extremely impatient.

You need power only to do something harmful. Otherwise, love is enough, and compassion is enough.

—Osho

CHAPTER 8

Scenes from a Life in Shambles

It is difficult to make a man miserable while he feels worthy of himself and claims kindred to the great God who made him.

—Abraham Lincoln

Being in an unhealthy relationship can wreck your internal compass. Forget True North—you can lose your way, so you don't know east from west, north from south, up from down.

That was how I felt—lost. I had no sense of direction any longer. The following stories are just snapshots from this tumultuous point in my life.

Gone but Not for Good

My Story

When Anthony left me, my daughter was only four years old, and my son was only a few months old. I would pray that my husband would be a loving husband and father and that my marriage and family would be healed. But a healing and reconciliation were not in the cards for us. After Anthony was no longer in our day-to-day lives, I worried about whether I could raise our two children alone. At first, I did not think that I could be a good mother, while my insides felt twisted and my heart defiantly continued to break. Most days, I was an actor, and it was one of the hardest roles that I have ever played. I felt like a terrible actress, and I would grade myself as doing a "good enough" job. But, on some days, I felt like a complete and total failure. And I do not like to fail. In school, I was the student that always had to earn an A in every class. I am a perfectionist. But over time, I discovered a strength inside of me that I did not know existed. I also learned to forgive my shortcomings, because I was doing the best that I could for my two children. After all, they were safe, fed, properly clothed, happy, going to school, attending Mass, involved in extra-curricular activities, and well-rested.

My Life Lesson

A very wise therapist once asked me to give her a million dollars. In fact, she demanded that I give her a million dollars, cash, by the end of the day. I said, "I cannot give you a million dollars." She asked me, "Why not?" I answered emphatically, "Because I do not have a million dollars to give you."

Many people don't get what they deserve, and many people don't deserve what they get. Every person is a sum of their experiences, so no spouse was raised exactly the way you were. And what you feel is right and just may not be the same morality or circumstance of the other person. Asking that other person to "be a good husband, wife, or parent" by your personal measuring stick is the same as my therapist asking me to give her a million dollars. *I did not have it to give.* And past partners did not either. *Frankly, neither did I.* Maybe these men did not have the emotional capability to relate to situations the same way that I did. Sometimes there are simply two different ways to view the world. This was a pivotal revelation for me. This is what ultimately led me to my forgiveness of both their and my behavior.

Single Parenting

I am sure you have seen the following play out with friends who have gotten divorced—or perhaps your own life. A couple splits up, and the parent who only has visitation, or less custodial time, suddenly acts like a college student or behaves immaturely. Maybe they go out constantly, or they do not fulfill their parenting obligations. Whatever the reason, one parent is the "responsible" one and the other views the divorce as a chance to sow their wild oats.

There have been times when the weight of parenting settled very heavily on my shoulders. That does not mean I resented this or would have had it any other way! Nonetheless, there were many times when I felt overwhelmed or even frightened by facing parenting issues alone. I can remember a time when my poor Gabi had recurring urinary tract infections. I needed to be vigilant and it didn't matter if I had plans or I wanted or needed to do something—she was my focus. Once, she was admitted to the hospital for two days for a bad bout of the rotavirus. I never left her and slept in a chair right next to the crib.

My Life Lesson

Priorities: When someone tells you that they are "too busy," it is not a reflection of their schedule. It reflects your position/place on their schedule. Action is what expresses priorities the best. Do what is right, not what is easy. Fun times will come and go, but your children will always be your children, and parents should be careful who they put first. Children should not have to be placed second, especially during a medical situation or other emergency. Lifestyles and activities can wait—emergencies cannot. Good parents will make sacrifices so that their children can have a good, healthy, and productive life. I will never forget the bonding that I experienced with my daughter during the times she was sick. Even though she was dreadfully ill, and unable to verbally communicate, because she was so drained; she hugged my parents and me all day long, instinctively knowing that we would never leave her. This is time that my parents and I will always cherish. We rocked her, sang to her, read to her, and loved her. She was so sick, yet still such a sweet little girl that held onto us like the lifelines that we were.

There are three things that leave and never return: words, time, and opportunities.

Let Your Past Make You Better, Not Bitter

My Story

Negativity was all-around me, any time that my ex-husband was present. He thought I was the sole problem in our marriage, and he often told me so.

Looking back now, I tell people that my first ex-husband did me the biggest favor by leaving me. When I was with him, I felt powerless over my situation, and I had no sense of who I was. Worse, I had zero self-worth. I began to feel disassociated with myself. My marriage was beginning to take control of me—literally and figuratively, in a one-two punch. I felt deeply disregarded and discounted as a human being. I was sapped of what little energy that I had left, after a full-time job that required over a three-hour commute a day, in addition to taking care of our two small children. I had a sense of crippling devaluation that was creeping ever so steady upon me, and it was invading my self-worth. This daily chronic stress caused my hair to fall out, insomnia, high blood pressure, exhaustion, weight gain, depression, and the list goes on. I believe that my pain was cumulative, which makes it difficult to recognize in the beginning. But I could not deny the physical changes that had manifested. There was not one event that got me to this demoralized and unrecognizable place. Rather, it was a series of ever-steady conflicts, that began to add up over time.

But, after Anthony left, I began to discover myself, to the point that my children now know their real mom. I am not longer a façade of who he wanted me to be. Moreover, I know who I am, and what I stand for. My children also learned that nobody has the right to control another person, either physically or emotionally. I was free to form my own opinion about my self-worth—not listen to what anyone else thought of me, or what they said about me. In the end, I was the only one who could give my children a happy mother, who loves life.

My Life Lesson

The moral to some of my personal stories is this: Unfortunately, not all couples are willing or capable of working together. This was the case for Anthony and me. But he seemingly gets along fabulously with his long-time girlfriend, other business associates, and various friends, which means that Anthony is obviously capable of getting along with other people. This is yet another reason that I think *we* were simply "mismatched" for one another. Anthony even told me that eventually I would be much happier with someone else. And he was right. This is one point that we both agreed on.

Couples become a cohesive unit when the two people recognize common goals, listen to one another, resolve conflicts appropriately, and make decisions based on the good of one another and their family. When one or both individuals have difficult personalities, disruptive results will occur, and this is not pleasant for anyone in their family. Both partners must be willing to encourage open communication, without repercussions. If one of the partners constantly overpowers the other one, then the atmosphere will almost always become emotionally charged. When this occurs, self-interest rules one of you, and self-preservation rules the other. Either way, there is no peace and harmony in the relationship. Realize now that you can be whole, all by yourself.

The absence of myself created a hole in my soul. And, you can't love yourself, or others, when you are empty inside. One of the greatest lessons that I learned, when I was thrust back into the single life, is that a person who does not value themselves—cannot value anyone else. More simply stated; it is not easy to find happiness in ourselves. But it is not possible to find it elsewhere.

Work on being in love with the person in the mirror, who has been through so much, but is still standing.

Exit Stage Left

My Story

There was no immediate warning, for me or my children, when my first husband decided to completely and permanently move out. He enlisted the help of his father to take what belongings he wanted, without consulting me, while I was at work. He departed our home, and our family, without so much as a note. I had no idea where he was or what he was thinking.

I will never forget the day that I came home, from that hard day at work, to find a half-emptied shell of our former family home. When I walked into our house that night after work, carrying one child in a car-seat and holding the other child's hand, the house looked transformed. I felt like I was in a dream, and I recall having a vivid feeling of being detached from myself. I had this strange feeling that every fiber inside of me was sending mixed electrical signals throughout my brain. I was in a heightened state of shock. I was observing my own life—but seemingly from someone else's body. I could not grasp that this was happening to me. All the hair stood up on my body, and my body began to quiver. My children both began crying uncontrollably. We had three televisions—but when I came home, not one of them was left behind. Therefore, I could not turn on *Teletubbies, Barney, Thomas the Tank Engine,* or any of our children's favorite and familiar shows on TV, to help soothe them.

I was doing everything in my power to just remain calm myself, but holding it together seemed like an insurmountable task. I was still very hormonal, as I had just given birth to our son. And to make matters worse, just a few short weeks earlier, I underwent surgery to remove an eight-pound fibroid tumor from my uterus. I was cut from side-to-side, and I was still in a lot of physical pain. I did not need any more pain in my life right then, especially not more emotional suffering. But no matter how much I wished it away, the pain still came. *Aside: I would like to point out that to Anthony's credit, he left his entire bedroom set, which was a saving grace for me. Because I was still recovering from my surgery, I could not have fathomed sleeping on the couch, while my abdomen was still healing. For that gesture, I will always be grateful.*

I was in shock and disbelief, and I was utterly devastated. My family had been forever severed. Standing in my half-empty kitchen, I felt as if I were completely alone in the world. I remember packing up my two children and driving to our local church. It was shadowy and raining outside. The church looked very different at night. It was very dark, with only the outside spotlights illuminating the buildings. But I could see the cross shining brightly atop the steeple, as if it were speaking directly to me, saying, "With my help, you will move from this darkness into the light." I immediately felt a calmness wash over me.

Although as soon as I got back to my half-empty home, I experienced that sinking feeling rushing all around me again. My heart was penetrable, and my thoughts were all over the place. I felt like I was being relentlessly slammed around in the deep dark currents, like prey in a gator's mouth. I felt like I could not breath. My house no longer felt like a home. Worse, Anthony could not hear me cry, as I was left alone to see all my dreams die. But, amid all my chaotic emotions, I instinctively somehow knew that my children and I would be all right, in time. I felt God carrying me, because I could not walk alone.

My Life Lesson

I learned that I was stronger than I thought, and my spirit had a resilience that I did not think I possessed. I believe that in your darkest hour, God gives you the strength to move through the pain. I also discovered that there can be silver-linings in every situation, if you look for it. The images of the cross on the church that evening were permanently etched into the recesses of my mind. Now, when I am faced with any situation that I feel is beyond my control, I am immediately taken to that calm place, and time stands still for me. I am gently reminded that I endured, and I am a fighter and a survivor.

> For I know the plans I have for you," declares the LORD, "plans to prosper you and not to harm you, plans to give you hope and a future.
>
> —*Jeremiah 29:11*

Keeping My Normal Work & Sleep Routine

My Story

By way of background, I have always professionally been involved in insurance, claims, safety, compliance, and risk management. The day after my husband left, I will never forget realizing that I had a critically important legal deposition, on one of our larger exposure liability insurance claims, the very next morning at work. What should I do? I decided that I would have to save my wallowing for a later date. I had to pull myself together. I had to forge ahead. This was much easier said than done. But somehow, on autopilot, I drove the hour and a half commute to work, and I successfully answered all the lawyer's questions, to fulfill my obligation to my employer.

The next workday was much more difficult. I was now undeniably single, with two children. I felt as though a ton of bricks had dropped on me, and the sheer weight buried me as a prisoner. I wasn't sure about how I was going to pay all the household bills on my own—or even where my ex had gone. So, for now, I was the only breadwinner, and I felt like I was the only parent of two innocent and needy young children. I had so many questions that I wanted answered. But it would take a long time to get my answers. *In fairness to my ex, he did continue to pay many of our household bills, even before the support order was formalized. And I will always remain grateful for this gesture.*

On my second day back at work, I dropped my kids off at my parents' house, and literally fell to my knees on their marble foyer floor. I was bawling uncontrollably. My parents were both consoling me and telling me that the best thing that I could do was to "keep my normal routine" and "go back to work." This was some serious Italian "tough love." Didn't they understand that I still felt paralyzed? So instead, I called one of my close friends at work, who also happened to be a paralegal there. I was looking to elicit a different response from her. She was extremely sympathetic, but then she said that one of our company lawyers and the president of our company, who was also an owner of the company, wanted to talk to me. I was petrified—after all, I wasn't at work. She transferred my call to our corporate counsel's office. The CEO, and my direct boss, answered the phone. He instructed me, "Come into work today." He further said, "I do not care how long it takes you to get here, just come into the office today." Because he was my boss and not my father or mother, it was the jolt that I needed to get me out of my state of bewilderment.

I do not remember anything about the drive to work that day, although I had taken the same route to work for approximately four years. But now, it felt was like I was in a trance, blindly traveling down unknown roads. But I do remember that when I got there, our corporate counsel and the owner that I had talked to earlier on the telephone, were waiting for me in the parking lot. They ushered me into the large conference room. I was an employee who always prided myself on being and looking the "corporate role." But this day, I looked like a complete disheveled mess. I mean, I gave "looking rough" a new name. I had not showered, and I had been crying all night. I had makeup streaming down my face, and my eyes were almost swollen shut from crying.

As I explained earlier, I had a very strong, yet fair and empathetic boss, who also just happened to be one of the owners of the company. As a director for his company, I reported directly to him. I will never forget how he reached out to me in my greatest time of need. As we were walking inside of the building, he reiterated to me that, "Hard times will always reveal true friends", and he reminded me that his company was a steadfast friend of mine. Hearing this changed the trajectory of my life. This revelation would surround me like a cloak of love, continually giving back to me, again and again.

After reaching the conference room at our corporate office, my boss and our lawyer both sat down with me. There was only a yellow legal pad of paper and a pen in front of them. They wrote down the very basic things that I needed to do, to move forward. They explained that this was my checklist, as I am a very organized and detail-oriented type of person. The list contained things like: Enlist the help of a counselor for yourself and your two children. Make an inventory of everything taken from the house. Get his name off of all of my credit cards immediately. Change the locks on the house (which my brother-in-law had already done for me). Hire a tough, seasoned lawyer (because they knew I had the tendency to be a pushover in my personal life). And, they provided me with a list of excellent and knowledgeable family-law lawyers, for the area where I resided. They provided me with some other practical advice too. They advised me to memorialize and categorize all of my household, childcare, and other expenses, to prepare for a future domestic relations order for child support. They also told me to file immediately, because child support could not begin until it was filed through the court and domestic relations. They told me to find my most recent tax returns, and they advised me to keep track of all the expenses that I was paying for our children alone (medical insurance, medical co-payments, formula, diapers, etc.).

The second thing that my boss did for me was humbling. He showed me true compassion. He had always been a very demanding yet understanding boss. But now, on occasion, he even asked his wife to come to my office, to talk to me. She was "checking in" to ensure that I was emotionally handling my new situation. She was an extremely spiritual woman, and this helped me immensely.

I held the type of management position that could not be ignored, because things could be overlooked that could grossly affect his business. And many times, when he walked into my office, I was blankly staring out my office window. I was having difficulty staying focused for long periods of time. I would quickly look up to him and say, "I am sorry. I promise that I will not let anything fall through the cracks." His response was this, "You are human, and you are going through an extremely difficult transition in your life. You *will* let some things fall through the cracks." Then, he chuckled and said to me, "Just don't let it be anything too major." He knew that I was a very conscientious employee, and that I would get the work all done, even if it required me doing it at home, after my children were asleep. But it was nice to know that I had my boss in my corner, and that losing my job was one less thing that I had to worry about.

My Life Lesson

My advice to anyone suffering through a transition period is to keep your same schedule, and keep on, keeping on. Let your job or your day-to-day routine allow you to regain your bearings again. And, it is okay to look forward in small time increments. Sometimes I would begin my workday, just praying to make it to lunch without having a meltdown. As time went by, the time that I spent ruminating and worrying about my impending divorce grew smaller and smaller. Remember that grief is a passage, not a place to stay.

Another important aspect of your recovery will be to stick to a regular sleep schedule. While sleep requirements vary slightly from person to person, most healthy adults need between seven to nine hours of sleep per night, to function at their best. Many nights I would lay awake, ruminating about my recent break-up. But over time, I found that a regular sleep schedule helped maintain and synchronize my sleep/wake cycle. I also read that people with the most regular sleep habits have reported fewer problems with depression. Do not take your cell phone to bed with you. Instead, if you can't fall asleep, then listen to soft music, take a warm bath, do some easy stretches, or read a book. And, if your insomnia continues, avoid caffeine as much as possible, especially before bed, because the effects of caffeine can last for many hours. I also found that using a diffuser in my bedroom helped to create a calm atmosphere. I would use Sage, because burning Sage has been a custom around the world, for thousands of years, and was used to get rid of negative energy. It's frequently still used in energy cleansing, as well as healing ceremonies. Many believe Sage helps neutralize and get rid of any "bad vibes" in your personal space. Palo Santo also has an aroma that can create a cleansing, uplifting atmosphere.

Don't pack up the sun and pull apart the moon. Life is too short to start your day with broken pieces. The secret to your recovery will be partly found in keeping to your daily routine.

The pain you feel today, will be the strength you feel tomorrow.

CHAPTER 9

Will I Ever be Happy Again? The Steps to Recovery

But the Lord stood with me and gave me strength.

—2 Timothy 4:17

Breakdown to Breakthrough

Surviving divorce is not easy. It also is not a straight line. You will find that you make progress forward, only to circle back and feel like you are starting all over again. Your emotions may also be all over the place. One minute you revel in your independence. Then next you are grieving. The next you are angry. But if you keep putting one foot in front of the other, you can make it from breakdown…to breakthrough.

My Story

Sometimes the worst place you can be is in your own head. But, the steps to recovery require you to face your demons. Most days, I felt as though I was sinking beneath love's overpowering weight. Can you relate to these feelings? Breakups can be hard, but here's how you can come out stronger than ever on the other side. Believe it or not, you will get over heartbreak, whether it is your first breakup or your hundredth. But at first, it will seem that you are on a wild bull. You will feel that this jarring ride will never end, and your bull will keep bucking and throwing you off course.

My Life Lesson

Part of your recovery is accepting that your life is in shambles, and *you* must change it. When you are at this point, you should thank God for closing doors that you may not have been strong enough to close for yourself. Because, the good news is that you will have doors opened that are even better for your life. Never think of your ex, for even a moment longer than is necessary. Focus on yourself and your children, if you have them. Push through the pain, until you successfully arrive at the other side. The other side is your recovery. You cannot get there if you harbor anger. Malice requires the sanction of the victim. Do not be the victim. Recovery peels back the painful layers and heals the gaping hole inside of you through connection, honesty, and hard work. In time, your heartbreak will provide you with the insight and motivation that you will need, to get through this. And, to love yourself is the beginning of a lifetime recovery.

> *Don't waste time watering and nourishing the weeds in your life. Water and nourish the flowers.*
>
> —*Lalah Delia*

Do Not Be a Penny Waiting for Change

Today is the day. If you are struggling with a painful breakup, today is the day to start remembering who you were, before someone else damaged your sense of worth. Or perhaps you just, like the friend

I referenced earlier in the book, realize you want a totally different future than your ex. Whatever the pain, know this: You are at the cross in the road. Which way should you go? You must choose one of two pains. The pain of discipline and taking the best long-term avenue of life. Or, the path of having another painful regret down the road, because you made another poor decision, while you were already knocked down and weak. I used to coin the phrase that I was, "Tired of being a penny waiting for change." Think about that. Have you ever received any change for a penny? Of course not.

Set higher standards for yourself. When I finally did this, I allowed my own conscience to guide me, and I remained true to my personal values. There is nothing wrong with wanting the best for yourself. Just because you set high standards does not mean the other person is "bad." I believe in the adage that there is someone for everyone. Because your ex is not *your* match does not mean they are not a match for someone else. Remember my friend whose ex didn't want children? He went on to marry a woman who did not want children and who did want to travel the world. My homebody friend married someone from a broken home—which made him value family even *more*, and they went on to have kids and happily love each other, still all these years later.

For those coming out of a toxic rainstorm of a relationship—dry off. Just in case you have forgotten today: You matter. You are worthy. You are enough. You will weather this storm. You will emerge a stronger and healthier person.

Take all the time that you need in your recovery process. You need to heal emotionally. Moving on will take more than a day, and more than a week. Direction is more important than speed. It takes a lot of little steps to be able to break free of your broken self. It is important to know that this is very normal. You are not alone in your quest to quickly get past this pain. But when God designed your life, it wasn't dependent on your being perfect. Your mistakes are not a surprise to him. You are on a journey. Try to enjoy the ups and downs of this life, because your time here is very limited. The seeds have already been planted for you to have a better life ahead, full of happiness, laughter, and love. Don't miss it, because you were preoccupied with rushing this step. Don't miss it, because you made important decisions too rashly, after a divorce or breakup.

I have another friend who got divorced and rushed into a relationship before the ink was even dry on her separation agreement. A wise friend of hers advised, "Take your time, or you may get yourself into another long-term relationship that will require extrication. Discover who you are and what you want first."

Remember: Many lessons in life are difficult, before they are easy. It is a progression, and you will eventually reach your emotional goals. There is no one *giant* step that does it. It will take a lot of tiny steps to get back on track again. You will not even realize the strides you are making day to day. However, when you look back after a month, and a year, you will see the enormous changes you have made. Never sacrifice your long-term gain because you do not want to work through your short-term pain. Most of you will begin to find glimmers of pleasure and meaning in your lives by six months after a loss—some sooner—some a little longer. Either way, there are better days ahead. This, I promise you. So, have faith and believe in yourself. Time does heal wounds.

Last thought: The enemy always fights the hardest, when they know that the Universe has something great in store for you.

> *Never allow someone to be your priority while allowing yourself to be their option.*
>
> **—Mark Twain**

> *Mountains know the secrets we need to learn. It might take time, and it might be hard, but if you just hold on long enough, you will find the strength to rise.*
>
> **—Tyler Knott Gregson**

Stages of Recovery—Take Comfort in Your Pain: It Breaks My Heart to See You Suffering

My Story

For many of my breakups, we would go back-and-forth on breaking up and staying together. The reason for this was simple. Nobody likes pain or the feeling of rejection, and I was no different. Many people also do not like change. I know I don't. I am a "creature of habit" in everything that I do. But, towards each final breakup, or the true end of my relationships, I realized that I was either unhappy, or pretending to be happy. I also came to the painstaking realization that my partner didn't truly love me, or I did not truly love my partner—or both. Initially, I did not accept this, but I did comprehend it.

I can remember crying for what felt like the entire day. Every moment felt like an eternity. I hated the weekends. Because I wasn't pre-occupied with work, I had more time to feel sorry for myself. I recall feeling like Muhammad Ali was punching me in the gut, all day—every day. I also recall that every time my telephone rang, I would pray that it was my ex-husband. And when it was anyone else on the other end of my telephone, I would instantly get upset and feel more depressed than I was before. This one-sided phenomenon changes over time. With each day of "no contact," you heal. Time is a great and wonderful healer. Unfortunately, you cannot rush this step.

My Life Lesson

Rejection is sometimes more difficult than death, because in death you are not rejected. I overextended my stay in relationships because I had invested time, energy, and love into building this happy and loving relationship. I also got to know my partner's family and friends, and it was all intermingled, making it more difficult to break away. Also, my boyfriends and/or husbands were also my friends. So that at least provided me with someone to talk to, socialize and do things with, especially because many of our friends were couples. So, not only was I losing a romantic relationship, but I was losing a confidant and anchor in life. That is precisely why I found this to be one of the hardest things that I have ever endured and overcome in my life.

Really pay attention to this next sentence. If a person no longer loves you, you cannot force them to. It does not matter how hard you try, or how muscular, skinny, pretty, handsome, wealthy, nice, giving, understanding, etc., you are. Beauty is in the eye of the beholder, and you cannot force love. It is important to keep sight of the fact that a good marriage takes two responsible adults who are both willing to still be together.

When you finally realize that you are worth more than settling on a mediocre relationship, then you will begin the road to recovery. You will begin to separate yourself from any mismatched partners. You will make the tough decisions that will help you become happy again.

A clear rejection is always better than a fake promise.

The Cold Hard Truth Is That Emotional Pain Is Difficult...Don't Mask It

Pain in this life is not avoidable, but the pain we create avoiding pain is avoidable.

—R.D. Laing, M.D.

My Story

My broken relationships have helped me become more compassionate to another's pain. Emotional discomfort won't kill you. It is what you do to avoid that pain that might harm or even kill you. And it will most definitely hinder your progress, on your road to joy.

Because you may be feeling pain in the very core of your being, you may be tempted to seek comfort, or mask your pain by numbing yourself. When I could not find a deeper sense of meaning, I would distract myself with some other pleasure. Some people try to cover their pain with alcohol, smoking, vaping, sleeping pills, gambling, random sex, or illicit substances. These choices could lead to even worse problems of addiction or even death. Active addiction has been described to me as "hell on earth". One former crack addict told me, "My drug addiction makes me feel like I am stumbling through life, constantly craving and suffering, while feeling completely numb." He went on to say, "I feel invisible to everyone in the outside world—like nobody even cares that I exist." You must surround yourself with healthy people. So, resist these other tempting choices, and persist in allowing your true pain to surface. Like so many of life's other challenges, experiencing and overcoming this pain could possibly reveal emotional depths and new perspectives that you never knew you were capable of.

Also, remember not to move too swiftly into a new relationship, and begin to separate your life from your ex's life. Make a pact with yourself to deal with the pain of your old relationship, before moving onto another one. This is called "facing reality." It is not always pleasant, but in the end, the trip will be worth the bumpy ride.

My Life Lesson

With me, sometimes everything would hit me all at once. I was up one day, and down the next. I would seemingly have it all together on Monday, but by the time Friday rolled around, I didn't have a clue how I would get through the weekend. I would literally feel like I was taking one step forward, and three giant steps back. Sometimes I felt like I had to restart my wellness program one-hundred times, and I got frustrated. But I kept moving forward, one day at a time.

I never realized how much strength it would take to pull myself out of this dark mental place that I was dwelling. But I am also living proof that you can, and will, be happy again. And you will not be left empty-handed. You will emerge a stronger person, because you successfully overcame something, that was vowing to destroy you. You will also emerge as a new person, who knows their true worth. And that is empowering.

> *Find a place inside where there is joy, and the joy will burn out the pain.*
>
> —*Joseph Campbell*

Know When to Ask for Help

The first few moments, days, or weeks following a breakup can seem debilitating. For some, ending a relationship means a loss of their identity, support system, and feelings of normalcy. Ending a relationship—even a mismatched one, can be incredibly challenging and emotionally draining. However, you do not have to do it alone. Know when to seek support if you need it. If feelings of grief, shame, guilt, or other negative emotions persist and begin affecting your daily life after a relationship ends, consider finding a qualified therapist or counselor who can help you process and acknowledge your feelings in a healthy way. A qualified mental health professional can help you examine the past relationship in a safe place. You will be free of judgement, while you work toward achieving a more complete sense of yourself, after the relationship has ended. Even if you feel like there is no hope after severing an important tie in your life, remember you can heal and you deserve a healthy relationship that meets your needs and complements you and your happiness.

> *Someday you're gonna look back on this moment of your life as such a sweet time of grieving. You'll see that you were in mourning and your heart was broken, but your life was changing...*
>
> —*Elizabeth Gilbert*

My Steps and Phases of Recovery

Elisabeth Kubler-Ross was a Swiss-American psychiatrist who came up with a theory on how people process grief. Originally, this was applied mainly to death—what happens when someone we love dies, and how do we deal with it. But these stages also very clearly apply to the end of relationships and the way we process and work through these difficult times.

My Story

1. Denial: In this phase, my heart trumped all other reason, while I was attempting to reconcile the idea of life without my partner. Even though I knew that each of my former relationships were over, I really didn't want to believe it. Against the better judgment of everyone around me, I couldn't help but entertain thoughts of things somehow working out for me and many of my exes. Disbelief plagued my every thought. I was not thinking clearly. For example, my first ex-husband explicitly told me that he was never coming back. Yet I continued to see hidden glimmers of hope, even though it was obvious to him, and everyone else, that our relationship was permanently severed. Yes, this is the phase where we are most susceptible to late-night texting, crying, and pleading with whatever Higher Power you believe in. Denial is the worst kind of lie…because it is the lie that you are telling yourself. And, denying the truth does not change the facts.

2. Bargaining: After most of my breakups, because I was a broken woman *and* I did not know my own self-worth, I was extremely susceptible to this stage. Bargaining often goes together with denial. Even though I knew that some of my past relationships were not healthy, I was still desperate to find any possible way to make these relationships work. I tried both negotiation and manipulation to get some of them to stay. (That is something that I am not proud to admit.) For example, I promised my first ex-husband that I would change. I would try to guilt him into staying, by telling him that he was hurting the children, our family, and even our family pet, by leaving. And, of course, this phase is not only limited to bargaining with your ex. I was also busy pleading to God. From what I have read, many people bargain with "The Powers That Be," promising to be a better person if only the ex will come back. During this stage, you may take a new interest in astrology or tarot cards like I did, hoping to read about a forecasted reunion. Sadly, I remember reading my horoscope every day at lunch. I was hoping for any small sign that my life would be okay. Lastly, you may enlist your friends and family to "talk some sense" into your ex during this time. It has been said that bargaining has neither friends, nor relations.

3. Anger: In the beginning of my recovery, some of my anger helped me. I allowed anger to be my motivator. In a way, my anger became my own private counselor and personal trainer. Because I had so much anger and frustration pent up inside of me, I would go to the gym to escape and rid myself of these overpowering feelings. I wanted to look better, feel better, and be better—mostly to spite my ex. But, unknowingly, I was making myself stronger in this process, and I began to want to recover for myself. So, if this stage can motivate you to become a better person—let it!

Anger can also manifest in many negative ways. You will ask yourself these questions, repeatedly (and this is very normal!). "How could he or she do this to me?" And, "How can he or she be so selfish?" You may even feel anger at whatever Higher Power you believe in, or at the Universe in general. My self-talk would repeatedly ask these types of questions; "Why can't anything ever work out for me?" and, "Why am I cursed?" You will even feel anger towards people or situations, just because they are somehow associated with your ex-partner or ex-spouse. I felt like I needed answers, and I wanted to "pin" the blame on someone. So, I convinced myself that other people were part of the reason that my ex "changed." I even got upset at my family and friends when they didn't agree with my anger. I remember going through our mutual friend list and thinking to myself, "I cannot believe that so-and-so still wants to be friends with him after what he did to me!" This is the phase when we think it's a great idea to tell anyone and everyone what a psycho-crazy person our ex was. This is also when we think it's crucial to send our ex harsh emails and texts, because we don't want him or her to think that they got away with anything...or that we care. Oddly, when you respond in this manner, it is definitely telling your ex that you are not over them—not even close! Don't give them that satisfaction. In the end, I found out that these anger-motivated things I was doing were all a way to camouflage my own pain. Nonetheless, this is a stage that I went through.

Another thing to remember is that it is fine for anger to be a motivating force at the beginning of your breakup, but if you nurture anger, indulge it, and so on, eventually it will be toxic. It won't help you and will instead fester and harm you, like an infected cut. Anger doesn't solve anything. Anger doesn't build anything. But...it can destroy everything.

4. Depression: Depression, like anger, festered and surfaced in many different forms for me. First, I felt tired all the time. I had to pry myself out of bed on the weekends. I remember not wanting to do anything but lay around without even showering. All this did was aggravate my feelings of being disconnected from people. Even when I was with my family and friends, I was on the verge of tears most of the time. My poor family and friends had to suffer with me. I had trouble sleeping at night, because my mind was always racing. I began to drink, socially, on the weekends that my ex had custody of our two children. I never drank in excess, but a few Coors Lights would numb some of my pain. But, *alcohol* is a *depressant,* which means it slows the function of the central nervous system. Alcohol blocks some of the messages trying to get to the brain. This alters a person's perceptions, emotions, movement, vision, and hearing. Alcohol was doing the opposite of what I wanted it to. I did not need to be indulging in any more "depressants."

It is hard for me to admit, but I also remember being sad and depressed, just by seeing other happy couples who were holding hands, laughing, kissing, or generally just having fun together. I thought I would never experience "that" connection again, and I yearned for it.

Hopelessness was the most pervasive and debilitating stage, for me personally. It is the one thing that led me to believe that nothing would ever, be or feel, different from how I felt then. Hopelessness makes it feel like you will never move on, and nothing will ever work out for you in the future. You will probably feel derailed, because your comfortable life was just uprooted. And your depression may try to convince you that you might never feel joyful again. This is not true. Do not buy into this garbage! Ultimately, depression will set you on a quest for something more—for love, wisdom, and justice.

The vast majority of people who experience a loss can recover on their own. Generally, I had trouble eating and sleeping, reduced interest in my daily routines, sadness, guilt, and many tearful outbursts. All of these symptoms were pointing to signs of depression, which my therapist told me were simply part of my healthy grieving process. But, when should you seek help? You should talk with your doctor or mental health professional if you experience any of these symptoms of bereavement-related depression: suicidal thoughts, persistent feelings of worthlessness, hopelessness, helplessness, ongoing guilt, marked mental and physical sluggishness, persistent trouble functioning, numbness, detachment, or you experience hallucinations. There is nothing shameful about seeking help. We all grieve differently. Everyone, no matter how big and strong, needs support sometimes. So, don't be afraid to ask for help when you need it. The National Suicide Prevention Lifeline is: USA 1-(800)-273-TALK (8255). This telephone number will provide you with 24/7 free and confidential support. Or, you can call 911 for emergencies in the United States.

5. Acceptance: Finally, this is the phase that we can make peace with our loss. In the beginning for me, acceptance was the art of mastering my energy and emotions, even when I was still restricted with pain. Acceptance did not come suddenly for me. This was a gradual understanding that came little bit by little bit. Looking back now, I think that I had this phase interspersed with some of the other phases.

Sometimes acceptance won't come on strong and involve a big blow-out party. My acceptance took its good old time. It intersected with some of my lingering sadness. But this stage entails making peace with the loss. This means that you must let go of the relationship and slowly move forward with your life. Personally, I really did not feel like this phase would *ever* come. If you feel this way too, that only means that you are probably still struggling in an earlier phase. It took me approximately one full year to get to this stage. And then it took me a few more years to fully accept that I did not need someone else to complete me. But I did need to accept my part in the breakup, and I needed to accept (and forgive) both of us—for our shortcomings. I replaced my expectation with acceptance. When I did this, I was able to begin my new renewed life. Happiness can only exist in acceptance.

My Life Lesson

To heal takes time, and grief isn't conquered in a perfectly straight line. I suspect that everyone is a little bit different, but I believe that you will "zig and zag" through each of the phases that I did, to completely rebuild yourself.

I also learned that even on the weekends, I needed to get up early, make my bed, take a shower, get dressed, and put on makeup for the day. It helped me "get going" every morning. Lying in bed only exacerbated my depression symptoms. Get outside! Bask in that sun, which will also provide your body with much-needed vitamin D.

At the time of your breakup, you may swear off love altogether, like I initially did. You may tell yourself that you will never love again. You may also convince yourself that you could never love anyone as much as you did this person. You cannot even fathom your future, let alone having someone else in it. I won't lie to you. You will need to pull up your big-girl and big-boy pants and get on with the hard work of your personal steps to recovery. Keeping this in mind, you are also grieving. So, dammit, cut yourself some slack!

When you go through a divorce it's like a death of loved one, except there is no funeral, complete with a large gathering of loved ones, full of sympathy and concern, to help you. Even if you're the one who initiated the divorce, you will still grieve. This is because you are not only mourning the loss of your marriage, you are also grieving the loss of your hopes and dreams, and what you thought your life was going to look like.

And you may be hesitant going forward into a new relationship. But, in time, as you heal, you will rebuild trust again with someone else if you want or desire to delve into another relationship. But if you do, the next person may not be your end-all, be-all. So, if you are aching right now, the pain will subside. And in time, the pain will be gone. You will feel all those highs again, that come from knowing and loving yourself and possibly a new love down the road. Most importantly, you will have a new and special relationship with your best friend. That best friend needs to be you! This is what will bring you peace, tranquility, and happiness. You will make a break-through, and when the timing is right for you to move forward, you will know. Beginning today, stop seeking out the storms and enjoy more fully the sunlight. Accentuate the positive and eliminate the negative, including any hurtful words that your ex may have spewed to you. Happiness is a result of you changing your frame of mind. In fact, happiness *is* a state of mind. Nobody else can make you happy. You will determine when you are willing to make a conscious decision to be happy again.

New beginnings are often disguised as painful endings. And, grief is like the ocean. It will come in different waves, ebbing and flowing. Sometimes you will feel overwhelmed, and sometimes you will feel calm. Either way, these are normal stages of recovering from your divorce.

The Lord is close to the brokenhearted and saves those who are crushed in spirit.

—Psalm 34:18

Use Me, But Don't Abuse Me: "Broken Wide Closed"

Real love begins, where nothing is expected in return.

My Story

A few short months before my first ex-husband moved out, I purchased a boat for "us". It was only in my name, because at the time, my work history was more consistent, and our home was only in my name, so I had collateral. My ex was also restarting a sole proprietorship. And because his business was new, it was more difficult for him to secure a loan. I wonder sometimes, if he knew then, that he was going to leave me. Because soon after I purchased the boat, he moved out. On reflection, I subconsciously felt uneasy about the state of our marriage. As a result, I made some foolish financial decisions. Shortly after he left me, I wondered why I didn't question this purchase or think about buying such an expensive item that I knew I would rarely use.

My Life Lesson

At this time, I had the good-paying job. I owned the house, which I purchased before we were married. And, out of my own frustration, I would admittedly throw these facts in his face, regularly. It was a cruel thing for me to do. I think it was a reaction to feeling inferior—being insulted. My parents used to tell my sister and me that when people feel inferior, they compensate in many ways. But one way is that they will diminish you, to make themselves feel bigger and better. One of my mother's favorite sayings is, "Blowing out someone else's candle, won't make yours shine any brighter." I suspect that this was my motive and my response for feeling used.

Looking back now, I also realize that part of my motivation behind purchasing the boat was to keep my husband from leaving me. I do not know what my ex was thinking or what his motivation was, but some people will only love you as much as they can use you. Their loyalty ends, where the benefits stop. You can see a person's true colors when you are no longer beneficial in their life. I was avoiding rejection at all cost; however, what I should have realized is that true love cannot be bought or sold. Do not allow anyone to use you for your "things", money, or what you can superficially provide to them.

Not everyone will appreciate what you do for them. You must figure out who is worth your kindness and who is just taking advantage of you.

Re-examine all you have been told. Dismiss what insults your soul.

—*Walt Whitman*

As I Was Recovering, I Still Suffered Vicariously Through My Children

My Story

My children were always my heart—and my weak spot. When they suffered, so did I. At one point, my ex sued me for custody—but I could very clearly show how involved a parent I was. I could name every teacher, every grade, their friends, their full medical history, their hobbies, their bedtime routine, their favorite foods—and the foods they hated.

I also documented every activity that my children missed out on, because of their father's schedule. He would rarely allow my children to participate in any activities during the nine-month boating season, if they were with him. This was because he owned a yacht in

Maryland, and he drove there every weekend, come hell or high water. Granted, it was an expensive monthly bill for him, that he paid twelve months of the year, but could only utilize it for nine months. At any rate, it didn't matter how nicely my children asked him. This caused my children (primarily my daughter) to miss many school dances, sporting events, friends' sleepovers, birthday parties, etc. My children could never make plans, because they knew their father would rarely stay back in their hometown for their activity, save the times that he stayed home because of our son's football games. But he rarely stayed in-state for any of my daughter's activities, parties, or requests. He would also not take my alternative offer to allow the child/children to stay with me, so that they did not miss out on a special event.

As I mentioned before, my view of having children was you move heaven and earth to make sure they are nurtured, cared for, and happy. There were numerous issues, which I will not go into because of privacy concerns, but I never felt that my ex-husband understood the need to keep my children's schedule. There were times when others noticed this disconnect—coaches, teachers, etc. But I felt that I needed to be one that provided our children with a sense of consistency.

Once, I had a close friend who was upset by his wife's clouded judgement, regarding putting their child first. When their son was about six years old, he had a big holiday event for his kindergarten class. My friend had packed a beautiful new outfit that he had purchased for him to wear, and he sent it with their son, to his mother's home. He explained to his ex-wife that this was the special outfit for their son's school Christmas show. Their son was young, and he was very enthusiastic about singing his Christmas songs, for both of his parents. He was also excited to don his new outfit. It was khaki pants, a light blue button-up collared shirt, with a dark blue sweater with a Christmas Bear on the front of it. Instead, his ex-wife sent him into school, in blue-jeans with a huge hole in the knee, that were way too tight and too short. I was at this Christmas show with our son, so I witnessed this firsthand. Their little boy was also wearing an over-sized tee-shirt, that had stains on it. You could tell that their son was extremely embarrassed, as he hid behind the other well-dressed and well-groomed children, as the kids sang for their parents. This should have been a wonderful experience for this small boy. But instead, he was so self-conscious and embarrassed, that he did not even sing the songs that he had practiced at home, repeatedly. Their son just wanted to shine in front of his parents, for ten minutes of his life. But this cherished moment was taken away from him. To make matters worse, his mother dropped him off at the school and immediately left. So, she was not even in the audience to support their son. And no matter how much his father tried to make things better and make excuses for his mother's absence, sometimes one parent cannot "fix" the pain, caused by the other one.

My Life Lesson

I believe that children should have the choice to be involved in at least some extra-curricular activities. Of course, this may not always be possible, due to financial restraints or work conflicts, other family parties or reunions, etc. But, when you can, I think this should be a priority for the parent. I believe that sports and other clubs provide children with a sense of belonging. It will also benefit their physical health, and they will learn more about discipline, time-management, getting along with other people, and working together. It will also foster their social life and mental health. So—let your children be involved. Let your children cultivate friendships. This time in their lives will be over in a blink of an eye, so make their school performances, dances, etc., special and important to you. Make these occasional-milestones ones that they will always cherish and remember, versus just experiencing regret over missing them.

It is also equally important to prioritize, plan, and maintain a schedule for your children. And, pickup and drop-off exchange times should be strictly adhered to. I think that children crave structure.

I learned that from great suffering, comes great triumph and love. I found out the lengths that I would go through for the safety, security, and happiness of my children. Most parents will do just about any-thing to protect and include their children.

You define what is important to you, by what you dedicate your time to. Injustice casts a shadow that could last a lifetime. Intervene. Get help. Seek family counseling and therapy if you realize there are issues of exclusion. If you are a parent, no matter how scary it might be, know you must fight for your children if need be. Children shouldn't have to sacrifice so that you can have the life that you want.

> *Love yourself enough to create an environment in your life that is conducive to the nourishment of your personal growth. Allow yourself to let go of the people, thoughts, and situations that poison your well-being. Cultivate a vibrant surrounding and commit yourself to making choices that will help you release the greatest expression of your unique beauty and purpose.*
>
> **—Dr. Steve Maraboli**

10

Infidelity and Cheating: All My Loose Ends Tied into a Knot

Even though on the outside it often looks like things are falling apart on us, on the inside, where God is making a new life, not a day goes by without his unfolding grace.

—2 Corinthians 4:16

Infidelity is a poison. It rocks you to your core, so you don't know who to believe or trust, and whether to even trust your own eyes or your own heart. Sometimes, the cheated-on partner is truly "the last to know" because they themselves are trusting or even naïve. Other times, there is a nagging feeling that something is not quite right. Unfortunately, when we are in an unhealthy relationship, we often stop trusting our gut. We second-guess ourselves.

Have you ever been cheated on? Do you know someone who's been cheated on? Chances are, the answer is yes. Today, cheating is unfortunately more common than ever. With hookup apps like Tinder, other secret cell-phone apps, and online dating sites—it's never been easier to cheat and get away with it. It is estimated that between 30 to 60 percent of all married people in the U.S. cheat on their spouse, and this number is even higher for people who are dating.

Infidelity is truly one of the worst experiences in any long-term partnership, causing agony and heartbreak and cracking the very foundation of a marriage. Now that I am in a relationship of great trust, it amazes me that I accepted untrustworthy partners. But I had many lessons to learn.

My Story

Wade and I both know what it feels like to be cheated on. This is one of the worst things that you could ever do to another person. It makes you feel worthless, dirty, and rejected. This occurred to us in previous relationships—not naming names or the specific relationships. But this has left long-term emotional effects on both of us, especially because we never received any sort of therapy to help us through these periods.

And to be completely candid, mostly in my younger years, before marriage, I also hurt people with my own disloyalties. I am certainly not perfect—not by a long-shot, and these few indiscretions still bother me to this day. Granted, they were all at the bitter end of relationships that had overstayed their welcome. But—that certainly does not excuse my behavior. Consequently, I must live with my own demons.

But the trauma caused *to us* by infidelity would affect every relationship decision we made going forward, until we met one another. Oddly, we did not question them. Instead, we began to question ourselves, and our own flaws became exacerbated, amplified and magnified. Personally, I would question my physical appearance. Was I pretty enough? Was I thin enough? Was my hair long enough? But we needed to understand that when our exes were having affairs, they were trying to fulfill their own need for love—and sometimes this was a result of how we were interacting with them, and sometimes it had nothing to do with us.

Wade and I both continued to choose the wrong partners, to some extent, because of self-protective behaviors that we had developed from the aftermath of these betrayals. We had many sleepless nights, and we ultimately ended up subconsciously choosing spouses that we felt were "safe" bets, for our second marriages. Love played a very small role in our marital decisions. We wanted someone that we thought would be faithful, regardless of whether we felt like we were in love with them. This was another agonizing truth that took us a long time to understand.

In part, the trauma of infidelity stems from the fact that the betrayed partner is all too often blindsided by this bombshell. Even when I suspected something may have been going on, I was still overwhelmed upon learning the full extent of my partner's behavior.

Adding insult to injury, it was not just anyone who caused this pain, loss, and hurt. It was the one person in this world that I felt the closest to. This was the one person that I thought would always "have my back," in good times and in bad.

I remember in my past relationships coming home and seeing that my things—makeup and personal belongings—were moved in my bedroom. Or that I once found clothes that we not mine in amongst the dry-cleaning. I recall once going to a coffee shop with my partner, and the waitress acted surprised by me being with him—because my ex clearly brought another woman to the coffee shop as a regular.

However, my exes were always extremely convincing, and they would accuse me of "making things up in my head." I remember one of my ex partners telling me that he could never cheat on me, blah blah blah. Truth be told, I was not really in love with him, but I was scared to leave him for an unknown situation. Back then, I did not have nearly enough love or respect for myself. And, I certainly did not have enough trust in my own abilities to go through life alone. I did not see that my ex was a weight on my shoulders. And later, when it became time to move on from my marriages, I could not even see that me and my children would be better off living apart from them.

My Life Lesson

Nothing, not even threat of death, has ever been able to stop people from cheating on each other. Cheating has always been a fact of life. Even though we know this, some of us are still looking around for that forever person and making that commitment with people whose history proves them unlikely to stay monogamous.

For most people affected by romantic infidelity by a spouse, the pain stems from shattered trust of the person that is supposed to be closest to them. It is not so much the extramarital sex or affair itself that causes the deepest pain. For the one being cheated on, this experience of profound and unexpected emotional and physical betrayal can be incredibly traumatic. Some studies have shown that the stress that women and men undergo when they find out a spouse or partner has cheated on them, is characteristic of post-traumatic stress disorder. Luckily for me, when my fears were confirmed about my various partner's infidelities, I had already broken my emotional tether to them.

I will repeat this, because it is very important. Your intuition is frequently one of the best indicators that something is wrong. You should trust your intuition. Because, it is also quite typical for a questioning spouse to have had his or her reality denied for years, by the unfaithful partner who insists that he or she was not cheating. They will use every excuse in the book to cover up their infidelity. For me, I overlooked my various partners growing absences, and I made excuses for them being pre-occupied or when they were unreachable for hours, while "working late." I would also believe them when they told me they were taking large cash withdrawals from the ATM, to get a better handle on their monthly monetary budgets. I noticed that our emotional and physical intimacy had faded, but I wrote that off to our busy schedules. I did not want to hear them when, on occasion, they would say that they "loved me—but were not in love with me." And, I certainly did not want to admit that anything was wrong when there was a sudden need for privacy, carried out by putting locks on their desk and password protectors on their computers and cell-phones. I also convinced myself that my own fears and suspicions were ridiculous and unfounded, even when they completely altered their work schedule, grooming habits, wardrobe, and suddenly become obsessed with a new exercise regime. *Please note that your significant other could display all these signs and still not be cheating. Only you know the true inner-workings of your relationship.*

One ex insisted that he was not acting any differently and that I was being "paranoid, mistrustful, and unfair." In this way, betrayed partners are made to feel as if *they* are the problem, as if *their emotional instability* is the issue, and they blame themselves. When your spouse or partner is armed with such elaborate and well-planned webs of lies and well-crafted defenses, you will eventually begin to doubt yourself. You will call into question your own intuition, because your thoughts and emotions are denied at every corner. This is all done, of course, so that your partner can continue cheating.

If you learn that your partner has cheated on you, I would strongly suggest that you do not keep that information inside. If you are not comfortable confronting your partner, then talk to a trusted friend, family member, pastor, or a therapist. Don't sit there alone with your fears and unsettled feelings. Reach out and find empathetic support. Just because someone has cheated on you, does not mean you are a fool. It just means that you trusted someone much more than they deserved.

It has been said that the adverse effects of a partner's betrayal can last over a year. Therefore, it is so important, not to jump right into another relationship if infidelity was the cause of your breakup. Neither Wade nor I heeded this advice. We did not wait, even against the advice of our parents and friends. We jumped into other relationships. And it is no surprise that these relationships were doomed from the beginning. We were both still feeling insecure, angry, hurt, betrayed, mistrustful, and lost. Because we were on this emotional roller-coaster, we were certainly in no position to jump tracks and choose another partner to date.

Like everything else that I discuss in my book, you can heal from the trauma of a cheating spouse or partner. Unfortunately, many betrayed spouses, despite the hurt and anger they feel, resent the idea that they might need help to deal with their feelings. Wade and I both felt like it was others' fault for cheating, so we convinced ourselves that we did not require any therapy. After all, they were the ones in the wrong, and they caused the hurt and pain, so "Let him/her get the help!" Instead, we would strongly urge you to seek help from a professional, immediately.

Learn to love yourself. You are no one's second choice. Do not give your love to someone who won't appreciate and honor it. Raise your standards. Most importantly, if someone continues to be disloyal to you, don't keep inviting that hurt back into your life. All it will do is get you heartache, loneliness, and grief.

A lot of marriages continue after the upheaval of an affair, although forty-percent of men and women admit that they are not on good terms with their spouses. You cannot change other people. Even if they appear to behave differently, many times it will not have staying power. Most people will go back to who they were *before* you tried to change them. Only time will tell. Remember that you can only change your own circumstances and yourself. You cannot "will" someone else to become faithful. And never underestimate another person's ability to make you feel guilty for *their* mistakes. Don't fall for their myriad of excuses. If you have decided to seek counseling for the indiscretion, and the mistreatment or cheating continues…have the strength to walk away.

All that is secret will eventually be brought into the open, and everything that is concealed will be brought to light and made known to all.

—Luke 8:17

Don't spend time beating on a wall, hoping it will transform into a door.

—Coco Chanel

11

Why Do We Stay in Abusive Relationships? Close the Gap Between Your Heart and Your Mind and Break Free of Your Broken Self

Never forget that once upon a time, in an unguarded moment, you recognized yourself as a friend.

—Elizabeth Gilbert

My Story

Why do good people stay in bad relationships? The answer to that question will be as varied as the people soul searching that very idea. I can share my story—and you may recognize bits and pieces of it. However, every person reading this book must answer that question for themselves. Once you discern the answer, you can go about healing, so you don't make that same mistake again.

You may be wondering why both Wade and I stayed in many of our unhealthy relationships for so long. There is no simple answer. When I began to really contemplate each of my former relationships, I realized that it was the sum-total of many reasons. It is quite complex. Each person may have several reasons, or varying degrees of motives.

I convinced myself that my first reason for staying was a practical one. I see now that it was probably just irrational thinking on my part. At the time, I felt that I was stuck in my relationship and could not leave because we economically depended on two incomes, not one. If it was only me, I would not have placed so much emphasis on this motive, because I earned a very competitive salary. But I had a four-year-old daughter and a newborn son to think about.

Admittedly, although I have not always attended Mass regularly, I have always considered myself to be a highly spiritual person, and I have felt God's intervention throughout my life. So, I know he is there. And I know he is listening. So, part of the reason that I did not want to get a divorce was because of my religious beliefs. In my church, I would no longer be able to receive the host during communion. I was told that I could get an annulment to resolve that issue. However, an annulment is a process that dissolves a couple's marriage in the eyes of the church. It restores a couple's status to how it was prior to the marriage, as though it had never taken place. An annulment treats the marriage as though it never existed. And I had two children born of this union. So, I felt that obtaining an annulment would be like saying that my children were not born out of love. This was just my own personal belief. Many people that I admire, respect, and who have children, have gotten annulments.

I also began to worry about the social stigma of being divorced. I was ashamed of my failure, and I felt like I would never again be worthy of love. And, I was deeply afraid of the thought of having to start my life over again, and I did not want to navigate it alone.

My mind was playing tricks on me too. I was rationalizing that staying in my marriage would be better for my two children. Wade told me that he did the same thing. We both overstayed our welcome, in large part, because of this guilt. We thought it was the right and moral thing to do for our children. What we failed to see is that sometimes the best reason to let go of an incompatible relationship is because your child or children are watching. Wade and I both agree that if it was just us (no children), we would have summoned the courage to leave our respective marriages, much sooner. Thoughts plagued our weary minds that our children would be better off coming from an intact home, rather than from a divided one. This was not sensible reasoning for Wade or me, mostly because of the many arguments and outbursts that continually ensued in both households.

But that is not to say that this isn't true for some families and some households. I would recommend getting family counseling before any decision is made to separate a family with children, no matter their age. Deep down, I knew that getting my children away from a volatile situation, and raising them as a single mother, was far better than the option to stay. In addition, all parents want their kids to find "the One." We want to mirror what our kids should be seeking in a relationship. Wade and I mirror that now. There is visible love and affection, handholding, and healthy conflict resolution. But previously our children did not see that in the houses they grew up in. However, regardless of whether our justifications were misguided, the belief that those justifications are true is sometimes more powerful than whether or not they really are.

Another deeper layer of why some people stay in the wrong marriages is the so-called "cycle of abuse." You are in the middle of an internal and external war. It is a two-front battle, between your own limitations and a fight to try to hold onto your dream of a good relationship and a harmonious family.

In a typical instance of domestic abuse, where one partner is abusive towards the other, it is said that abuse tends to occur periodically (cyclically), rather than constantly (all the time). There is no clear beginning of manipulation, and it arbitrarily and progressively worsens over time. Each time there is usually some "trigger point" or event that occurs, to set the outburst into motion. Sometimes this event is not even real. It is imagined or spun, by either person. But whether it was real or imagined, the result is frequently irritation and anger.

For many, the antagonism can appear in many ways. Sometimes, abuse can be verbal, physical—or emotional overload. I have read that many times the aggressor will either force sex on their spouse or withhold it. I was on the side of being alienated, left alone, deserted, and made to feel unloved and unworthy of sex. Here is the big problem: Shortly after the incensed event stops, the abuser usually expresses some sign of remorse or guilt, in a futile attempt for your "forgiveness."

If we were under constant siege, it would have been easy to leave because none of us are meant to withstand long bouts of abuse. We are emotional beings who need love and affection to thrive. Most of the time the aggressor will vow to never allow this to happen again. But we are many times enticed by the age-old "makeup sex," and so we convince ourselves that we are loved once again. And then things seem to be back on track—temporarily.

For Wade and me, our situations left us walking on eggshells, many times because of our own insecurities. Affection and sex were not a big part of our prior lives. I know I "settled" for whatever crumbs of affection were given to me. In my case, I continued to fool myself, because my exes also had many redeeming qualities. Granted, in many of my past relationships, these characteristics were not revealed to me very often, but when they were, I was pulled back into the relationship... hook, line, and sinker.

For example, at the christening of our baby boy, Savino, Anthony gave a very endearing speech about me. It left my cousins, who only knew Anthony superficially, in tears. People that only knew us as a couple, from the outside, thought we had a solid and even loving marriage. Anthony always rose to the occasion in public. I suppose, much like me, he did not want his persona, or his public marriage and family image tarnished. But this is how a wrong marriage can appear good to the outside world. *Only* the two people in the relationship really know all the salacious details.

At this time, my life consisted of only high-highs and low-lows. There was no middle ground, so I never felt like I could catch my breath, and I always felt off-balanced and on the defensive. My emotional state was always on high alert, because I never knew whether it was going to be a good day or a bad day. Looking back now, *my* uncertainty probably heightened many of our arguments. To this day, I don't believe that his entire speech was disingenuous, because I was able to see the good side of him. He said things like, "I love my wife more than anyone in this world, and she went through life-threatening months of her pregnancy to ensure the safe delivery of our son." And, "I will love her forever for her sacrifice to our family." Moments like this, that were few and far between, kept me in this cycle of deceptive love.

My Life Lesson

Inevitably, in truly unhealthy relationships, the calm periods always end, with the beginning of another cycle of abuse. Again, the user feels angry, disrespected, or treated poorly in some way, starting the cycle all over again. The abuser will never be satisfied, no matter how pretty or handsome you are, how much you do for them, how much you do for the children, how much money you bring into the marriage, etc. This list goes on and on (and on). It will be an endless well of giving on your part, and an endless taking on the part of the abuser. Therefore, it works quite well for them. *You give. They take.* Repeat this cycle, over and over again, until you are so worn down that you literally have zero self-worth. In the end, sometimes the person who tries to keep everyone happy is the loneliest and most exhausted person in the world. And it is when your guard is down, that you could relapse into allowing other people to get comfortable disrespecting you.

You must stop using your guilt and pain as a badge of honor. You are not alone. Many other people have felt (and are feeling) just like you do right now. I remember feeling that I somehow deserved what happened to me. That was not true for me, and it is not true for you.

So, stop carrying this ancient useless guilt around with you. Unpack it! What are you waiting for?

Some people are motivated to generate validations about their respective spouses, because they desperately want to believe that each argument is a "one-time" thing, even when they know it isn't. Because if it was an isolated incident—things would eventually get better. Wade and I tended to look through rose-colored glasses, and we focused on the few good aspects of the relationships. We convinced ourselves that our relationships were good, and that everyone has relationships chock-full of issues, stress, and problems. We were not emotionally equipped to see the truth about our prior respective relationships. I know now that I stayed in some of my relationships *only* because I was clinging to the past. I needed to judge my relationships based on how we *actually* interacted, rather than relying on a glorified and false portrait—one that I so desperately wanted to paint.

It is not uncommon for family and friends to believe your significant other is great, because of what they perceive from the outside. This is wonderful, if they are a great person. But if not, this misconception may be something that you have to deal with. A close friend of mine even had her own parents take the side of her ex-husband, when they divorced. They were so convinced that he was a great person—they could not get past their own lack of discernment, to see the truth. Remember that perception is not always reality. And people in the peripheral, may fall victim to your ex-partner's façade.

Wade and I had fooled much of the outside world, and others perceived that our past relationships were at least good enough—or even loving. Worse, we had fooled ourselves, because we had very low self-esteem. So, the irrational thoughts such as, "I don't deserve any better" were glazed over in our minds.

Deceit is the false road to happiness; and all the joys we travel through to vice, like fairy banquets, vanish when we touch them.

—Aaron Hill

And the very hairs on your head are all numbered. So, don't be afraid; you are more valuable to God than a whole flock of sparrows.

—Luke 12:7

12

Feeling Helpless and Sunk Beneath Love's Weight: Addicted to the Wrong Love

"It was a mistake," you said. But the cruel thing was, it felt like the mistake was mine, for trusting you.

—David Levithan

As I wrote previously, the only two people who know what is going on in a marriage are those very two people. I think from the outside, my marriages looked one way. But trapped inside it was very different. I felt like I was in one of those funhouse mazes—only it was anything but fun. It was disorienting, each time I made a turn, or looked one place or the other, the funhouse glass was distorted, and I did not know what to believe.

My Story

In my first home, there was constant yelling. My ex would yell at me for any and everything. And, admittedly, I would yell back. We were the stereotypical "hot-headed Italians." We got to the point where neither one of us could control our verbal outbursts. I remember him throwing things—at *me*, at the wall. I felt like he was a volcano—and at any moment, for any reason, he could erupt.

When I was going through group therapy, I learned that frightening verbal, emotional, and physical abuse is going on behind closed doors all around us. I found myself feeling less frightened, and feeling stronger, as I learned I was not alone. One woman in my group told this next story. It will be forever etched in the recesses of my mind, because I was so disturbed by it.

She vividly recollected that during an argument with her ex-husband—it escalated. She explicitly recalled a time when her ex-husband and she got into an argument coming home from a wedding. He was upset because she was tired. She revealed to us that she was sick and almost seven months pregnant, so she asked him to leave the reception early. She told us that he was pissed. Once they were in his car, the argument escalated, and he began speeding and swerving in-and-out of traffic. She said that she was afraid for herself and their unborn child. So, she begged him to slow down. He slammed on the brakes and pulled over to the side of the highway. He screamed at her, "Get out!" She did as she was commanded. It was dark outside and pouring down rain. They were at least three miles from their house. She described the horror of getting her pregnant body over the cement median and crossing over two lanes of traffic coming in the opposite direction. Visibility was very poor this night. One man stopped to help her. And she described the horrified look on his face, as he realized that she was extremely pregnant and out in the rainstorm alone, at night. Ultimately, she passed on the Good Samaritan's offer of assistance because she did not know him. She explained to our group that the known path to get home, albeit precarious, was better than risking the unknown. By the time that she reached her home, she was soaked and exhausted. And when she arrived there, the doors were all locked. She did not have a key; after all, she had left with her husband, who did have the house key. She also did not have a cell phone. So, she sat outside for hours, crying and begging, into the damp night air for mercy. She revealed to us that it was many hours before her ex-husband finally let her into their home.

This lady went on to explain that her ex-husband would do this same exact thing to his own mother, when she "got on his nerves." She explained that his mother was extremely fearful of driving on highways. And her mother-in-law would wince when her son would speed around cars, in erratic lane-changes. She told us that it bothered him when his mother would voice her fears and concern when he was driving. So, in response to this, he once dumped his own mother out in a sketchy suburb of Pittsburgh, for her to navigate her way home, with no money and no cell phone.

But these are just a couple of stories. Sadly, you need only watch the news or browse a news site to see countless examples of unhealthy relationships that end in tragedy. If you met me, I suspect that you may not think I am the type of woman you'd expect to be involved in an unhealthy relationship. I have held a management position in the corporate business world for the past twenty years. I am extremely assertive at my job, and I am very competent at how I earn my living. Yet, I became a prisoner in my personal life, and I felt trapped in a relationship that was not healthy. It can happen to anyone, regardless of your color, race, gender, sexual preferences, religious background, economic background, etc.

People who knew me superficially would think, "She seems so powerful. Surely, she has the strength and resolve to leave him, especially because she is not dependent on him financially." But toxic relationships are hewn from all walks of life. Again, this is important enough to reiterate it. There is no discrimination. You can be targeted if you are rich or poor, educated or non-educated, female or male, straight or gay, strong or weak, or any ethnicity or religious affiliation. Therefore, the person stuck in the cycle of abuse is not always what we perceive as fragile or powerless.

My Life Lesson

People tend to think that a person being abused or mistreated could just make the "easy decision" to leave. They erroneously believe that you are choosing to stay with an abuser for some reason. They cannot reconcile their vision of a strong and powerful person being powerless to leave a bad situation. Many people get blamed for staying. There is a shared confusion in society about this issue, and that compounds the problem. But the truth is that we have yet, as a society, to come to terms with the dynamics of abuse.

It does not matter if your partner makes you out to be the "bad guy," just because you walked away from their mistreatment and drama. Let them deal with what they have created. Be at peace with yourself, and continue to avoid conflict. It is almost always the person with the dirty hands that is pointing their righteous fingers at another.

Had I listened to my parents, before I got married, or had I taken my own advice, I could have avoided a lot of pain, for both myself and many of my previous partners. Like a thunderstorm, it started with low rumbling, but my life ended in total devastation. My first marriage started out mediocre at best and went downhill quickly. My second marriage started off strong, but it also suffered a slow downward spiral. Many wrong marriages can have the propensity to escalate into both physical and emotional abuse. So, if a relationship does not nourish your soul…let it go. Life is about balance. Be kind, but do not allow others to misuse you. Trust, but don't get deceived. Be content, but never stop believing in yourself and what you deserve. And realize, there is always a way to happiness—if you are committed to it.

Abuse victims do not stay for the pain. They stay for the "idea of love." Or, they stay, because they are afraid to leave. Or, their self-esteem is so damaged that they are not thinking clearly—so they stay.

Looking back, I do not believe that I was ever in love with Anthony. I was in love with the idea of being in love. I was in love with the idea of feeling that warmth and excitement that *should* be associated with true love.

The thing is to free one's self: to let it find its dimensions, not be impeded.

—*Virginia Woolf*

Low Self-Esteem:
You Are Not Damaged Goods

My Story

I suffered from immeasurable worry and sadness. I worried that I would never find love again. I did not want to be alone forever. I felt that I had so much love to give, but it was not being accepted, or reciprocated, by my partners. In fact, I knew that my partners did not really know me, much less love me. I also believed that I was "damaged goods." Many people in this situation have expressed that they believed that they did not deserve any better than to be continually degraded and told they were worthless, useless, and never doing enough. I, too, did not think that I deserved a better relationship. Instinctively people know that they must break away and find a new safe haven—but that is easier said than done. The way that many people are barely living…should never be a viable option.

My Life Lesson

For some people who do not break away from abusive partners, they may find that abuse escalates to dangerous proportions. Abusive partners may stalk victims who try to leave them, beat them severely, or otherwise attempt to control their ability to exit the relationship. If they don't threaten to kill or harm the victim or the children, they may threaten to harm themselves, and by so doing, guilt the victim into feeling sympathy for them. And then they may stay to prevent the threatened suicide from happening. So, if you are in this type of abusive relationship, you need to get both the law involved and any community outreach programs available to you.

The bottom line is that usually the combination of low self-esteem, with the intermittent positive attention (often in the wake of an argument), fear, and disguised manipulation, convinces many victims to stay put. And, every time a victim forgives an abuser, that abuser is reinforced for being abusive, and it becomes that much more likely that the enraged person will become abusive again in the future. The net effect is that the abuse tends to continue forever, until the victim finds the courage to leave or is abused to death (e.g., murdered, in the most serious, violent cases). This truth is frequently lost on both the abuser and the victim.

During my breakup recoveries, I spent a lot of time shrouded in a dark sadness. But I realized that there is a sacredness in tears. They are not a mark of weakness but a symbol of strength and change. Only people who can love deeply can also suffer great sorrow. Grief will eventually lead us to the pathway of healing. And when I began to heal, I realized that it is not what you *are* that is holding you back. Rather, it is what you think you are *not* that is your worst obstacle.

And through counseling, I was taught that old wounds sometimes take a very long time to heal. The hurt must be exposed again and again, to get any effective resolution. But, as with anything in life, if you work at it hard and long enough, you will bear the fruits of your labor in a healthier you. You will expose your wounds, clean them, and finally let them heal.

> *You are not what others think you are. You are what God knows you are.*
>
> **—Shannon L. Alder**

> *Never bend your head. Hold it high. Look the world straight in the eye.*
>
> **—Helen Keller**

The Straw that Breaks the Camel's Back

My Story

Many relationships end with what I will call the "boiling point" or "trigger incident"—that one final act or incident that finally causes the relationship to implode. This occurred to me—and it's a common phenomenon. For years in these marriages, the pot had been quaking, steaming, and boiling over. This unstable setting occurs, until one isolated incident blows the lid off, and it forces the breakup, which was inevitable. I never had the courage to initiate either of my divorces. And for many others, it is basically decided for them. For some, it is initiated because the police respond after an altercation. For others, they may literally catch a spouse "in the act" of cheating. And many others are prompted after public altercations, where words yelled could never be taken back. In still other cases, there is simply a breaking point, and only the person who reaches that point knows what it is. For example, I know someone whose husband constantly belittled and put her down. She accepted his insults, how he criticized her appearance, her parents, and even mocked her in public. Until the day he told her she was a "lousy mother." For her, devoted to her child, that was the straw that broke the proverbial camel's back. She could not forgive that remark as she had forgiven countless other insults. As she said, "Tell me I am a terrible cook, that I need to lose twenty pounds, you name it. But do not tell me I am not a good mom."

My Life Lesson

If you know that your relationship is way past the point of reconciliation, it may be time, with support and counseling, to make the break. You have so much more life left to live. Grab your happiness! In both Wade's and my scenarios, there were plenty of warning signs and foreshadowing of dismal things to come. So, before something worse or ominous occurs to you, try to end your bad relationship. If you initiate things while both people are still calm, you may avoid additional pain of your pot boiling over like we experienced.

Where Did My Self-Esteem Go? Crumbs of Love

The worst loneliness is not to be comfortable with yourself.

—*Mark Twain*

My Story

My current husband, Wade, is the "All-American" man. He has defined good looks, with an athletic stature at six feet tall, weighing in at 225 pounds, which is pure muscle. He is extremely intelligent, likeable, charming, witty, kind, and he has a very giving nature. Yet, he was very insecure in relationships. In everything else in life, he is extremely confident. However, when it came to standing-up for himself in a relationship, he was incapable.

So, this man who had it all, felt like he was drowning most of his adult life. He describes it as always feeling like he was at the crossroads of numb and lonely. He never had or experienced real, reciprocating love. Wade said that when he would return home after a long day at school or work, he felt like he was facing defeat instead of victory. He was not immune to the other person's unhappiness, and this only fueled his thoughts that he was a failure, especially because his entire goal was to make his significant other happy. He felt overwhelmed and exhausted most of the time, in trying to please his various partners, and he felt powerless to get what he needed. He was so tired and alone that he admittedly began to have clouded judgment, regarding personal decisions. He was not thinking clearly. He describes it to me as being so overwhelmed that he was literally "out of decision-making ability."

I had the exact same insecurities, frustrations, and self-loathing.

Sadly, many people took advantage of this flaw. We were visibly "love-starved." Day-to-day chores, responsibilities, and niceties became expected by some of our partners, rather than appreciated. We just wanted to be accepted and loved, even though others in our lives may not have been able, or willing, to reciprocate it. Regardless, we dutifully fulfilled our "roles" that we thought we were supposed to be playing. This scenario is not fair to either partner. This type of relationship eventually results in one-sidedness and a wide cavern of pain.

Wade and I have talked many hours about how we accepted these little parcels or "crumbs" of love and acceptance from our exes. When you begin this type of justification, it is your own insecurities rearing their ugly head. We rationalized that this made all the rest of the time spent with our ex-partners okay.

Wade and I had a myriad of low-self-esteem issues that kept us paralyzed and willing to accept something that was merely "good enough." We both lost our personal self-worth (in relationships) in our early years, probably in high school or college. We were forever scarred from prior relationships that included painful infidelities. Our subconscious minds took over and told us that this is all that we deserved. And, because we were so hurt in the past, we both chose "a safe love" in our second marriages. We did this to avoid getting hurt. We thought that being "in love" was not paramount or critical to our marriages. We were looking for companionship, and we were looking for someone who would not hurt us. This path did not work out for us either. You must be *in love* with the person that you spend the rest of your life with. Mediocrity will not last. So, we found ourselves back in another unfulfilling relationship. How terrible to be called attractive, smart, and strong, but end up being alone every night.

We used to crave "acceptance" from our partners. We needed to feel appreciated and loved in order to thrive. But the harder we tried to please our partners, the more we seemed to be looking from the outside in. We not only didn't know ourselves anymore, but our exes had even less of an idea of who we truly were.

My Life Lesson

Never waste your time trying to explain yourself, or who you are, to people who are explicitly committed to misunderstanding you. If you get to this point, *you are out of decision-making ability.* Therefore, you will allow people to manipulate you. For Wade, he once allowed a girlfriend to move into his home because she seemed to offer a tiny morsel of help. Admittedly, he was so overrun, that he took that small offering over his own long-term happiness. Trust me. It is much easier to get rid of a mismatched mate now, versus trying to get them to move out later, or worse...you marry them. Then, the breakup is exponentially more difficult. And, you will avoid the emotionless abyss that will follow you around (day-to-day) during this type of relationship. This is a one-sided relationship. One person gives. The other person takes.

If things are bad a large percentage of the time, for an extended period, you cannot "will" things to get better. We both kept thinking that our partners would go back to who we "thought" they were in the very beginning stages of our respective relationships. We were so desperate to avoid being alone, that we did not even know the people that we professed our love and devotion to. And, they did not know us. Later in life, when we were unhappy in our partner-relationships, we discovered that we *were* always happy around our children. So, this is where we placed our focus. Our children were like boomerangs. We would give our unconditional love to them, and they would return it. So, we focused most of our time and attention there. But children grow up, and though you can remain close, it is not their role to be your primary relationship.

I cannot say this enough: the kindest thing that Anthony ever did for me, was to leave me. Wade says the exact same thing about many of his exes. We were both holding on for dear life to relationships that were never really ours to begin with. We rationalized it by thinking we were sacrificing our own happiness for the sake of our children. So, we suffered through year after year, of loveless relationships. We felt like sea-creatures that no longer had their pretty seashell exterior. We had lost our protective outer layer. And as a result, we hardened over time. We were both unrecognizable to people that knew us best. And that is no way to live life.

As you get older, you also change your way of thinking. I used to think that the worst thing in life was to end up unaccepted, or alone. It's not. The worst thing in life is to end up with people who make you feel unwanted and unworthy of their love. If you are reading this now, you have survived 100 percent of your worst days. And, you will continue to improve your emotional health with each passing day.

The more you love yourself, the less nonsense you will tolerate.

I have no right to say or do anything that diminishes a man in his own eyes. What matters is not what I think of him but what he thinks of himself. Hurting a man in his dignity is a crime.

—Antoine de Saint-Exupéry

13

The Plateau:
You Cannot Heal What
You Cannot Feel

Friendship—my definition—is built on two things. Respect and trust.

—Stieg Larsson

My Story

Just prior to meeting one another, Wade and I were ending relationships in which we were "going along, to get along." It was like we were in the land of the *Walking Dead*. We didn't even realize how unhappy we were until that "one" person came along and made us feel alive (each other). Would you rather have mostly highs, with very few lows, or have your life be a steady drumbeat of the same old-same old? Sometimes you do not know how well you have it until you have it bad. Conversely, sometimes you don't know how bad you have it, until something good comes along. So, do not settle, because then you may find yourself in an unhappy marriage when "the right one" comes along. To love someone and to tolerate someone are two completely different things.

During our quest to salvage our marriages, Wade and I both desperately wanted to escape the "plateau living" to which we had become accustomed. Those flat-line moments in life can be a real soul-sucker. But most people can elevate out of this downward dive before it's too late. A healthy couple can determine where they want to be, even if they are currently stuck at a level below their desired goal. But for us, it seemed like no matter what we did, we were never able to improve our relationships. For years, we were living without much feeling or emotion. I believe that we became used to this. That numb nothingness became our normal. We began to feel destined to a life in a purgatory of perpetual plateauing, with very few "high moments" in our lives. After attempting marriage counseling, we realized that we could not improve our situations, and we knew that change was inevitable. We had to make difficult changes in order to thrive once again. We decided that if we could not figure a way through the cement wall of this unsustainable mediocrity, and level up to the life that we wanted, then maybe the painful road to separation was an option.

Whenever I hit plateaus in my life, my first response was to look for something new and exciting that I could do. I'd think, "If I only find the right workout or the right planning system, my life will change, and I can start making progress in my marriage again." And sometimes people look to others, outside of their relationships, to fulfill their emptiness. Sometimes people become perpetual motion machines, just making their lives so busy—often around their children's lives and activities—that they don't have time to be still and be in the moment. The reason is obvious—in the "moment" is misery. But any of these distractions are merely temporary "fixes."

My Life Lesson

A new love will not heal a past emotional pain. Many people enter a relationship with the wrong person, because they believe that it will spare them the risk of becoming emotionally involved with others, thus eliminating the risk of pain, rejection, and disappointment. Therefore, it is not uncommon for two people to enter a relationship with different levels of risk and security. But like Wade and me, the person with the lower threshold for risk of getting hurt, will soon feel empty inside; they will feel that there is not sufficient challenge, change, or love in the relationship to keep it going. *And, you cannot heal what you cannot feel.*

The person who has the higher threshold for hurt will become like a sponge, soaking up all the sadness and misery. And if only one of you is truly "in love," it is that person who will feel that they are never doing enough to "keep" their partner with them. And, this is not fair to them. There must be a balance, because when a relationship is unbalanced, it can lead to potentially damaging consequences.

Great relationships are not just about security and feeling comfortable. If you have been hurt before, you cannot go into a relationship trying to minimize risks to your heart. Yes, we all want to feel safe in our relationships. But, if this is the only string left holding the fabric of your love together, you may be left feeling very stagnant.

You can build all the walls you want, essentially constructing a fortress of protective structures around your emotions. But, at times, too much of a good thing can be a bad thing. These walls could result in long-term undesirable consequences like boredom, restlessness, resentment, and depression. Moreover, if you are unwilling to love your spouse physically, as well as emotionally, you will succumb to a flatlining of intimacy.

Sometimes changing things up can help us break through a plateau, but in my experience, it is just a waste of time searching for that new "magic-bullet" that will change your life for the better. We tend to sometimes grossly overestimate the pleasure brought forth by new experiences and underestimate the power of *finding meaning* in current ones. So instead of spending time on searching for something new, start focusing on the basics. For example, when Wade would hit a plateau with his weight-lifting, he would reduce the weight, focus on his form, and slowly start adding weight again. It is the same concept for relationships. Go back to the basics. Remember what brought you together in the first place. Can any of those feelings be salvaged? On numerous occasions, I've found that even when you're advanced at something, delving back into the basics can give you fresh insights that help you progress even further.

During this time, don't have the tendency to feel that your relationship plateau is permanent. Your goal is to ameliorate the problem and get your relationship back on track. You should force yourself to think of this plateau as temporary. You need to figure out a way with your partner to eventually get past this, which most of the time requires a bit of hard work and a lot of compromise.

To cultivate this attitude, reflect on a time where you felt you had reached the end of your development in some area, only to later bust through the plateau. If it was possible then, it's possible now.

Neither Wade nor I like to fail. But, when you and your partner are not meant to be, then no amount of work, love, or fortitude can make them love you, or you love them. You may be able to reconcile to the point of loving and respecting them as your friend, or your children's parent, but a love needs all aspects to flourish. You cannot "will" yourself to be attracted to someone sexually. Trust me, Wade and I have both tried it. If it is wrong on an emotional level, it will be wrong on a physical level too.

Find Your Solace

My Story

Right before the end of my second marriage, which I initiated, I can remember running at 4:30 a.m. every single morning, on my treadmill. I would tiptoe down the long, lonely, empty, and dark hallways of my home, ensuring not to awaken my children or my second husband.

This was my only alone-time during the day. It was sacred to me. I would take this time to listen to my favorite Christian music, and literally run and cry. I did this for almost six months straight, because it lifted my pain, if even just for that one hour. I tell everyone that it was only with the help of my family and friends that I got through my ordeals. I also give praise to a musical group called, Casting Crowns, and the singer, Todd Agnew. The words to all their songs seemed to apply to me—and me alone. As I look back on it now, I see that it was God speaking to me through their songs. I held onto these songs like an anchor in the sea. These songs gave me hope.

I saw no way out of this relationship. We would have to sell the house. And, it needed money poured into it, because in today's market, buyers are looking for "move-in" condition. We had a small dog that ruined the carpet in three rooms, which would all have to be replaced. The paint would have to be neutralized, from the deep maroons and dark browns that I favored, to beiges and whites.

After living there for ten years, I had accumulated a *lot* of *stuff*. How would I ever go through everything? Pack everything? I was now commuting approximately three hours every day, to and from work. I had a daughter in high school and a son in middle school. Their biological father was not in the picture during this time. Finally, my second husband was working extremely long hours, and he was mostly working night-shift. So, he left for work before I got home in the evening. And I left for work in the morning, before he was done with his job. All of these things led to my "perfect storm" of isolation and bearing the burden of all things during this time, including all of the children's needs.

My Life Lesson

You can find joy in the little moments every day. And, don't ever underestimate the power of music. I found such joy and solace in my favorite songs because they were uplifting and gave me hope. I felt a connection with my favorite artists. The power of their songs made me feel as though I was understood in my grief and pain. I was able to relate to other human beings by the lyrics of their songs. And, my daughter, Gabi, once told me that if you sing Christian songs, it is like praying twice. I always loved that analogy.

One good thing about music—when it hits you, you feel no pain.

—Bob Marley

14

The Toughest Critic and Finding Support

The loneliest moment in someone's life is when they are watching their whole world fall apart, and all they can do is stare blankly.

—*F. Scott Fitzgerald*

Sometimes, amid a divorce, our harshest critic will be the voice in our heads. As I shared earlier, I am quite certain my beloved parents would have *much* rather I canceled my weddings, than suffer the pain from my marriages. As a parent now myself, of course I see that. But that is the wisdom of growing up and growing older. I could not "see" that when I was a young woman.

This chapter is not only about that inner critic. It is also about that person who wants to make everyone happy. That was me—and I know I am not the only one.

Breathe In, Breathe Out, and Move On!

My Story

I have always been the type of person who had to get straight A's in school and understand every nuance of every situation. When I would watch a movie, my parents teased me that I would ask a hundred different questions, five minutes into the movie. I have been described as a very "concrete sequential" personality type—meaning I like a lot of "order." This is good and bad. (Please learn from me.)

Because I felt that I needed answers to make my little universe whole, I wasted a lot of time trying to change my ex-partners and trying to understand the "whys" and "why nots" of my failed relationships. My past relationship rejections catapulted me into a whole new obsession to figure it out. This slowed down my recovery progress. I finally realized that I probably would never get some of the answers that I was seeking. I will never fully understand my mistreatment and, to some extent, why I "fired back" and mistreated them. Because of this, I was holding onto anger, resentment, sadness, and fear, and I would ruminate (a lot) about why and how someone could treat me (and later, me and my innocent children) a certain way.

I was looking for "closure". But I would not get that from anyone, except me. One more text from your ex, one more email, or one more telephone call, will not help you. Get busy with your own healing and stop looking for your ex to help you recover. In a few months, things that you are sad or upset about now, will seem foreign to you. Things that made you panic, or cry, will no longer hold the meaning that it once did.

My Life Lesson

When I entered my past relationships—they were with the wrong people, until I met Wade. But, I too, was the wrong person, because I wasn't my true authentic self, and I had never let go of my past pain. Let it hurt. Let it bleed. But then, let it heal. And by all means...let it go! Deal with the pain, but again, *let it go*! Let go of that proverbial anchor that is weighing you down. Let go of toxic, judgmental, and negative people. When you let go, you will create space for better things to enter your life.

Another aspect of letting go is to stop looking back. It can be extremely tempting to keep, and look at, all the old relics of a past relationship. Doing so, however, may prevent you from moving on with your life. If you must keep the old love letters, texts, e-mails, movie ticket stubs, photographs, stuffed animals, or romantic gifts, you may want to store them somewhere out of sight until you're ready to move on. It isn't uncommon to only hold on to the good memories of an ex and completely shut out the bad memories. Maintain your perspective by remembering both sides of the experience. Remind yourself of the good times, but don't forget those bad times or you could end up forgetting why the relationship ended in the first place.

Sometimes love also has a way of clouding your perception, which often makes it difficult to a see someone for who they really are. If you really want to get out of an unhealthy relationship, you must be willing to take off your rose-colored glasses and look at the person objectively. Consider talking with a close family member or friend or even finding a therapist to help you look at the relationship impartially. Do not make the age-old mistake of looking back. You may begin to blame and doubt yourself, or only remember and fantasize about the good times. Your other relationships ended for a reason. (Now, there are some exceptions to this rule. Maybe you met the love-of-your-life too early in life, and you had to experience more, before understanding that they were your one "big love." But unless you parted as friends, or because one of you moved out of the area, etc., then leave well-enough alone and leave the past in the past.)

Remembering why the relationship was unhealthy and focusing instead on what you want (and deserve), in a relationship can be empowering.

Know your worth. Know what you deserve. And know when it is time to move on.

Blame Games Are Just That—A Game! Forgiveness is a Decision

Don't stay stuck in blame games either. Living with pent-up anger means that fury will eventually wrap itself around your soul, like a serpent does around its prey's neck. You cannot focus on blame. Every saint has a past, and every sinner has a future. It is easy to want to give all the problematic culpability to your ex, their family, or even to yourself. Blaming someone or something will keep you in a holding pattern of your own misery. You will remain stuck in your bad and broken divorce or breakup forever. Do not give him or her that power over you. Let go of them and the life you once had. Get on the path of healing. Build a better life for yourself and your children (if you have them).

Sometimes we want to place blame anywhere but with ourselves. When you feel this way towards your ex, it becomes even more difficult to accept, understand, and forgive their imperfections and limitations. It doesn't matter if you feel that the other person "got one over on you." And, it doesn't matter if the other person tries to act as though this is a competition, constantly flaunting that they "won." It doesn't matter if *they* feel that they were "right or justified" in their actions towards you, including abuse, ignorance, mean-spiritedness, rivalry, cheating, jealousy, vindictiveness, or even the breakup itself.

What is important is to forgive your ex, even if you truly feel that they do not deserve this mercy. The point is that *you* deserve *peace*. Holding a grudge won't make you stronger. It will make you weak and bitter. So, absolve them, and forgive yourself. This is the first step in healing. Better things are coming your way. Be happy. Set yourself free! Your relationship with *you* holds the magic key to your new life.

I used to silently repeat this as a mantra of mine, when doing yoga, "*Reach for peace.*"

For me, it's no longer about wishing that the Universe takes revenge on any of my exes, for what I perceive they did to me. It's about praying for their well-being and happiness. It's about hoping that they find the help that they may need, just as I have found the help that I needed. It is about hoping that they each find (or have found) the kind of love that they couldn't have with me. It is about wishing that our experiences help each of us to grow and become someone that another would be lucky to have. Hopefully, it becomes about wanting to be better people. Now, I can finally say that I wish everyone in my past, a lifetime of love, without pain.

Most of us walk without chains, yet we aren't free. We tether ourselves to past regrets, sadness, and personal failures. In this way, the past serves as a prison, and you are the enslaved prisoner. But you have the combination to unlock the prison vault and arrive in the present moment. However, that requires forgiveness. Then you will breathe in a new life. So, take that step to arrive in the "here and now" versus dredging up the past bitterness. There is sunshine just waiting for you to bask in.

Hate cannot drive out hate—only love and forgiveness can. So, if you think that imparting revenge will provide you with any peace whatsoever, think again! Revenge only keeps you tied to your ex. I've heard many wicked vengeance stories, from both recently divorced men and women. But there is only one way out of the craziness of it all. You must let it all go. Get out of the boxing ring, put down your gloves, and get on with your recovery. You will emerge from your breakup or divorce with a much happier life.

My Life Lesson

A valuable lesson that I learned was about forgiveness. You need to forgive yourself. And you need to forgive your ex. This may sound very strange to some of you, and I understand that this is not an easy task. You do not have to be friends with your ex, but through forgiveness, you will no longer allow them to drain *your* emotional energy.

It's hard to end a marriage without some degree of anger, resentment, disappointment, or guilt creeping in. But, being archenemies of your ex is unnecessary. Most people, given the choice, want to have an amicable divorce. Yet intense emotions and misunderstandings can lead to anger, grief, fear, and mistrust, making it difficult to get along. Let's face it. You didn't get along when you were married, which is probably why you are divorcing. So, this is not an easy task. But it can be done. In the face of these strong and painful feelings, it can be hard to cooperate and co-parent effectively. Even Anthony and I are putting our differences aside, now, for the sake of our children.

Forgiveness is for your benefit. Do not worry if the byproduct helps your ex as well. If you are both happy, then you and your children are the real winners. Forgiveness does not mean that you are condoning your ex partner's bad behavior. But rather, it means that you are making peace with the wrongs done to you, and that you did to them, once and for all. If someone seems to get away with doing something wrong, maybe God is just giving them a chance to make it right. Be patient. Forgiveness will do something even more strange to you. For me, it minimized the helpless "victim" mentality that I had. I was able to reclaim my power and my life. Forgiveness has also allowed me to let go of blame, anger, and grief too. I acknowledged all those emotions, and then I left those anchors behind. I made myself move forward. In doing this, I helped myself and my children. The major conflicts were eliminated. And, I will reiterate what I stated earlier in the book. The pleasure of revenge is short-lived. Trust me. The best revenge is to forgive them and live a happy life.

Let no man pull you low enough to hate him.

—Martin Luther King, Jr.

Forgiveness is an attribute of the strong.

—*Mahatma Gandhi*

Surround Yourself with Your Support People

My Story

When you connect with people who are good for you, you feel it. This is a big deal. I was very fortunate to have extremely close friends and a loving family that helped me through these most difficult times in my life. I was also fortunate to have an understanding boss and co-workers, who were instrumental in my healing. These are the people who had faith in me when I did not have faith in myself. My family and closest friends did not judge the way, or how long, I was grieving. I never felt isolated. They were not critical of me, my mindset, my appearance, or my many tears, which were my coping mechanisms of choice. They allowed me to cry and scream, without urging me to be more patient and pious. They allowed me to keep my self-respect intact by always finding time to listen to me. And I love to rehash things, repeatedly, so many of them were listening to my same fears, questions, and sadness, on a daily basis. They provided me with compassion and sympathy way before they imparted their advice. Initially, I was not ready for advice.

Selfishly, it was also comforting to me that I could see that they too, were pained by my grief. It let me see how important I was to these treasured few. These are the people who gave me empathy, along with wings when I could not fly. (Hell, there were some days that I felt like a feeble old woman, who didn't want to crawl, much less fly.) The older I get, the more selective I have become of who is in my inner circle. I would rather have two half-dollars than one hundred pennies. However, every single person who extended a hand to me when I was at my lowest, will forever be a part of my extended family.

Wade tells me all the time, that a big mistake he made was not talking about his problems more with his trusted family and friends. He said that his parents and his aunt and uncle would ask him about his relationships all the time. They were interested. They cared. But he hid from his perceived failures. He told me that because he never opened-up about many of his shortcomings, they still haunt him to this day. He would only discuss the superficial things that were marring his life, because he was embarrassed to fully disclose all the unpleasant details. He did not embrace all his emotions. He did not embrace his perceived weaknesses. If he had, he would have realized that his support system could have acted like an internal compass, pointing him in a different and better direction.

Alternatively, when I was at my weakest, I talked all the time. I talked about my problems and my seeming failures to my trusted inner circle. Conversely, Wade held most of his thoughts and emotions inside. Looking back now, he believes that this is a major reason that he may have never successfully pushed all the way through his issues. He believes there was no resolution from his first failed relationship in high school, to his last, almost six years ago at the time of this writing, because he never openly discussed the real issues.

To add to our own insecurities, for a very long time, we both listened to the steady humming of acquaintances who did not know us or our exes. It seemed that everyone around us was telling us everything was "all right" or "hang in there, and it will get better." We heard repeatedly, "This is how marriage is for everyone." Have you ever heard of the saying, "Birds of a feather, flock together"? It was as if these superficial friends had poor relationships and encouraged us to think it was just fine that our relationships were deteriorating too. And there were the jokesters who would reply, "Everyone knows that marriage sucks." And we would see the cartoons and movies that referred to marriage as the "good old ball and chain." With that much negative stigma surrounding marriage, it is no wonder that we sometimes think that all marriages are bad.

I quickly learned that I should only confide in my family and closest friends. These are the people who will tell me what I *need* to hear, not what I *want* to hear. My parents have always been straight-shooters, as were my tried-and-true friends. So, I listened intently and gratefully with an open mind. But my heart had an altogether different agenda. Even though I knew what they were saying was true, I was not ready to hear some of what they were telling me. This is okay. You can only absorb so much at one time. Later, as I let their words marinate in my mind, I slowly realized that they were right.

My Life Lesson

If you have family or true friends, you may need them, as you travel this journey of healing. Respect the people who find time for you in their busy schedules, but lean on the people who never look at their schedule in your time of need. Choose the friends and family who reach out to you when you are quiet and not actively seeking their help. These are the ones who really know you. They are the ones who will love you enough to be honest with what you *need* to hear, versus what you may *want* to hear. Do not get distracted by the people who are only curious. Chances are, they just want your juicy story for gossip. At first it was difficult for me, but I learned to ignore these types of acquaintances. Set your mind on a steadfast course. Get yourself to a place that makes you happy and whole. I would never have gotten through my ordeals without my cherished friends and family. (A shout-out to each of you! You know who you are!)

We all have hidden pieces of ourselves that we are sometimes not willing to share with others. These are the secret gardens of our personalities. Most of the time, we only allow other people to see a glimpse of who we really are, and what we are thinking and feeling. But, when you find yourself in troubled times, this is when you need to allow others into those hidden places, so that they are better equipped to help you. Just by talking about your situation, you will feel better.

None of us can make a change until we are ready to do it ourselves. Relationship criticism is not always easy to hear, especially from your inner circle. I know I'm guilty of doing this. I would frequently ask my family and friends for advice on my relationships. I told them that I wanted "constructive criticism," when really, I just wanted some positive affirmation, on any aspect of my relationships, big or small.

Learning to accept criticism is something that simply takes discipline and practice. First you must work on taking the criticism into consideration. Then you work on shortening the time between your initial reaction of, "What?!" and "There's nothing wrong with what I did!"—with remaining objective and calm.

As with anything, the more you practice this, the easier it will become habit. And soon, you will be able to calmly reflect and see if there's value in the criticism. (I suppose the next stage is to skip that momentary urge to plug your ears. But I'm not there yet myself!)

It takes two people to enter a marriage, and it also takes those same two people to enter a divorce. Neither should ever be taken lightly. If you part ways, for your own happiness, let your past be a lesson, not a life sentence. That choice is up to you. Learn from your family and friends' advice, and your past mistakes.

Once you are truly mindful of your own wants and desires, and you know how to express them in a healthy manner, your relationship goals will become very clear to you. This may include learning from people you meet along your journey. I truly believe people are put in our path to teach us important life lessons.

If you feel stuck in your relationship, before doing anything drastic, seek out an outside marriage counselor, life coach, or other professional mentor, who won't pull any punches and will give you the honest criticism that you need to improve. Maybe look for someone who has gone through what you have, so that they have firsthand knowledge of how to get through this tough time. They can lead by experience, and not just provide another opinion. Too many opinions will overwhelm you. This is not to say that you shouldn't still talk to, and confide in, your family and friends. Quite the contrary. You should still do that, but be sure you are being totally forthright about where you are on the scale of recovery. And reassure them when you are ready for their honest feedback.

The kind of help that I eventually found was a life coach. I was done with therapists, because I didn't want to "talk about it" anymore. I had spent so many unhappy years complaining, before my divorces, that I was all "talked out." I wanted a conventional path to happiness. I wanted (and needed) assistance on rebuilding my life. My life coach helped guide and encourage me, with a specific plan, to transition back into my new single life. She helped me pinpoint my obstacles and challenges, and she prepared a simple course of action. Because of my personality, I adapt best with a sequential plan of outlined steps, for my personal accountability. My coach taught me that every positive change in my life would begin with a clear unequivocal decision, to either start doing something, or stop doing something.

During your path to recovery, you will sometimes feel like you are "going backwards" in your progress. My coach reminded me that sometimes I would face difficulties, not because I was doing something wrong, but because I was doing something right. Initially, my progress and change were sometimes painful. But when I look around at the life I have now, at the *love* I have now, I am certain that those growing pains were well worth it.

One of the greatest gifts of life is friendship—and I have received it.

—Hubert H. Humphrey

We are free to change. And love changes us.

—Walter Mosley

15

Before You Choose Again:
Red Light, Green Light...
Proceed with Caution

There are many twists and turns to ending a relationship and moving on. Even if your relationship was not distressing, or if your divorce or separation does not involve children, there is a period of time when you will be very vulnerable. For me, the months after separation often felt like the hardest time.

Before you start a deep relationship with someone else, it is important to figure out what failed in the relationship you are ending.

My Story

Whenever we lose a relationship, even if it was terrible and dysfunctional, there will be a sense of loss and mourning. This is when I felt unbearable darkness. We grieve the lost hopes and dreams, and the future we'll never have with this person, especially if you have children. When I was in the thick of my grieving process, it seemed as if I would always feel despondent, even though I knew on a rational level that I wouldn't. This is when you will wish all your memories would just fade away. *This is the recovery stage.* You have struck rock bottom. Things cannot get much worse for you. You must be careful not to have a preconceived notion that happiness is in the next place, the next job, or the next partner; otherwise, you will never find it. It will be elusive because, *true happiness comes from within yourself.*

My Life Lesson

Rock bottom will teach you lessons that mountain tops never will.

This is the most difficult stage. I cannot sugar-coat this section. I know. *I know.* You feel miserable. And none of us want to feel depressed all the time. But your emotions will take more to suppress than to address. And, the best way out, will always be to cut directly through. So, face this challenge of learning to make better life decisions head-on. Lay down your old chains. They were not providing you with any security anyhow.

Everything happens for a reason, and mercy will always find you... right where you are. The time with your ex has served you in some positive way. Maybe it provided you with perspective on what to look for in your next relationship and what not to tolerate. You are preparing yourself for better and brighter days. These broken relationships actual "lift" you to the next level. Our most important lessons are usually learned in our "down cycle." Remind yourself that good love conquers; it does not divide. You are broken right now. That is not love. You are feeling the pain of the shattered remnants of your past life. Even after the darkness, your heart can and will love again, even if that love only consists of loving yourself. Your life isn't falling apart...it is falling into place.

In Japan, when objects break, they are often repaired with gold. The flaw is a unique piece of the object's history. This adds to its beauty. Although you will feel broken, consider this: During this stage of the recovery process, the shattered pieces can become as beautiful as a fragmented stained-glass window. This is the part where it will require your blood, sweat, tears, and hard work. Spiritual growth is the result of devastation, and the process will be messy.

But, in the end you will speak with your own voice, walk your own path fiercely, stand tall with grace and dignity, and above all else, you will fight for yourself. Some of the people that have been anchors in your prior life will not even recognize this new and improved you, because you will have put all the broken pieces back together differently—but better. You will learn to breathe in love and blow out the regret and pain.

Did you know that your heart affects your mental clarity, creativity, and personal effectiveness? You need to take time to repair your heart, and you need to know you can trust your heart in the future. Because you have had some failed relationships does not give you permission to start doubting yourself. The tricky part is that sometimes, it does not know any better. But every mistake can be a new opportunity, because you can learn and grow from it, if you choose to view it that way. Your heart can point you to a direction that challenges your old way of thinking. It may require you to change how you view life and love. It will take a lot of strength and courage to do this, but you need to focus on the end-game.

And, damn it…Get back up! Seek the light! Stop dragging your heart around. Pack up your fear, get healthy, and know you will one day trust and follow your heart again. You will love again. You will be loved again. Sometimes the smallest step in the right direction ends up being the biggest step of your life. Tiptoe if you must, but take that first step.

It is time to stop spinning the hamster wheel. It is time to change courses. Be your own compass. Be your own weather vane. Point yourself in a new, positive, and healthy direction. I believe that everything in life is interconnected.

It is also my belief that there is no such thing as "coincidence." So, trust that you are where you are supposed to be at this very moment. You need to take this time to focus on mastering the chaos that is all around you and that is inside of you. You need to stop throwing yourself into the flames of the fire and become the fire itself.

This time in your life will not be simple.

You will not get over your broken heart by ceasing to love altogether. However, you will recover by creating a new life for yourself, where it is easier to love yourself. If you do not create this new life, then the past mistakes and factors will eventually catch up to you again. The cycle of your pain will never end.

Nothing worth anything is ever easy. The only way to live is to accept each moment of your past as an unrepeatable lesson. Love has never met a lost cause. So, wear your scars as reminders of your past. Get to know your own limitations and begin to understand all the positive attributes that make you special. These difficult times are what help to define you as a person. Think about it this way. If everything in life came easy to you, or worked out on your first try, where is the self-satisfaction in that? As you make your plans and proceed with what seems like the impossible task of rebuilding yourself and your life; gather all your strength and summon your courage! Be fearless in the pursuit of YOU. F.E.A.R. has two meanings: "Forget Everything and Run" or "Face Everything and Rise!" The choice is yours. So, *rise!*

And I am a firm believer that "laughter is the best medicine." So, go where the belly-laughs are. This may be your best friend's house, or a comedy club in a city near you. If you look, you will always find a reason to laugh. It may not be an instant fix to all your current problems, but it will surely make your life a little better, as you sort through it. We don't laugh because we are happy; we are happy because we laugh.

Something very beautiful happens to people when their world has fallen apart. There is a humility, nobility, and higher intelligence that emerges at just the point when our knees hit the floor.

—Marianne Williamson

How to Put Humpty-Dumpy Back Together Again: Once You Were Lost, But Now You Are Found

My Story

During Wade's past relationships, he said that he tolerated too much because of his weakened state of mind and emotions. I did the exact same thing in my previous partnerships. We forgot about our own feelings and emotional well-being, because we were overwhelmed with grief, loneliness, and pain. Specifically, when you are in this state of mind, you will tolerate a lot more criticism, nagging, anger, etc. and become very passive in your role. We just did not have the strength to fight every battle anymore. So, over time, we slowly started to become more and more distant from our exes, and we felt an emotionless void. We liken it to "Humpty Dumpty." The only problem is that we were both very cracked and damaged. We felt that we could not be put back together again. At least, not without help.

My Life Lesson

Lost love is like a natural disaster. It will leave you running for cover or running away from your situation. Breakups and divorce are the earthquake. Your life just violently shakes. You *can* stop the quaking. But first you must understand that what you allow—is what will continue.

But, how does someone begin the healing process? You must accept your life exactly as it is, because the quality of your life completely depends on the quality of your relationship with *yourself.* You are lost now, but this is not permanent. Trust me. You will find yourself again. I am living proof that you can go from feeling like a "zero" to a "hero", if you put in the tough work required to love yourself.

Do what is difficult, and life will be easy. Do what is easy, and life will be difficult.

And there is another important lesson that I learned along the way. You cannot rush this healing process. It will take time. And, more than likely, it will take the help of a professional. After a few weeks, it will become easier, and after a few months, you will begin to normalize. In time, I began to embrace and enjoy spending time getting to know myself. But again, there is no "instant gratification" for this process in your healing. This is not a race to the finish line. You need to get this part right. Slow and steady will win this race. And this time off by yourself should not begin until you and your significant other are completely separated (not cohabitating together anymore). You can only punch into this time clock once you are completely on your own.

As I look back on my life, I realize that every time I thought I was being rejected from something good, I was being redirected to something better. Do you really want to remain paralyzed by your emotions, where you are forever controlled by your failures, as life passes you by? I hope your answer is a resounding "No!" Because, you certainly deserve happiness. But, until you get control over your emotions and thoughts, your life will not be your own.

Also, don't waste another second of your life because you are afraid that you will make another mistake. Failure is a very normal part of life. We learn from our faults, and each time we stand back up afterwards, we are stronger for it. This is a tough lesson, but an important one, so I will repeat myself. Do not continue to get upset or anxious about your ex (or other people or situations). They are powerless without your reaction. You have someone better to focus your time and attention on. Yourself!

You will never heal, until you stop glorifying the ended relationship. It ended for a reason. Write those reasons down if you must, and read them repeatedly, until you are at peace with your decision. Avoid places that will bring back nostalgia, and if a special song comes on the radio, by George, change the channel!

Whenever you feel unloved, unimportant, or insecure, remember to whom you belong.

—Ephesians 2:19-22

16

Put Yourself First: Lost in Love, But Now I Am Found

Coming out of a bad relationship is a bit like a bear awakening after hibernating all winter. It's a process to wake up that part of you again, and it can be hard to shake off the winter chill you once felt. Spring may be here, but until you love yourself, first and foremost, it's difficult to move on in a healthy manner.

My Story

After my breakups and divorce(s), I was so frustrated because things would happen to me, and I knew I *should* be happy. But I got to the point where I was numb to most everything around me, other than my career, my family, and my friends. Joyful situations would occur, but I couldn't feel them like everyone else. It always felt shallow and temporary. In fact, it wasn't until I was willing to own the part that I played in my failed relationships, forgive myself, and forgive my exes, that I reclaimed my power. In fact, I felt so liberated and free, because the thousand-pound weight had been lifted from my shoulders. Nobody will have the power to control how I feel, ever again. I finally realized that I could survive (and thrive) on my own. My happiness was not dependent on living with someone else—or based upon someone else's choices.

My Life Lesson

You must first love yourself. And, you must give yourself permission to fail. It does not mean that you are "damaged goods." Instead of avoiding the things that are hardest for you to cope with, you must meet them head-on!

So instead of seeing failure as a negative thing, think of your failures as stepping stones to success. You are planting seeds that will one day be a beautiful and bountiful harvest. You are investing in yourself, and this is a good thing. Take time to nurture yourself and your daily habits. If you choose to learn from your failures, they can bring you closer to your goal of becoming healthy and whole. You will not instantly be successful at changing your self-talk. But you need to learn to be positive and not worry about what others think or say about you. To improve, we must constantly push ourselves beyond where we think our limits are; then, we must pay attention to how and why we fail. I no longer have the most respect for the strongest among us; rather, I respect the one that never gives up. Be "that" person. Respect yourself enough to keep your own personal resolve for a life full of love, happiness, and peace.

I realized only after I was in a healthy relationship that I was "feeling good about feeling bad." I was so used upheaval in my life, that when things were *not* crazy and out-of-control, I felt like things were sinking even deeper into my abyss. Being sad, worried, argumentative, alone, etc., became my normal. It became my solace, so I had to reprogram my mind. I would start arguments with my new man to make myself feel better, and I noticed that my children also seemed off-kilter in the calm too. It was the *absence* of stress that was now creating my uneasiness. I had become addicted to my own stress hormones. The good news is that you can begin new behaviors, and research suggests that it only takes approximately twenty-one days to form a habit—a better routine.

Once a breakup or divorce gets off to a rocky start, the situation can quickly spiral down. Many people find themselves caught in vicious cycles of hurt, anger and retaliation, even when they don't want to be. The "War of the Roses" was only funny in the movies. Engaging in these "battles to the finish" will just cause you more angst, and it will steal your energy, not to mention that it will cost you a lot of money in legal fees. The good news is that it is never too late to change gears. And, the *only* way that I have found this possible in my own life is through forgiveness, loving yourself, and knowing your worth.

> *Don't worry about people who do you wrong. God sees it all. A false witness will not go unpunished, and the one who lies with every breath will not escape.*
>
> **—Proverbs 19:5**

The Looking Glass Is an Excellent Litmus Test: Dark Shadows and Light Reflections

My Story

In the beginning stages of my breakups and divorces, I literally could not look myself in the mirror. If I stared at myself for too long, I became very uncomfortable. This is because I did not really know who I was, and I was not comfortable in my own skin. And at this point, I was walking around in the darkness, so that I did not have to face my reality. As time marched on, it became a little easier to glance into my own eyes and into my soul, to discover myself.

Try passing an upscale storefront without stopping to catch a glimpse of your reflection. You first stare at all the fancy and expensive things that you can buy inside. But then you see your own reflection or image. I saw only a fragment of who I really was. It was a smaller image of my former self. There was the elusive question that demanded an answer. How did I get here? I was an emotionless human, with dark circles under my eyes, and stress marks appearing where I had never noticed them before. I felt dirty, covered in years of unhappiness, denial, and unworthiness. I saw all the years that I had wasted—sadly glancing back at me. I thought to myself, "Look at what you have become, Francine." I would always turn away from my reflection very quickly, only to end up following my shadow, which was void of my former self. I had become a shell of who I used to be. I was desperately searching for those feelings of self-love, security, and desire—to become myself again. I wondered if I had fallen too far, to ever be loved or love again? I was searching for hope in my own reflection. But all I saw and felt was this empty shadow that always loomed in front of me. I dreamed of a day that I could become who I wanted to be. I desperately wanted my reflection to provide me with strength and optimism—if even just for the split-second that I looked at myself. I also needed reassurance that I would eventually make a good final choice for my life partner.

I used to be embarrassed and ashamed of all my broken parts. But I am not anymore. I have learned that even when I was in pieces, I had value and was worth something to both myself, and the right person.

My Life Lesson

To begin to rely on your own decisions regarding relationships and who is a good match for you, you must possess self-confidence and self-reliance. Self-confidence and self-reliance are at the heart of finding yourself. If you don't have a solid sense of self-worth, you'll mostly listen to what others say about your life. You will be tempted and swayed by their insistence on what is best for you. Learn to believe in yourself and trust your own feelings. Remember, be patient with yourself and confident in your abilities. Everything will come with time. Time is your friend.

The truth is that other people's perceptions of you are really a reflection of themselves. You are not being fair to yourself if you care more about what other people think of you. You must put your own well-being first and foremost.

Your own reflection doesn't become scary until you are alone and clear-minded. We have all walked down the street and caught a glimpse of ourselves in the storefront window. Do you notice that your shadow follows and jogs ahead at times but just shows an outline of your physical appearance, without any details? It is when you take the time to look at the windows that you pass and see yourself that you begin to understand what you have become.

I needed to wake up. I needed to lift my head and look around. I needed to face my demons and love myself.

Being happy is a very personal thing, and it really does not have anything to do with another person. It all centers around you. Looking at yourself is a scary thing, especially when you have made the types of mistakes in relationships like I have. This true introspection initially made me cringe in disbelief. So, I began throwing all these failures to my shadow, so that I would not have to deal with them. This allowed me to still superficially and quickly look at my reflection. But, you should be able to stare at yourself in the mirror for as long as you can stand there. I could not do that, until I met my failures head-on.

Don't worry about hurting my feelings, because I guarantee you, that not one bit of my self- esteem is tied up in your acceptance.

—Dr. Phil

17

Three Strikes, You're Out: Time to Learn Which People to Avoid

When you do things from your soul, you feel a river moving in you, a joy.

—Rumi

The next stage of my journey involved learning to watch out for the red flags in relationships that had been waving in full sight before—but I had somehow ignored them. This was my time to dig deep and learn to love myself.

It is important that you see things as they *are*, not as you want them to be. If you are a loving person, or an optimist, you will try to always see the best in others. While this is a beautiful trait, it needs to be tempered with caution and realism.

My Story

I realized that I could not be victimized in a relationship unless I gave the other person power over me to do so. This time I was going to be in control. Because I became emotionally healthy, I promised myself that at "three strikes," they were out! I made a promise to myself, and I created my own "Baseball of Red Flags." In my next relationship, if I saw any of the red flags, I would write them down in a journal. Then, I could evaluate the traits that could possibly destroy, infringe, or damage my trust, respect, or love for the other person. If the other person exhibited any of these negative behaviors again, I would again write it down. This would be their strike, as they were up to bat. If my partner did anything that caused me pain for a third time, it would be their final swing. "You're out!"—you are done. Wade and I will never again allow anyone to steal our happiness. We have had our share of thieves that took way more from, and out of us, than any person ever has a right to.

I made this pledge to myself, just prior to meeting Wade. And guess what? My journal is full of empty pages, because when you find the right person, there are no red flags.

My Life Lesson

These were some of the red flags that I had written down, and that I was arming myself with:

1. **Avoid Liars**. *If you tell the truth, you don't have to remember anything.*—**Mark Twain.** For any relationship to work, honesty is an important ingredient. Don't be fooled by a pretty person, who harbors ugly secrets. If you catch them lying, move on! These people make untrue statements, with the intent to deceive. I think sometimes they begin to believe their own lies, and therefore, you would be living in a very lonely world, built on promises—constructed by *their* lies. When lies replace the

truth, people will get hurt. Do not let that person be you. And remember, if someone is willing to lie *for* you, they will also lie *to* you. Honesty is a very expensive gift. Don't expect it from cheap people.

2. **Avoid Narcissists**. When these people discover the center of the Universe, they will be very disappointed that they are not it. These people are extremely controlling, and their moods can oscillate abruptly, for no apparent reason. They are quick to become angry, and they sometimes use threats of violence to maintain control over you. They may break objects in one of their fits of anger. They will also use verbal abuse and demeaning cut-downs to deteriorate your self-esteem. Most everything these people do is deniable, by them. They always have an excuse or explanation for themselves, and they are extremely defensive. They rarely, if ever, admit they are wrong. They will violate your boundaries. They will undermine you, and your accomplishments are acknowledged only to the extent that they can take credit for them. They will minimize, discount, or ignore your opinions or experiences. They will insinuate that you are unstable, knocking you off-balance—how else would you believe their lies about you? They are extremely envious, self-absorbed, and self-centered. If you are in the limelight, they will try to spoil it for you. They will manipulate your emotions to feed on your pain. They will find fault in almost everything you do, and you will always be wrong. They are selfish and willful. They will isolate you from your family and friends. And, there is often a history of battering. No one should tolerate this type of unhealthy relationship, especially if their partner doesn't even recognize there is a problem. The National Domestic Violence Hotline in the United States is: **1-800-799-SAFE**. Although these partners' love is fake, the pain it causes is real. So, I urge you to call this number if you or someone you know is in an unsafe or unhealthy relationship.

3. **Avoid Hypocrites**. These are the cognizant deceivers, the imposters, and the pretenders. Be cautious of people whose actions

don't match their words. If this person is gossiping about other people to you, you can be assured that they are talking about you to other people, too. These are the people that lie with sincerity, and act in contradiction to their stated beliefs or feelings, while pointing their finger at someone else. These are the people who judge other people, as if they have never transgressed themselves. The true hypocrite is the one who puts on a false appearance of virtue and ceases to perceive his or her own deception.

4. **Avoid Victims**. These are the whiners; the people who are always wronged, and never by their own hand. These are people who live in the past, with stories of "woe is me." They cannot or will not let go of pain or hurt that someone else has previously caused to them, and you will bear the brunt of their high and heavy walls.

5. **Avoid Fence-Sitters**. These are people who are wishy-washy. My father used to tell my sister and me, "You have to stand for something, or you will fall for anything." And, "United we stand, but divided we fall." You want someone in your life willing to jump that fence to be with you. Hell, you want someone who would capture the moon for you.

6. **Avoid Angry People**. These are the negative people, and they will always feed on your reaction. And worse, if they see that they are affecting you in a negative way, they will continue doing or saying it. Do not allow these people to drag you down to their level. These people thrive on conflict. The battle they are fighting is not with you, it is with themselves. Listen closely when people are angry, because that is when their real personality and their truth comes out.

7. **Avoid Selfish People**. These are the ones that are self-absorbed and lack consideration for others. These people are chiefly concerned with their own profit or gain. And, they will go to all lengths to get what they want, with total disregard for you. These

are the crabs in the boiling pot that will claw you, until you go under with them. The saying, "misery loves company" is quoted so often for a reason.

8. **Avoid Jealous and Envious People**: A little jealousy is normal. In fact, at times a little jealousy ensures we do not take our partner for granted. But unhealthy jealousy is a terrible trait. It is a sign of insecurity, weakness, and obsession. The jealous are possessed by a bad omen and a gloomy spirit, both at the same time. Anyone that is extremely jealous of you will always try to bring you down to their level. The reasons for this are simple. Because they either see you as a threat, they hate themselves, or they want to be you. And finally, your misery is their joy.

9. **Avoid Manipulators:** These people will use guilt as their weapon to get you to do things for them. These are the people that will over-flatter you in a way that is not sincere. They continually use your own words against you, by twisting what you say to their benefit. This leaves you on the defensive, while they are off the hook. And, if you confront them with something that they did wrong, they will turn the tables on you. They will bring up something that you did wrong in the past, to take the focus off themselves. These people are cold and distant, and they will take things and affection away from you if you don't do what they want you to do. They will say and do horrible things, and then they will tell you that they were only joking or you're being overly sensitive.

If you have been victimized by any of the above types of "red flag" people in the past, you must confront these issues. They're not going to go away on their own. They might be coloring your approach to daily life, causing you to live up to *their* expectations, instead of your own. Start trusting your own judgment and decision-making processes, mistakes and all.

The Double Bind: Damned If You Do, and Damned If You Don't

I am giving the "double bind" its own subtitle, because I had never heard of it, until Wade described it to me. And, I guarantee if you have a failing or failed relationship, you have experienced this at one point or another. A double bind is a form of control, that is also an emotionally distressing dilemma, but it lacks open intimidation. So, it is a strong manipulation tactic used to box the other person into a "no-win" situation. It is when you are given repeated contradictory instructions, and these instructions are enforced by a threat of some sort of punishment (explicit or implicit). It is also compounded by the fact that you are not allowed to discuss the contradiction, and you cannot leave the situation. In short, it is when words and actions don't match. An example of this is if a co-parent continually chastises you because you are not sharing "equal responsibilities" in raising your children, yet you are not given equal rights by that same co-parent. It is a no-win situation for you. Another example might be a partner who wants you to always "look your best." But then when you dress up, do your hair and makeup (or for a man, hit the gym, to look fit), the person accuses you of doing so for the attention of other people. You cannot win.

So, my friends, be on the lookout for the dreaded *double bind*. This creates a situation in which a successful response to one message, results in a failed response to the other (and vice versa). This is done so that you will automatically be wrong, regardless of your response. A third example of this is if your ex attempts to shame you for trying to "buy" your child's love and affection, because you purchased a warm winter coat that your child needed. Conversely, a few weeks later, that same ex criticizes you for not ever spending any extra money on your child (above and beyond child support). Your ex will then complain that they do not have enough money to purchase necessary items for the children. Abracadabra! You are trapped! In your co-parent's twisted mind, you lose no matter what decision you make. Either you are a manipulator, or you are greedy.

My Story

Both Wade and I have extensive examples of the "double bind" in our own past relationships.

For example, when Anthony left me, he told me that he "did not want or love me anymore." However, I did not tell Anthony that I remarried my second husband, until after the ceremony. I did this predominantly out of fear that he may ruin our day, either by withholding the children from the ceremony or that he would show up and somehow disrupt the day. When he came later that evening, to pick up our two minor children (eight years old and four years old) for his custodial time, the children were very excited about the day's events. So, they ran outside to tell their dad the "good news." Anthony then asked my daughter to go back inside and ask me to come outside to talk with him. I will never forget his response. He began to cry and hug me. I felt him shaking. It was one of those awkward hugs that lasts a little too long. He then whispered, "I had no idea that you were even considering remarrying." You see, I believe that Anthony did not want me, but on some unconscious level, *maybe* he did not want anyone else to have me either. Or, maybe he was genuinely happy for me. I will probably never know. But I also suppose that a shocking thing to him was that I found someone who loved me again. I am only guessing, but I think in his mind, nobody else would ever want or love me—much less marry me.

My Life Lesson

If someone is telling you that they love you, but their actions are telling you a completely different story. (i.e., they tell you they love only you, but they are cheating on you, with another partner, or they are emotionally or physically abusing you.), you should rethink your situation. And, if your partner expects you to meet their wants, needs, and desires, without them explicitly telling you what those wants, needs, and desires are, this could be a double bind being served to you.

Have you ever heard your partner say, "I don't want you to do it because I asked you to, I want you to do it because you want to"? Human interaction is extremely complex. In this scenario, you are placed in a real predicament. If you acquiesce and do what your partner asks you to do, they think you are doing it only because they asked. If you do nothing, then you are not meeting his or her wants, needs, and desires. And worse, if you tell them that you do not agree with what they are asking you to do, out of principle, or you say that you are too busy at that moment, because of work or other reasons, then your partner will think this is your indication that you no longer love them.

There is a learned helplessness that comes with the double bind. What I mean by this is that whenever we are continuously placed in a "no-win" situation, the relationship will begin to break down. *The one that can never be right* will begin to feel apathy, and they will eventually give up on trying to please their partner. It gets very tiresome to always be wrong. Both Wade and I had very little victories in our past relationships, because we were continually incorrect, no matter what we did, or how hard we tried to please our previous partners. This is a dangerous situation, because you are "dammed if you do", and "damned if you don't." If someone constantly feels that whatever decision they make will be wrong, because of the conflicting messages received from the other person, they will emotionally shut down and stop trying.

> *It is easy to see how quickly some expectations become layered, competitive and conflicting. This is how the shame-web works. We have very few realistic options that allow us to meet any of these expectations. Most of the options that we do have feel like a "double bind." Marilyn Frye describes a double bind as "a situation in which options are very limited, and all of them expose us to penalty, censure or deprivation."*
>
> **—Brené Brown**

Distinguish Your Own
Thoughts: "Never Settle"

My Story

I quickly realized that I really knew nothing about myself. I always seemed to morph myself into what I thought others wanted me to be. I am a people-pleaser at heart. Directly following my breakups and divorce(s), I could probably only tell you superficial things about myself, for example, that my favorite color was purple and that I love nachos. I never really delved deep enough into my own psyche to get to really know myself. I felt superficial. I often wondered about the very substance of my being. I did not know what I really enjoyed doing in my spare time. I knew my general political views on world news was conservative. Otherwise, I knew very little about my position on things, other than my career. I have always had a keen business sense and savvy, which is probably why I was never able to be swayed in that area of my life. However, if you are anything like me, I had many other frailties and insecurities, when it came to myself.

As far back as I can remember, I was never without a boyfriend or husband. One relationship rolled into the next. I put all my energy into my relationships. I morphed my likes and dislikes to coincide with my partner's favorite pastimes, views, and agendas. That was good in one way, but in other ways it was detrimental. If you are not experiencing new things for yourself, then you are remaining stagnant. But if you are not staying true to your own identity and authentic self, you will never be truly happy. You will also not have anything new and exciting to bring *to* the relationship with your significant other. And the worst part is that your partner will never really know the real you. Try not to focus *only* on your partner. Focus on yourself as well. I find that most of the time, if you are looking through a microscope at someone 24/7, you are bound to become weary, tired, resentful, and bored. So, invest in them, but also invest in your own interests, thoughts, and outside activities.

You must also learn to distinguish your thoughts from the thoughts of others. For me, I was on autopilot. I had a daily routine that I was familiar with, and I am not the type of person that relishes change of any kind. In fact, I was on autopilot most of my life: Go to college, get a job, get married, have children, think this, that, and boom! Time passes by quickly, and things get away from you. That's all well and good, and it gets the job done certainly, but it doesn't allow room for *you* and your own passions.

My Life Lesson

Remove all your masks and discover your authentic identity. Sit down with yourself. Come up with a few beliefs that aren't based on what you are told to think, or what you think others want you to do or believe. Base these principles about yourself on your true inner thoughts, goals, and dreams. We all have them. Now, what do you think? Is your list different from the life you are living?

Society has a very covert way of handing the "misguided," condemning the "losers," idolizing the "beautiful," and alienating the "lonely." But these describing words have no basis. Think about what *you* believe to be good and bad parts of yourself, your past relationships, and what part you played in them. Do not rely on what anyone else has told you. Everything changes when you start to emit your own thoughts and ideas, rather than absorbing these from the people around you. You need to make your own imprint for your life, your values, your morals, and what you believe in. You cannot receive these things from anyone else.

The authentic self is the soul made visible.

Authenticity is the daily practice of letting go of who we think we are supposed to be—and embracing who we are.

—**Brene Brown**

18

Positive Self-Talk, Healing, and Moving, Grooving— And Giving—Your Way Back To Health

Sometimes your joy is the source of your smile, but sometimes your smile can be the source of your joy.

—*Thich Nhat Hanh*

I can only speak of my own experiences as a woman and as a mother, but to be honest, women are very often the last people on their own "to-do" list. I am sure there are men who are this way as well. Between work and housework, running kids to activities, and all the responsibilities of life, it is easy to think there is no time for "you." But the truth is you need to carve out time for you, especially if you are coming out of a bad relationship.

My Story

I took up yoga for the first time during one of my separations, and it helped me immensely. I could immerse myself in quiet time and solitude. I learned to breathe in the "good shit" and exhale the "bullshit." This meditation time allowed me to engulf my soul into the light. Give yourself permission for this special self-time and space, to get away from the expectations, the conversations, social media, your cell phone, the noise, the media, your children, and the pressures of day-to-day life. I used this alone time to think about myself and how I could better who I had become.

I would focus on one mantra and repeat that to myself over-and-over again. For example, I would say "I am kind and giving," or "You can do this," or "You are enough," or "You are stronger than you think." You get the point. These positive mantras began to take hold of who I was becoming. Whatever you do, move away from anything that distracts you from contemplating your life and where you want it to go. In solitude, you should feel independent and self-sufficient, not lonely, needy, or afraid. Focusing on the negative aspects of your life is a surefire way to keep you connected and tied to your past.

Talk to yourself like you would to someone you love.

—**Brenè Brown**

My Doctor, My Friend

One of my best purchases when I was separated was a great pair of Bose headphones. I began to jog after work. This helped to release endorphins, and it also was making me healthy again. I also found that I could sleep better after I had been outside in the fresh air. Now this did not come easily for me. In the beginning, my friend (Jamie), who also happens to be my family doctor, came over and literally dragged me out of my bed. (And I loved to sleep, because it was my only relief from sadness, anger, and loneliness.) Jamie had purchased a Garmin watch for me, and she would come over to my house a few times a week and "make me" walk with her. Then she said she would be tracking my progress on-line, so I began to upload my daily walks onto my laptop. At first, I did this because I did not want to let her down, and I certainly did not want to be embarrassed that I wasn't doing my daily exercise. But after time, I began to crave it. I was doing this for me, and only me. The best side effect was that I was also losing weight and feeling stronger than ever. This feeling alone is so empowering that it exudes self-confidence. When I would run, I remember feeling like the headwind that used to hold me back, was now the tailwind that was pushing me (and my running shoes) forward.

My Life Lesson

Sometimes it is easier to do something—anything—rather than sit still and be stagnant.

Now, you should be at a point to at least seek out a few of your very own passions. Try your best to shift your focus from your incompatible relationship—back to yourself. Consider trying new things or putting your energy into a hobby you've neglected. Be passionately crazy for what you love. Be a little innocent with yourself. Go ahead, don't limit yourself. You will probably believe in something or see beauty in something that you didn't before. You should do it no matter what anyone else thinks. If you have found something that is worthy of your best efforts, sacrifice, and tears, then you have found the most important pursuit of your life. Often, that pursuit can lead you to something ultimately fulfilling. The key here is to realize that *it doesn't matter what it is*. For me it was to volunteer at a local food shelter, walk the dogs looking for permanent homes, at our town's animal shelter, indulge in my love of photography, attend guitar lessons, and take painting classes. There is no scale when it comes to passion. You either feel it or you don't; no activity is better than any other. When you find something that draws you out of bed in the morning, cling to that.

Get involved in local activities. Decide what you want to do. Write it down and formulate a plan. And then work your plan every day. Join a gym. Take a public speaking class. Sign up for a dance lesson. Plant yourself on a park bench to watch the world and the beautiful nature all around you. Take a photography class. Learn to play the piano, or another musical instrument. Learn to make jewelry. Go swimming. Bake something. Ride your bicycle. Breathe life in. Do anything that interests you. This may take you awhile, especially if you have never focused inward before. Now Wade and I try new things together. For example, we recently took ballroom dance classes. It was a fun exercise, and we both enjoyed learning all the various dances, like the foxtrot, tango, waltz, etc. We would practice at home, and it gave us something different to talk about.

Most importantly, work on your relationship with yourself. Focus on cultivating self-love and respect. Remind yourself that you are worthy of love and that you deserve a healthy relationship.

> *Do your little bit of good where you are; it's those little bits of good put together that overwhelm the world.*
>
> **—Desmond Tutu**

> *When you recover or discover something that nourishes your soul and brings joy, care enough about yourself to make room for it in your life.*
>
> **—Jean Shinoda Bolen**

In Giving—We Receive and Heal

My Story

I came from a long lineage of giving people. My parents are the epitome of this. So, this was engrained in me from a very early age, with stories about my maternal grandfather, who was a medical doctor in the small town of Punxsutawney, Pennsylvania. He died before I was born, yet he is still referred to in his town as "The Good Doctor." He was dubbed with this nickname because if someone did not have the money for his in-home doctor visit or the required prescriptive medication they needed to heal their ailments, he would pay for it himself. Or, my grandfather would allow patients or their families to "trade" in-kind, for just about anything they had to offer, like a home-made meal. He would suggest these "trades" to his patients that he knew could not afford his bill. He did this so that these hard-working folks would not have to feel embarrassed for not having the money to pay him. He left them with both their medicine and their pride. My maternal grandmother, "Nana," as we affectionately called her, was a registered nurse. Sometimes, she would accompany him on his rounds, after working a full shift at the hospital. So, my grandparents, a doctor and a nurse, both worked extremely hard, but they lived very frugally so that they could help others.

On the other side of my lineage, my father became his family's "head of the household" when he was a senior in high school. His father suddenly and unexpectedly passed away. My father worked two, and sometimes three jobs, to help support himself, his mother, and his sister, at the age of sixteen. This grueling work schedule continued through college, where he majored in civil engineering at Penn State University. Because his sister was divorced, and his mother was a stay-at-home mother, who was hard-working, but unskilled like most women of her generation, my father helped take care of them. He was also a father-figure to his sister's two boys, until the boys were old enough to take care of things. My cousins were also extremely hard-working young men, who did not have the luxuries afforded to them that some do, so they worked from a very early age. And they worked hard to help support their mother and grandmother. Our family was extremely close-knit, on both sides. We did not take life, a roof over our heads, or a hot meal, for granted. We all worked together, to help those who could not fully help themselves.

And my mother is a saint, at least in my mind. She is the most giving person that I have ever met. She always has a kind word for everyone, and she lives the word of the Bible. She never speaks ill-will of anyone, even those who deserve her anger and resentment. She is always looking for the good in people. My mother taught me that in giving she receives a peaceful joy. And she explains to me that this is how she knows she is nearing the truth of why she is on this earth. She has dedicated her entire life to raising her family, and she and my father did whatever was needed for my sister, me, and her four grandchildren.

In fact, when my sister and I were in high school, we would leave at one p.m., every day. This was approved by our school district, so that my mother could drive us, two hours, one-way, to get to our private gymnastics' classes. There were only a handful of gymnastics clubs that had coaches and teams that operated at the competitive level that we trained. She would have dinner prepared and packed for us, and we would eat in the car. She would help us with our homework, during our commute. And, she also taught gymnastics to the beginner gymnasts, for most of the five to six hours that we were training. Afterwards, she would drive us the two hours back home. We would arrive home anywhere between ten and eleven p.m. She did this every single day, sans Wednesdays, for six years.

It was also my mother that I credit for inspiring my daughter, in her service to others. My mother got my daughter, Gabi, and her cousin, involved in the local soup kitchen at a very early age. And, my daughter continued this giving, during her high school years, at our local parochial school. She was recognized for logging in *triple* the required service hours, which was approximately two hundred hours-of-service more than the students were required to serve to graduate. Every single weekend, she would spend approximately five to fifteen hours giving of her time to others, for nothing tangible in return. But Gabi would always tell me that she was receiving something far more precious than money or things. She said that it made her soul feel good, and you could see it on her tired face, at the end of every one of her "service days."

My Life Lesson

My complaints, drama, victim-mentality, whining, crying, and blaming never got me one step closer to finding, what seemed for me, to be elusive happiness. You should look outside of yourself to begin your healing process. It is my personal belief that we are not blessed so that we can have more. Instead, we are blessed, so that we can give to others. Do this to heal yourself, and if you have children, take them with you on this journey of giving. I believe that when you focus on being a blessing to others, God will make sure that you are always blessed in abundance. I have felt his profound blessings in the feelings that I receive, when I am a grateful servant to others. I learned that the best medicine for despair is service. We rise by lifting others.

If you're having trouble letting go of the past, consider getting involved in a charity or cause that you feel passionate about. Doing this will not only occupy your time and mind, as you process feelings and let go of the relationship, but it can also help shift your focus to something bigger than yourself. Studies have shown volunteering can significantly improve your overall well-being. This can also provide a new perspective and help you feel good—as you also help your community. Giving back to others is extremely valuable, but helping others also offers you the opportunity to help you learn more about yourself. You will also gain valuable life experiences that will take the focus off you and your current difficulties.

Another positive thing about volunteering or working for a charitable cause is that you will meet other selfless interesting people. These are the salt-of-the-earth people that you could forge lasting friendships with. Your anxiety may be temporarily still weighing you down, but a kind word or deed, to or for another, can cheer you up. You will make an impact on the people that you are helping, and your fellow volunteers can possibly provide you with new insights on life and conquering true happiness. Your fellow volunteers may also offer different perspectives and ways to look at situations. So, take time to listen to others. Absorb what others might have to say and offer. And if that is not enough, when you make even small sacrifices in the name of others, for nothing in return, you will begin to feel a peace and happiness that you may have never felt before.

Get the kids involved. They are never too young to help the less fortunate, sick, or elderly. They will quickly realize that the pleasure of giving, without any expectations, is more rewarding than expecting without giving. And I believe that this is the source of true and organic happiness. From young children to matured adults, there seems to be a growing need for material things. It has taken on a great importance in many people's lives—as if it were a necessity of life. It seems to me that the demand for such material purchases has corrupted the definition of pure happiness, and it has given us an artificial sense of being content and satisfied with our lives—which is temporary, at best.

A few years ago, my daughter played her guitar at a local retirement home. She came home with tears in her eyes, and she said, "Mom, there was this elderly woman in a wheelchair who looked up at me." And, after the last song, she said in a gravelly voice, "You've made my day. This means so much." My daughter then said, "No one had ever thanked me in such a way for doing something so small, and she was a stranger no less!" She will carry that feeling of love with her, always. That love is always cloaked around her, like her favorite childhood "pink blankie" that she still sleeps with today. We too can wrap ourselves up in these little moments. And, we can draw upon these moments, when life gets us down.

Use your God-given gifts to serve others.

—1 Peter 4:10

Giving without expectation, leads to receiving without limitation.

—Charles F. Glassman

You Give Power to What Has Power Over You

The most wasted of all days is one without laughter.

—*Nicolas Chamfort*

My Story

My father's favorite quote is, "Life is an attitude, so you better adopt a good one." This is how I learned that our minds will always believe everything we tell it. Feed it hope. Feed it truth. Feed it forgiveness, and feed it love. If you want to be happy, you must be happy on purpose. If truth be told, during this time in my recovery, my daily "self-talk" was always negative. You must force yourself to find positive attributes about yourself and accentuate them and eliminate the negative. Work on being in love with the person in the mirror. At first it may feel very uncomfortable. I felt so silly looking at myself in the mirror, telling myself, "I love you." Sometimes, so much so, that I would burst out laughing at the ridiculousness of it all. But, then again, a smile did change the way my entire body felt. It felt good to laugh, especially at myself.

Attitude is a choice. Optimism is a choice. Respect is a choice. Self-love is a choice. Therefore, personal happiness is ultimately a choice... *your* choice. Whatever choice you make—makes you.

My Life Lesson

Shut the door to your past and put a padlock on it! Slam it shut, if you must, but make a clean break. Do not look back. As you go through this transformation, do not ever accept feeling left out, abnormal, or unhappy, just because you are facing a temporary adversity. I will say that again. It is *temporary*. I would cry every night. I would literally have a reoccurring "pity party" for myself, after I put my children to bed. All this did was make my eyes puffy in the morning and make me more tired than I already was. You need to move forward, getting on with life. You will not find salvation in the darkness. You can rise from anything. Nothing is permanent. You are not stuck. You have choices. You can think new thoughts. You can experience and learn new things. You can create new and healthy habits. All that really matters is that you decide to change today. In the beginning, you will feel bad "minute to minute," but as the days pass, the time that you feel good will increase. You will not notice it at first, because the change is gradual, but it will happen. And then before you know it, you will be happy longer than you are unhappy.

You do not need permission to rewrite your story or to be happy. We often tend to place the weight of our identities into our self-professed life stories. We believe we are what we continually do and tell ourselves. Hell, I even made the mistake of believing what other people said or thought about me was the end-all and the be-all. Examine your story and rewrite it in a more empowering way to start making positive changes in your life. If you continually tell yourself you lost your soul mate and you're destined to be alone and unhappy, you might struggle to hang on to a relationship that is no longer serving you. Reframe your story and consider the fact this relationship may have just been one step on the journey toward an even better relationship in the future.

And you? When will you begin the interesting journey into yourself, so your attitude begins to change? Let go of the negative you now, so that you can experience inner peace. Yesterday is not ours to recover, but tomorrow is ours to win or lose. Believe that what you seek is seeking you...and you will find it. In every moment, we are the ones who get to choose our attitude. Choose wisely.

Ships don't sink because of the water around them; ships sink because of the water that gets in them. Don't let what is happening around you get inside of you and weigh you down.

Write to Expose the Wrong

I found it helpful to write down all my feelings and my major milestones. I listed all my past accomplishments and memorialized them with pen and paper. Next, I thought about how each of those events shaped or affected who I am today. When life brings triumphs or problems, it shapes our belief system and makes us think differently, but it also makes us *who we are*. These things in your list are organically *you*. Remember your growing accomplishments and how they changed you for the better. And take time to set new goals for yourself, including focusing on your relationship goals.

Entertaining this activity of self-realization will help prepare you to begin again with a clean slate. You must develop your own moral guidelines, of what you are willing to accept and not accept in your next relationship. But most importantly, you must practice sticking to it. For me, I had so many bad habits and making excuses for others' behavior and wrongdoings, that it took a lot to overcome my own conduct. But I do remember getting stronger every day, as I searched for that evasive "inner peace." It truly does begin the moment that you choose *not* to allow another person or situation to control your emotions.

My Life Lesson

Stop spinning that bad-movie reel throughout your mind. You cannot rewrite the dialogue of your story to this point, no matter how much you wish you could. And you also cannot change someone else. Finally, do not organize and attend a daily pity-party for yourself. Recovery and happiness will not be found in wallowing. It's about clarification and identification of issues. These issues might be keeping you from reaching your present potential and letting your true self blossom.

Spend a little time making a timeline and clarifying when you were the happiest and the saddest. You want to replicate the happy times. A timeline is an incredibly objective method for marking down past occurrences in your life that you consider to be major. You can look at them as formation blocks and as learning experiences along your timeline. Keep your timeline simple, real, and condensed to the major effects or lessons learned from each past incident.

When analyzing negative past experiences, focus on what you learned from them. Everyone has these blips in their timeline but exaggerating or ignoring them won't help you. Instead, recognize that these experiences shaped you into a better version of yourself.

Lastly, it may help you to write all your feelings in a letter, to your ex, even if you have no intention of sending it. You can choose to give this letter to your former partner or destroy it when you're finished. The point of the letter is to allow you to release your feelings. Writing or journaling can help you reflect on the relationship as a whole, while giving you a way to further your mental and emotional wellness.

> *Absorb what is useful, reject what is useless, and add what is specifically your own.*
>
> **—Bruce Lee**

Daily Mantras and Mentors

My Story

My yoga class taught me to fill my void, with not only relaxation rituals, but also with positive affirmations. I had a journal beside my bed. I would wake up to blank pages, and I would try to fill the paper with my pain—and words of comfort. I would often recite Joel Osteen or some other inspirational speaker, or even write down parts of scripture from the Bible. Soon, my journal was full of good things that I could refer to in my times of need. I was getting out my frustrations and my unhappiness through my words. I was no longer trying to cover it up with all my self-imposed pain-releasers, like cigarettes, overeating, staying out too late, weekend drinking, and so on. I no longer was going to accept living with my conscience flying somewhere in the wind. I would set a demarcation line, and not cross it.

My positive inspirations and that journal quite literally helped me change my mindset. I tried to write down things I was grateful for—even in the midst of heartache. My children were healthy. I had a great sister and parents. I would repeatedly tell myself, "You are worthy of being happy." If your attitude is filled with gratitude, there will be no stopping you.

My Life Lesson

As a quick overview so far: Be kind to yourself. Try not to stress yourself about things that you cannot control. Control the things you can. Maintain your daily schedule. Go to work. Go to school. Go to bed early. Love yourself. Forgive your ex. Do not interrupt your calendar because of a break-up or divorce. Resolve that argument with that friend. Get everything out of the way, to clear up the path to "me" time. You may also find that having all your other affairs in order will help expedite the process to grabbing a firm hold on your identity. And allow yourself to be silently drawn by the strange pull of what you really love. It will never lead you astray.

You are at the point now where you may want to find yourself a mentor. A support system is key to any self-improvement tactic. Not a lot of people will understand what you're going through and will brush off your broaching the topic as a flash-in-the-pan moodiness. You must surround yourself with those who only lift you higher. Release all things that do not serve you well. Only take advice from someone that you are willing to trade places with. While it is true that soul-searching can only be done by you, having a mentor will be an incredible resource when you hit those unavoidable bumps in the road.

Seek out someone you trust who has a definite sense of self. Those professionals will help you be free to be your authentic self. When we surround ourselves with positive influential people, we are clearing the negativity that attempts to engulf us. We are making room to welcome the good and the positive with a renewed energy and attitude. Doing this not only enriches our lives, but it will surround us in a supportive and healing space. This will foster your growth, and the growth of your children.

Use this mentor as a sounding board, too, for what you come up against. The outlet will surely come in handy. This person will become your lifeline in times of trouble.

But, like anything else, after a while, you may not need to call upon them. Let them know the process you're starting to undertake. Explain to them that you respect them, and that you would like to utilize them as a source of strength, as you complete your self-realization journey. Ask them questions. Learn from them. Find out what grounds them, and how they stay true to themselves, their ideologies, and moralities.

A sweet friendship refreshes the soul.

—Proverbs 27:9

My religion is very simple. My religion is kindness.

—Dalai Lama

19

You Do Not Need Anyone's Approval: Happiness Comes from Within

A man cannot be comfortable without his own approval.

—Mark Twain

While men can also suffer from the need for approval, women are often told to be "nice" throughout their lives. After all, we are thought of as the nurturers, the mothers, the "kind" ones. As such, we may feel the need for people to "like" us.

Sometimes—for men and women—this struggle can go all the way back to childhood. Perhaps we moved a lot because of a parent in the armed services, so friends were hard to make. Maybe we were bullied for being different. Whatever the reason, wanting people to approve of us is a deep-seated need and fear for many of us.

My Story

Something that I still struggle with is the need to feel accepted by everyone. Let go of your need for approval. I have now realized that some people will think poorly of me, no matter what I do, even if that is an ex-partner or ex-spouse of mine. Chances are that they did not support you when you were married, so they will most likely not approve of you now that you are separated or divorced. Stop looking for something that may never be there. It's important to forget about what everyone else thinks, because you cannot please everyone. Own who you are. And if people do not understand why you are getting separated or divorced, remember that if they are your true friends and loving family, they should want you to be happy and whole. And while you might not want to disappoint them, remember that this is your life. If you continue to exist just to fulfill other people's ideas of who you should be, you'll never know who you really are. This thought is aptly summed up by Raymond Hull: *He who trims himself to suit everyone will soon whittle himself away.*

There is an Ed Sheeran song entitled "Save Myself." This song beautifully describes the pain that I went through, with both of my divorces. I love the lyrics, because they are powerful words, with a powerful lesson.

Ed Sheeran has captured the essence of what happens if you allow yourself to succumb to everyone else around you, at the expense of your own well-being. He speaks of us as either radiating good energy—or draining others in the world. He also sings of the scars that remain of our pain.

You do not need to end up with more scars, so put yourself first. It is the same reason that airlines ask you to put the oxygen mask on yourself first, so that you can help those around you. You will be no good to anyone else if you do not ensure that you love yourself, first and foremost.

Ed Sheeran's song ends with the idea that if you are not right for someone else, you will be left behind—and before moving on, you have to love yourself. Nothing could be truer.

My Life Lesson

Realize that some people will become jealous, afraid, or overwhelmed when a person changes their usual habits. So, when you grow, mature, and become more self-loving, some of your prior acquaintances will run from it, while others will embrace it. The ones who don't like it or feel that it is a threat to the relationship you've always had with them, aren't worth your time right now. You cannot allow yourself to get dragged into another person's drama. It's okay if everyone does not embrace the "new you." This reminds me of a famous quote by Rumi: "If you are irritated by every rub, how will your mirror ever be polished?"

Your change may also be forcing others to take a cold hard look at themselves, and they may not like what they see. Give these people space and compassion; they may come around in time. If they don't, leave them be. You don't need them to be happy. Do not remain imprisoned by wanting to make everyone else contented or comfortable, when the door is wide open to your self-awakening.

The point to this is that we all battle one kind of insecurity or another. You will need to have "trigger points" for yourself, as you move forward in this process. Because it is when you begin to feel very uncomfortable, depressed or lonely that you could relapse. You may try to find that quick-fix for happiness, at the bottom of a drink on the rocks, or you may call an old flame that you know isn't right for you, just because you are temporarily uncomfortable. You have exes for a reason. Stay away. They didn't support or approve of you then. Find yourself a new trap door to prevent you from hitting bottom.

A technique that helped me stop one of my bad habits—worrying what other people think—was simple. I would put a loose rubber band around my wrist. Anytime that I would think negative thoughts or begin to question my decisions regarding my breakup/divorces, I would snap the rubber band against my wrist. Over time, when I would feel that tiny sting of the band snapping against my wrist, I would force myself to rethink my emotional state. Although not the same, it was a Pavlov's dog theory, which studied respondent's classical conditioning. Pavlov's dog refers to a learning procedure, in which a stimulus (in this case food), was paired with a previously neutral stimulus (in this case a bell). In this study, when someone rang a bell, the dogs were fed. The neutral stimulus began to elicit a physical response from the dogs in the study. The dogs would salivate when they heard the bell. Similarly, my rubber band method, was an effective tool for me. The rubber band helped me stop what I was doing or thinking, and change course. Overtime, my rubber band would help me to elicit a more positive emotional outlook or pathway.

The unknown is scary, but that is precisely why you must keep your resolve and focus on moving forward. You can look towards a new and healthy relationship, even if that is just with yourself, for the time being. I have learned not to be fearful of the future. I accomplish this by trying to do what is right, moral, and just, for me and my family, and I never intentionally set out to hurt someone else. This way, even if I fail, I still possess my self-respect and dignity.

If you can "give happiness to yourself," without taking away something, from someone else, and you can do that *without* a significant other, then you are probably on a good course to recovery. Claim your destiny by developing inner equanimity, self-discipline, and perseverance. Too many people get wrapped up in the idea that someone else can make them happy. Or, they believe that pleasing someone else will make them happy, but I found that this just isn't so. I've learned this lesson the hard way. And it's a lot easier to be happily single, or happily married (whichever you decide), if *you* are first happy. The time you spend getting to know yourself will be profitable and for your own good. It is always best when you know what *you* want out of life…and love.

Keep the people in your life who truly love you, motivate you, encourage you, inspire you, enhance you, and make you happy.

Love yourself first and everything else falls into line. You really have to love yourself to get anything done in this world.

—Lucille Ball

Success without happiness is failure.

—Tony Robbins

20

Choosing Again:
How Do You Know if the
Person is Right for You?

After you have successfully gotten to really know yourself, then and only then, should you think about entering the dating world again. At times, this process was a paradox for me. Because I felt like I was broken but into many beautiful pieces. Because, in having my heart severed, I found myself, a little at a time.

Love is just a word until someone comes along and gives it meaning. Do I believe in soul mates? I never did. I thought love depended on where you lived, what your interests were, and that there was no larger scheme of life acting serendipitously to "arrange" your lives to cross paths. I thought that someone could love multiple people, depending on your circumstances.

It is so cliché, but the saying, "You will know when it is the right one," is true. The problem is that I always thought my next boyfriend was "the One." It felt right to me, and I ignored all the warning signs, and all the good advice that my parents offered me. I knew better. But what I have learned is…I did not know better.

But all of that changed when I met my third (and final) husband, Wade. We had crossed paths many times throughout our lives, but we both missed the signs that we should be together, until one day it was made so clear that there could be no denying our love.

My Life Lesson

Don't look for love. Let it find you, after you learn to love yourself. What you seek is seeking you.

You have loved hard, but you may have been misguided in the past. This time, you are going to adopt the, "Do not be hard, but take no prisoners" attitude. You want, and have, so much love to give, because you now know how it feels to be loved so little in return. Perhaps you did not change at all, yet your relationship still ended. Instead, the other person in the relationship with you just never knew you. Maybe you did change—for the better—becoming an independent person. Maybe you were betrayed. Every single failed relationship has its own story. Now, only you can change your situation.

Take personal responsibility for your happiness. Do not place blame on anything or anyone. No one else can make you happy. Do not become stuck in the cyclone of pain and the wicked "blame games." These competitions with your ex will only drain you. There is no way back to the life you once had. You are in the driver's seat. You will determine your own destiny. Remember that you will attract what you want by *being* what you want.

So, how do you know if someone is right for you? This type of love will immediately feel eternal and pure. This love will feel *drastically different*. The difference will be so powerful and overwhelming that you will not be able to mistake it. For me, this feeling far surpassed my prior understanding of love. This love will even unselfishly love your selfish tendencies.

I compare this inherent new sense of "true love" to when I was pregnant. I was fixated on the signs of labor. I was certain that I would *not* "know" when I should call my doctor to head to the hospital to deliver my firstborn. I was certain that I would be delivering my baby at home. But, when the time came, I instinctively knew. Just like every other mother "just knows." Your mind, body, and spirit provide you with intuitive, emotional, and physical signs. When you find true love, it will be such a vast difference between any relationship that you have previously been involved in, that you will absolutely know it. Nobody will have to tell you. Everything that you experience will be better. It is not an incremental change, but a night and day difference. So, if you have not felt that "ah-ha, world-changing moment" then you need to keep looking.

My love is selfish. I cannot breathe without you.

—*John Keats*

From the Pot to the Frying Pan: Don't Exchange One Set of Problems for Another

My Story

They say it takes approximately half the time you are with someone to completely get over them. For me, it took a little more time for *complete* peace. (I must like to wallow and dance in the dark.) The hardest lesson that Wade and I have both learned is that when you find pure love, you will never again live with the deep-rooted void that we both suffered with for so long. We were devoid of love in our relationships, and this is no way for anyone to live their lives.

After my first failed marriage, I was looking for the "exact opposite" of my first spouse. This caused me to have "tunnel vision." Where did this lead me? I chose wrong, *again*. One similarity Wade and I shared is that we were both ravenously starving for attention, affection, and faithfulness. In fact, we were desperate for it. And, desperate people will do desperate things.

I should have taken more time off before I jumped into another relationship. And Wade should have sought out therapy to help himself, prior to marrying a second time. His "stages" of recovery included: keeping to himself, not talking about his relationship or the infidelities he suffered through in previous relationships and forging on through endless hours of work. He tells me that whenever he experienced relationship breakups, he never looked back, not even to heal himself. It was permanent. He did not waver on his decisions, and he did not look back, not even for counseling or understanding on why the relationship derailed. So, we both set ourselves up for more heartbreak. Love is a journey that you want to be filled with positivity. You do not deserve another puppeteer that is constantly pulling your strings, or vice versa. And you do not need more "butting of two heads" that must be subdued every day. You probably still feel like love is a now a wall that you must somehow get over. However, you will never get there without introspection.

My Life Lesson

One of the worst things that I did, when I was hurt by my first ex-husband, was to compound the damage, by hurting myself a second time. How did I do this? I got married for a second time— too soon. Because of this, I left myself dealing with not only rejection and bereavement from my first divorce, but I began to doubt my decision-making ability altogether. Too often in my pain and confusion, I impulsively did the wrong thing, instead of thinking things all the way through. I didn't feel that I deserved to be helped, so I allowed anger, guilt, resentment, loneliness, and pain to seep into my psyche, and I made other wrong relationship decisions. But real love cannot be built on fake emotions or rash decisions.

In hindsight, what Wade and I should have done was to take time for ourselves, to properly grieve the loss of our respective relationships. Instead, we both impetuously jumped into our second marriages, without getting the therapy and help that we both so desperately needed. It was not fair to us, and it was not fair to our second spouses. I believe that before anyone can completely move on, they must let go of their past ghosts, or they will continue to haunt you. Wade should have invested time with a professional counselor, and I should have remained in therapy longer, at least until these professionals felt good about our mental and emotional states. But, neither of us felt we needed this help. Let me assure you. We did. And chances are… you may too. There is nothing to be embarrassed about. You are not a weak person because you were in a relationship that failed, or you are seeking therapy. Some of the strongest people that I know have been through breakups and divorces, some of them multiple. Be proud of yourself for how hard you are trying.

> *Pain is like water. It finds a way to push through any seal. There's no way to stop it. Sometimes you must let yourself sink inside of it before you can learn how to swim to the surface.*
>
> **—Katie Kacvinsky**

Too Fast, Too Soon (Ping-Pong—Rebound!)

Rebound relationships are defined by more than just speed. A person who is rebounding may be trying to avoid their feelings about their recent breakup. Fixating on someone new is a great way to do that. I have surmised that in a rebound-relationship, there is no space and time to process the truth of the past love. Therefore, the rebounder uses the technique of denial, along with moving on quickly, to stop their feelings. The pitfall is that they might be moving so fast, they never stop to learn, or grow, from what was left behind.

If you have spent years in an unhealthy relationship, like we did, you will feel like you are ready to make up for lost time. That is normal. But just because it is typical does not make it right. Wade and

I also wanted to prove to our family and friends that we "could get it right the second time." This sense of urgency and desire caused us to both to rush in the wrong direction.

What Wade and I did not understand was that our "rebound relationships" were not going to make up for the shortcomings and mistakes of our prior partners, nor were they going to fill that unfathomable hole inside of our own hearts. And this will probably not fill the deep gap inside of you right now either. It took me approximately one year to even accept losing Anthony. But I began dating within six months of our divorce. This is not a good idea.

After Anthony left me, I was coming out of a relationship that was unhealthy, so the first "nice" guy that I dated became my second husband. The problem with that scenario is that emotionally, he was not the right man for me either. He was soft-hearted but was indecisive and not a "planner." Consequently, I made every decision, and as a result, I became very difficult and temperamental. The marriage felt like a burden instead of a help to me. I was exhausted most of the time. I had to figure out all our bills, budgets, and finances. Sometimes, I felt like I had three children instead of two. This type of burden is not fun, especially if you have two jobs: raising your children and working outside of the home. However, I will say that we are still friends today. He is an extremely sweet and giving man but just not the right man for me, and I believe that I was not the right woman for him.

My Life Lesson

Right after a divorce, I suspect that many people try to numb the pain by quickly getting involved with someone else. That is just a bandage over a wound that needs time to heal. Slow down and take the time to get to know who *you* are again. Rebound relationships will usually never solve your emptiness and loss. And a rebound does not necessarily only refer to a time reference. In my opinion, it also refers to anyone who enters a relationship but is not properly healed from a past one, regardless of the amount of time that has elapsed in between them. So, in this context, Wade and I both chose wrong, when we entered the infamous "rebound relationships."

To recap, I would define a rebound relationship as one that occurs shortly after the breakup of a significant love relationship, or before you are completely healed from a prior romance. Generally, a rebound relationship will only serve as a short-term distraction. But it is usually only that—a distraction. What you are doing is trying to connect with another person, to mask the full emotional pain of your recent breakup or divorce. I say this with a warning. Usually, someone ends up being used and hurt as a result. If you are in a relationship to distract yourself from the pain of a broken heart, then you are using another person. More than likely, when that person has served their purpose you will move on, leaving them to pick up the pieces, as you are trying to do right now. Be honest with your new relationship partner about your intentions and ask them to be honest with you. Hell, maybe your rebound is rebounding with you. You don't want to be left behind once he or she decides to move on. Take measures to protect your heart, especially now.

Rebounds are a misguided attempt to move on. Even so, I personally know many people that jump right back into the dating scene, because they do not want to be alone. I did it, and Wade did it. It's a quick fix, and not a long-term solution. If you can accept a "rebound relationship" for what it is, then it may serve some short-term purpose. It will certainly be more fun than dealing with the misery of your recent heartache. However, it will only delay the inevitable. But you will eventually still have to "pay the piper" and put in the hard time of coping with your past lost love. Sleeping with someone new, while you are in search of your self-worth, will not bring back your confidence and happiness. It will only temporarily make you feel good—right before making you feel bad.

So, be very careful when you come out of a relationship, especially if it involved infidelity or abuse. You cannot expect your new partner to be able to "fix" the pain that you experienced in the old relationship. Unfortunately, it just doesn't work that way. It may only create more problems for you down the road. I discuss what I refer to as the Pendulum Effect, later in the book. In short, this is when you go too far to the opposite side of the love-pendulum, attempting to escape the same love mistakes of your past, but end up with another mismatch.

Above all else, guard your heart, for everything you do flows from it.

—**Proverbs 4:23**

Being Alone Versus Feeling Lonely: Change Isn't Always Easy, But Sometimes it is Necessary

My Story

My biggest heartache with both of my divorces was the crippling feelings of emptiness. It was disorienting not to have my partner anymore, especially after years of marriage. If you are like me, you probably can appreciate exactly what I am talking about. It's a hollow energy that you can't shake. For me personally, this was the most distressing part of my two divorces. And to make things worse, if you are still residing where they used to live with you, or visit you, the pitfalls seem endless. You look at where they used to sit, eat, play, etc. It is a loss like no other, because you are all alone. But not really. You still are with yourself. The quality of your life completely depends on the quality of your relationship with *you*. There are no perfect waves, so emerge from the deep sadness in your own sea-of-misery.

Many of my poor relationship choices stemmed from one damming personality trait that I had. I have never been the type of person that could be alone. My entire life, one relationship would end, and

I would roll right into another one. For me, the idea of being alone conjures up a sense of sadness. Maybe it's the sense of boredom, or the feelings of isolation, or being forced to confront my own thoughts. If this is difficult for you as well, you must get over this hurdle to be able to choose a partner who is healthy and good, both for and with you. To create a life that you love, you must either discover or rediscover yourself, and you must do this now.

It had never occurred to me that my own independence was strength, while my dependence on a man, was my weakness. And when I look back over my life now, if I could change one thing, it would be this: I would realize sooner, that even by myself, I was a strong person. I feel very sad that I was ignorant to this concept for so long. If you are at this crossroads, choose to love yourself. Choose to put yourself first. Choose to be comfortable in your own skin.

I struggled from a fear of loneliness for as long as I can remember. As an adult I was uncomfortable even going into our local Wawa convenience store by myself. I always felt like a fish-out-of-water. I am not sure where this comes from, but maybe it was because I grew up in a wonderfully close Italian household, in the small town of Indiana, in the suburbs of Western Pennsylvania. It was a town where everyone knew everyone else. It was the quintessential close-knit town that we have all read about or seen in a movie. And feelings ran deep in our small community, because everything becomes personal when people truly care about one another. I was rarely alone. There was a profound comfort for me, knowing everyone around us. Through my family and the people in our small community, I was accessible to a town that positively reflected and rejoiced in my personal strengths and successes. I always had someone to share in my joys and sorrows. I think that we all have a small built-in craving for this. We all seek, in at least a small measure, a level of acceptance and recognition, by others, to help us feel included. And my family and friends in our community provided this to, and for, me.

On any given fall weekend, you could hear the high school football game being announced at our local field, and you can be certain that most of the town's people would be there cheering on our hometown team. I was a cheerleader, and I was always surrounded by lots of friends and other people who cared about me. And I was always cheering for one of my two boyfriends in high school. First, I dated the star quarterback, and later the star and captain of the defense. Because my graduating class was not that large, everyone knew everyone. And for the most part, everyone was friends with everyone. I was never alone. So, I began to wonder where my fear of being alone came from. Perhaps it is *because* I was rarely ever alone as a young adult.

My supposition is that loneliness is a very normal part of our existence. But, after high school, whenever I was in an unhealthy relationship, I would become overwhelmed and scared of the prospects of being alone. So, when my heart was broken by someone, I would immediately seek another romantic relationship, no matter how superficial it was. Therefore, the state of many of my relationships was like trying to squeeze that round peg into the square hole. It never fit. Wade tells me that he escaped his loneliness by becoming a workaholic. He started his first business when he was in high school. Wade remembers being afraid that his various partners would leave him, and he did not want to be left alone with feelings of rejection and abandonment.

Now that I am in a mature and healthy relationship, and I love myself, I am better equipped to deal with those pesky negative thoughts of being isolated and alone. The reason for this is simple. The answer is at the core root of how I feel about myself. I love myself. My own self-image is finally healthy.

For months after Anthony left, I woke up, every single day, very depressed. I would wonder what I did wrong to deserve this isolation and loneliness. I would look at other couples, when I was out-and-about, and wonder what they possessed that I did not. I would wonder if they were looking at me and judging me for being alone. My logical brain knew that they were complete strangers; therefore, how would they know that my marriage had failed? But I also wondered if anyone could see past my tough exterior and see all the pain and anguish that I was trying so desperately to hold in. Deep down, I did want someone to notice me. I wanted someone to care about the pain I was experiencing. I needed validation. What I didn't know then was that the key to unlocking this began with me.

When my parents told me to focus on my self-esteem, I heeded their good advice. I consciously made a dramatic change. I began to spend time with just me. I desperately wanted to be done feeling lonely. As I said earlier in the book, I got up early in the morning, before everyone else, and I would just sit in bed alone with myself. I would meditate, read, or journal, before I would exercise. That thirty minutes I gave myself was an unbelievable gift. It gave me the space to turn off the noisy dialogue in my head and just be present with me. I could gauge the day's events and prepare for any of my known "stressors" before they happened. Just like anything in life, preparation is the key to success. So, I began to prepare for my emotional well-being, first thing every morning. And I began to enjoy this "me time." It is not selfish to take care of yourself. It is selfish not to. Unfortunately, I did not learn this important lesson until I was forty-five years old. Don't wait this long. Begin to understand and accept this immediately.

My Life Lesson

The only person that I ever "lost" and needed back…was myself.

Have you taken a good look at yourself lately? If you were honest, I would bet that most of you reading this book could probably tell me that you are, at least to some extent, avoiding yourself. I did. I had gained an extra twenty-five pounds, and I hated my shape. My clothing did not fit me right, so I had all the tricks in the world to hide my real self, both physically and emotionally. It never occurred to me that someone I once loved was right here, inside of me. Allow yourself to get in touch with the essence of who you really are, underneath all the baggage. It is that person who will help you move forward to a meaningful life, whether you are alone or not.

Greatness is sometimes forged in pain and discomfort. And weakness waits for those who settle for content. There really is a purpose for our pain. These symptoms are to warn us of possible derailments of our life. As you are sliding sideways, the pain is there to wake you up. It is there to make you change your course.

Most change begins with an uncomfortable feeling or situation. You must push past the negative thoughts and hesitations and just take the plunge. It is like when you first jump into a swimming pool or a river, when you know it is going to be chillingly cold. Everyone knows that once you jump in the water, and get over the discomfort of being cold momentarily, you are going to have a blast. Your body adapts to its surroundings, and you do not even notice it's cold anymore. The same is true for pushing through an emotional hurdle.

Loneliness can cause serious hurt and pain. It acts on the same parts of the brain as physical pain. I believe that loneliness is mostly caused from feelings of disconnection or rejection. And these emotions can be elicited whether you are single or married. This is what makes loneliness so insidious. It is the demon that hides, unlike smoking, over-eating, or alcohol abuse, which are all issues that are plainly seen and recognized. With the age of social media, loneliness is becoming a real issue. Again, simply being alone, is not a symptom. We all have a drive for social connectivity, and some are getting it superficially through social media, like Facebook, Instagram, Snapchat, and Twitter. But this is not the same as a real relationship.

So here are some tips that I used to face my loneliness:

- I would talk to people that I did not know, in places like Wawa, when I was on my lunch break. I would cognitively smile at others, and I would usually get a greeting back.
- I would schedule face-to-face interaction with my family and friends. No cell phones were allowed. Do you know that doing this will boost your production of endorphins, which are the brain chemicals that ease pain and enhance wellbeing?

- Use social media wisely. If you are simply using social medial to post photographs of yourself and your family, always smiling, on vacations, chances are that you will not authentically connect with anyone. It should be used purposefully, and for short periods of time. When you charge your cell phone at night, put it in another room, away from your bed. If you wake up, and you check your phone, before you have sat up, you are addicted to something that is sucking the life out of you. Change your habits now.

- I got to know my neighbors. I would invite my neighbors over for coffee or tea. Being with these ladies took away some of my feelings of isolation. They were experiencing many of the same issues that I was, regarding childrearing, etc. So, I did not feel alone in my strife.

- I took this time to organize and clean my home. I found that I was much happier living in an orderly home, without clutter.

- I would visit animal rescue centers in my area. Most of these shelters needed people to walk the dogs that were up for adoption. Animals are a therapeutic way to feel better. Pet therapy is something being utilized more and more, to help animals and humans heal themselves.

- I got to know my creative side. I took some art classes, which helped me feel connected, without having to talk directly about myself.

- I would hug…a lot. Hugging is powerful medicine. It cues our brains to release oxytocin, which helps strengthen social bonds.

I believe that humans need connections with other people. But first, it is important to remember that there is a difference between being alone and feeling lonely. They're two separate and distinct concepts. The main difference that I have found is that being alone is a metaphysical description. On the other hand, loneliness is a feeling that is associated with being alone, and it is often experienced as negative and painful. You can be alone and happy, or you can be alone and lonely or unhappy. What I have learned through the years is that the idea of being alone is what you make of it. Your outlook on life is changed by your attitude towards it. So, if we assume that loneliness is a normal part of everyone's life from time to time, then what other forces affect how we view it? Along with outside forces and events that have made you who you are today, your biological makeup is also a big factor. All your past experiences are part of who can "cut rope" on a bad relationship, and who hangs on until the bitter end, even when the relationship is bad.

I also think that your individual personality type and genetic makeup is also a big factor when it comes to who experiences discomfort from being alone. Introverts may find alone time more desirable than extroverts. If you're an extrovert, you are comfortable and feel compelled to be around other people and you typically do not like to be alone. It is just the way you are genetically set up.

At the end of the day, whether you're an introvert or an extrovert, all humans experience feelings of loneliness. And many do so during the times they are physically alone. But it doesn't have to be that way. You can also feel alone even if you are in the same room with someone else. And if you have experienced a bad relationship then you know exactly what I am talking about. And I think that is worse.

Along with the realization that I suffered from loneliness, I also finally understood that I have always been in love with the idea of being in love, and all that it entails. When I got down to "brass-tacks" on why this was, I came to the sad awareness that I did not want to be alone. Every person needs time alone, whether they're introverted or extroverted, single or in a relationship, young or old. Solitude is time for rejuvenation and self-talk, for utter peace, and for realizing that purposeful "loneliness" is not a bad place to be, but rather, a liberating part of your overall existence. Once you learn to control your mind, the Universe will give back to you, making you unbreakable and irresistibly magical. You will become the magnet that everyone else is drawn to.

Elevation requires separation. To be happy when you are alone, you must discover who you are. You also need to take time off. Specifically, this means time off from the dating-world. Date yourself. Take your parents, children, and friends on dates. This is crucial, especially if you decide that you want to enter another romantic relationship. Even my family-law lawyer gave me friendly advice, telling me, "Get some therapy and wait before jumping back into another serious relationship." He had seen many of his clients make the same mistake again…and again. He represented many of the same clients, on multiple divorces. I felt like he instinctively knew that I wasn't ready to enter any other romantic relationship—not yet. Meanwhile, I thought I was in total control, and I thought I was making sound decisions. Well, folks, I wasn't. I got engaged again too soon, and I got entwined in a marriage that would eventually unravel into divorce number *two*. I should have listened to my attorney.

You may need to draw upon the strength of your family, friends, or other loved ones, until you are strong enough to decipher when you are truly "ready" to date again. Use those resources to calm yourself down and know that you will be just fine when you are alone. This is not a permanent state, unless you choose to be alone, which is great too. These feelings are temporary, but they are also necessary steps for you to become healthy.

My last point on this matter is that you will not be any good to anyone, including yourself, if you do not know who you are. And you must be alone to really get to know yourself. You must be comfortable in your own skin *before* you will have a successful relationship. Love yourself. Forgive yourself. Take time to get to know you and all the wonderful things that make you unique and special. There is nothing more freeing and empowering than learning to like your own company. Who knows, maybe you will decide that you are so happy being with yourself, your family, and your friends, that you may choose not to enter another romantic relationship.

I will end this chapter, where I began. Learn to be alone, eat alone and sleep alone. During this time, you will learn about yourself. You will begin to cultivate your own dreams, your own beliefs, your own striking clarity, and you will figure out what inspires and motivates you. Remember that sometimes you must give up on certain people, not because you don't care, but because they don't. Sometimes, you must forget what you feel and remember what you deserve. Maturity is learning to walk away from situations and people that threaten your self-respect, peace-of-mind, values, morals and self-worth. People think that being alone makes you lonely, but I do not buy into that theory. Rather, I believe that being surrounded by the wrong people is the loneliest place in the world.

Love when you are ready, not when you are lonely. Do not rush love, and never settle for any reason.

> *No relationship can ever be a substitute for your soul. You alone are your own friend.*
>
> **—Osho**

> *The most terrible poverty is loneliness and the feeling of being unloved.*
>
> **—Mother Teresa**

21

Stop Ruminating:
Live in Each Moment

*All true artists, whether they know it or not, create from a place
of no-mind, from inner stillness.*

—Eckhart Tolle

I am one of those people who, by nature, worries and thinks a lot. I
am pretty sure I was born that way.

But in my quest to heal myself, I needed to stop some of those
thoughts from racing around my head. Instead, I needed to learn to
be in the now—to live in each moment. I now think learning to be
"still" opened the space needed to eventually let Wade into my life—
the way real love is supposed to be.

My Story

Imagine if we obsessed about the things we loved about ourselves—
versus worrying about things we cannot change.

When I finally looked around, sat down, and cried a little, I began
to clear my head. I realized that I possessed the control, to turn my

life around. I had the power to "walk away" from my past, all along. I realized that I was the only person who could put my broken relationships behind me, and move forward into the light, away from the dark lonely place that I had been dwelling for so long. When this reality struck me, I vowed to steer clear of the dim, foggy, murky marsh, that had once sucked me in, as my safe-haven. I would no longer allow myself to be transfixed by the negative.

When you are by yourself, watch your thoughts. Because eventually, your thoughts will become your actions. And many times, actions become habits. What you do every day, regardless of the outside pressures, is what makes up your character. So, if your thoughts are virtuous and positive, then it will eventually lead you down the road to a clear conscious and a desirable character. The one thing that separates you from everyone else, is your thoughts, your voice, your mind, and your vision. And, only you can alter the ending to your own story.

I have always been the type of person who ruminates on things, especially tragedy. Part of my job is to adjudicate serious automobile accidents. Over the years, I have processed five fatal accidents. I would get the scene photographs, the autopsy photographs, and view the outside and inside of the car, which had become someone's temporary tomb. I would replay the accident repeatedly, in my head. This sometimes, lasted years. There are still some accident locations, when I pass them today, still stir up all those gory and sad details—the images come rushing back. Unfortunately, I am the same way with my personal life. As a result, I remember asking my parents and closest friends the same questions about my failed relationships, over and over, ad nauseum. I just could not let it go. I needed answers, to the unknown. I was not satisfied without answers, so I became transfixed on every aspect of the failed relationship, including how the other person was moving on with their lives. This was not healthy for me. My parents would sometimes have to snap me out of my trance, because some days, it was all-consuming.

I needed to realize that life exists in the present moment. I had to make a conscious effort to choose to live in the present, rather than getting lost in my past mistakes and nostalgia.

My Life Lesson

For me, turning to the Bible helped tremendously. I placed my trust in my family, myself, and God. I have always believed in the pure love and wisdom of his teachings. God has always been one step ahead of me. In time, he has revealed his plan. So, I now trust in his plan, even if that means that I must prayerfully wait and be patient. This very day was on his mind, before the world had seen mankind. He knows all our hearts well. And, long before my birth, I believe that he had a purpose for me. I trust that writing this book was part of his bigger plan for me.

I also found that if you truly live in the moment, often, the result will be far more positive than you anticipated. By "living-in-the-moment," I mean that you are completely involved in an activity for its own sake. Many people exercise to gain this Zen feeling, and maybe this will work for you as well. But, whatever the activity, you will need to find something that absorbs your attention fully (not watching television though). It should be something that you look forward to, and that can take your mind off your struggles. You may not find your go-to activity immediately, but keep looking for it. It is not elusive. You will find it, and once you do, keep that activity a priority of your everyday life.

My son once said that he heard someone say, "Rejection breeds obsession." This is true, and I personally had to fight my urge to obsess over my past. So, when you are alone, try very hard not to ruminate about the negative aspects of your current situation or your ex and how they are living their lives. *You* are the most influential person that you will talk to all day. Give affirmation to yourself. Your self-talk can be negative or positive. In optimism, there is magic. In pessimism, there is the vast abyss of nothingness. So, try changing your thoughts. Get a positive good attitude. You will instantly feel much better. Your brain can either be your best friend, or your worst enemy. Reprogram your mind. Go out and live your life with joy. Live in each moment, for it can never be repeated. Do not sit at home, in a dark room, feeling sorry for yourself. Chances are greater that you will meet someone "out and about" anyhow versus pining over someone in your room because you are afraid to be alone.

It personally brings me comfort believing that God knows what each of us needs, and when we need it. I have trust that he knows how to put us at the right place, at the right time. No matter how good or bad your life is, wake up each morning and be thankful you are alive.

He knows my name. He knows my every thought. He sees each tear that falls and hears me when I call.

—John 10:3

The moment was all; the moment was enough.

—Virginia Woolf, The Waves

22

My Four Love Experiences

The greatest happiness of life is the conviction that we are loved; loved for ourselves, or rather, loved in spite of ourselves.

— *Victor Hugo*

Personally, I have experienced four different types of "love" in my life. Only one of those loves is healthy. Previously, I thought that I was in love at least a dozen times, until I met Wade. And these relationships elicited all the same responses from me, until I met him.

I believe that I needed each of these loves for a different reason, depending on what was going on in my life, at that moment in time. I know that as my life was in metamorphosis stages, I would choose different partners, with different strengths and weaknesses. Obviously, I did this subconsciously. But as I look back now, it becomes very clear. I will try to explain the four very different love-relationships that I experienced.

Puppy Love: My First Love Experiences

My Story

My very first love would be characterized as "puppy love," and it occurred when I was very young; in fact, I was only a sophomore in high school. This is the idealistic love. Lots of people get married because they think they're in love. "In love" is a loaded term, and most of us go through some phase of being infatuated with our romantic partners, but infatuation isn't a mature love. And some people, when under the spell of infatuation, commit to marriage.

My first relationship was the one that seemed the most like fairy-tales that we read as children. I loved him in a way that you can only do in your first romance. For me, it was the kind of love that doesn't know any better and doesn't want to. It is dizzying, foolish, and fierce. For some, I think that this love is misinterpreted. For some, I believe this first love is sometimes not love, but rather, infatuation. I think that infatuation tends to feed more on the need to be loved, than to actively love someone else. It is self-centered. This is the love that appeals to every fiber of our being. It is this relationship that we tend to look back and compare every other relationship to.

I had two serious boyfriends in high school. I thought each was the love of my lifetime.

My first high school boyfriend and I entered this first relationship with the belief that this would be our only love, and so it didn't matter if it didn't feel quite right, or if we found ourselves having to swallow down personal truths to make it work. Because deep down, we believed that this is what love was supposed to be, and we also had nothing to compare it to. I remember thinking at the time, that this love mattered the most. This was my end-all, be-all.

Puppy love is also the first time your "love relationship" is viewed by others. You want people to think that the two of you are "good together," at all costs. If your love looks right, then it is right. Right? Wrong.

Generally, at this age, we are not as surefooted at voicing our own beliefs, wants, and desires. At the young age of fifteen and sixteen years old, I can now see that I transformed myself a little, to "fit" each of my long-term high school relationships.

My first two young loves were very similar. I have only wonderful memories from my two high school crushes. These were the types of love where I had nothing else to compare it to. I had no historical references. Because of this, I did not really know what I was looking for in a romantic partner. My list of boyfriend-qualities in high school consisted of wanting someone who was athletic, and if they played football, so much the better. Of course, I wanted someone who was ultra-attractive in their physical appearance. (Or, "hawt," as kids today refer to it.) And it went without saying that I was also looking for someone who was popular and smart. Did you notice the one quality that I left out back then? I never really thought that how they treated me was a box that needed to be checked. I was fortunate, because both of my high school boyfriends were very respectful and sweet to me.

I suppose that my first two high school romantic relationships were like some of yours. I thought the sun rose and set with these two boys. I thought they were perfect. I daydreamed about marrying them, and all my paper-covered school books had their names, in hearts, scribbled all over them. I would meet them in-between classes to exchange notes or kisses, at one of our lockers. (When I was in high school, there were no cell phones, so we would pass written notes back and forth.) It was in these first love relationships that I would declare, "When I marry so-and-so, I'll never get divorced." And, "When I get married, it will be forever, because our relationship is perfect." And looking back at my first two young loves, things were damned near perfect. That was—until I went to college. Now there was a separation of time and distance, which presented new challenges that I now understood relationships had to withstand.

As I got older, I also discovered that I was very naïve at this tender age, regarding true love. At that young age, I did not fully understand what real-life responsibilities and stress looked like. Because we were in high school and lived with our respective parents, there were no mortgages to pay, and we had no children together. There were no health or medical issues to overcome. There was no work stress. Our biggest worries were getting good grades, exceling at sports, going on college visits, and deciding what outfit to wear to the next dance. My parents worried about those real-life issues, behind closed doors. I also had no idea what the future held, for me, or for them. I was clueless that people could evolve over time, especially in the next ten years. This is precisely why I believe that you should be at least in your late twenties, before you even consider tying the knot. The promises that you make at such a young age, may become the burdens and great disappointments of your later life. Love always feels like it's going to last forever, initially. But that excitement may eventually taper off. At that point, you had better actually like one another and have important life goals in common. Otherwise, you are in for a very rough ride.

After my first high school boyfriend broke up with me, I was devastated. I remember lying on the floor of my bedroom, listening to depressing love songs on my cassette-tape player, all weekend long. My favorites were REO Speedwagon's songs, "Keep on Loving You" and "Time for Me to Fly." (I was too busy with schoolwork, gymnastics, track, and cheerleading during the week, to spend too much time wiping back my tears, but I made up for lost time when I was home.)

ASIDE: I remained close friends with both of my first loves. Today, I am still friends with one of them, as well as his lovely mother and other members of his family. Sadly, my other first love is no longer with us, on this earth. He was killed serving our great nation, as a navy pilot (lieutenant commander). May he rest in peace. However, before his tragic incident, I also kept in touch with him, his mother, and his older brother. I wish that all breakups would end this way... civil and without drama.

Sometimes when I was young, I would listen to everyone's opinion, except my own. But, in college I began to realize what my personal boundaries were. (I am not saying that I always stayed within those lines, because obviously I didn't, but I began to formulate what I would accept and what I would not accept in a relationship.) After two divorces, I completely realized that going outside of those demarcation lines would eventually lead me to an unhappy life. As young adults, many people think that marriage is the way to happiness. When you are younger, most of us are looking for someone that matches us "well enough," to make us happy. But, to have a great relationship, you must be happy with yourself before you find a life partner.

Looking back, I honestly believe that either of my high school relationships could have worked out. But seeing their beautiful wives and children now, I see why those connections didn't work.

My Life Lesson

There is one serious point that people tend to forget about marriage. A marriage involves two people. So, it won't matter what your intentions are if either you or your partner matures past the relationship. And often this happens after the teenage years, into the mid-twenties. So, there should not be a rush to get married. I know a few high school romances will last, and I personally know some of these couples that are still happily married today. My parents are two of those lucky people. But most high school or college relationships probably won't last over time. In my experience, people change and grow a lot from the ages of eighteen to twenty-five. This is usually the age that young adults are living on their own, for the first time. They are beginning to learn about themselves, with minimal parental influence.

It is this first love that will sometimes bring the heart-shattering pain, when it does not work out. The pain is so intense that there are days that you think your heart will literally implode from sadness. You feel like your entire world has ended, while the rest of the world has the audacity to keep on going. You feel that knot in the pit of your stomach, alongside your pounding heart, making you feel that you will most surely die of a slow and painful death. Unless you marry your first love, you will have to push past this pain too. Wade experienced this trauma when he was getting ready to be commissioned from the United States Military Academy. And I was in high school when my very first breakup occurred. And, to the then-teenage me, the heartbreak might have been the most important thing that ever happened in my life. It showed me that there are various faces of love—and loss.

Even amid your pain, certain things must march on, including you and your life. In a later chapter, we will discuss mechanisms to get over this wrenching heartache.

> *A man is lucky if he is the first love of a woman. A woman is lucky if she is the last love of a man.*
>
> **—Charles Dickens**

Forced Love: My Second Love Experience—My First Marriage

My Story

The second type of love that I experienced, was a hard and almost forced love. This is the love that taught me the hardest lessons of my life. This is the love where I somehow convinced myself that it was okay to "settle."

This is the kind of love that hurts; whether through lies, pain, deceit, or manipulation. One of the many problems with this type of love is that you begin to feel unworthy and that mistreatment is the only treatment that you deserve. This is never true.

I married my second love-type, as a step to the next milestone, because I thought I was ready to start a family. So, I suppose I chose the best available option open for myself. Now I was making choices out of the need to learn lessons. Looking back, I almost felt like I was "playing house."

My first husband, Anthony, looked "great on paper," but I really did not have anything in common with him, and we did not get along. (Unless by "get along," you are referring to two hot-headed Italians trying to live together with almost daily arguments over both the big issues and the mundane.) In my case, our backgrounds were so grossly different that the moral compass was too polarized, on too many issues, for us to ever be considered a good match. Unbeknownst to me, this life-decision would turn out to be too much of a constant tug-of-war for us to accomplish anything together. Litmus Test: If you go on a vacation with your partner, and you cannot get along there, this is a red flag.

But this did not prevent me from holding on by my fingernails to make it work. My second love became a draining repetitive cycle. I prayed that somehow the ending to our story would be different, or that we could change one another, or "grow" into love. Yet, each time we tried, it somehow always ended up worse.

My Life Lesson

Most of the time this type of love is unhealthy, unbalanced, or narcissistic even. In my first marriage, there were many emotional, mental, and even physical abuses or manipulations in this relationship, from both sides. There always seemed to be drama at every turn. This is exactly what keeps us addicted to this storyline, because it's the emotional rollercoaster of extreme highs and lows, and like a junkie trying to get a fix, we stick through the lows with the expectation of the next high.

With this kind of sick and distorted love, trying to make it work becomes more important than whether it should. I was always walking on eggshells, just so I did not upset the proverbial applecart. It's the love that we wished was right, and for many of us, there are now children involved. This controlling behavior is true for men and women. Many self-absorbed people control their partners like puppets. They use anger, fear, and withdrawal of love and sex to keep them "in line." They can make the lives of their partners a living hell if they want to. And the worst part is that their partners believe that they deserve every bit of it.

These types of people are professional actors when they are in the public eye. They have the innate ability to fool many people into believing that they are righteous, upstanding, moral, and honest, leaving their partners feeling even more bewildered and confused.

A real victim will search for help because they cannot stand the pain and suffering. A narcissist or other controlling individual will make up stories of "abuse" that they have endured.

They will usually play the role of the victim, and they will seek pity from everyone around them.

> *What you do in front of people is nothing if you are not living the same life at home, behind closed doors.*
>
> —*Matthew 6:5-7*

The Pendulum Effect: My Third Love—My Second Marriage

My Story

The third type of love that I experienced was a slow and steady heart-break, consisting of high-pressure and loneliness. If you are anything like me, you are finished with people that are anything like your first ex-spouse. I wanted something completely different this time around. But because I was so focused on dating someone who was completely opposite of Anthony, I ended up choosing wrong again.

Pendulum Effect: What I experienced as my third type of love, I refer to as the Pendulum Effect. This is when you go too far to the opposite side of the love-pendulum, and you end up with another mismatch. The pendulum stays balanced, by being in the middle and having equal weights on either side. You need to think of yourself as one of the weights, and your new romantic partner will be your counter-balance. I was ultra-focused on making sure that I did not attract the same guy, no matter what! But in doing this, I chose a "safe" love. Because of this phenomenon, I know a lot of people who married their spouse, even though they were not certain that they were "in love." Some even tied the knot knowing they weren't.

First and Foremost, It's Safer to be Loved, than to Love

Although I have nothing terrible to say about my second husband, we did not share a magnetic attraction. He was a very nice guy, so this was a very "safe" love for me. This "safe" love, as I call it, occurred when I was still hurt and scarred from one of my previous loves. So, I built a solid fortress around my heart. Nobody ever wants to feel "that" pain again. I am talking about the grief that comes with a breakup, especially if you are the one that is left behind. It is like a BOGO (buy-one, get one free) sale. Breakups and heartaches just go together.

My Life Lesson

As humans, we try to avoid that sinking feeling in the pit of our stomach, that feels like we will suffocate in a pool of sadness and disbelief. Because that pain is so incredibly cruel, and it takes so long to become healthy and happy again, sometimes people subconsciously choose a partner that they know is not right for them. They choose someone who is a "nice guy" or "nice girl," but that they are not sexually attracted to. They may think that they are "above" that other person, which is their way of protecting themselves from being dumped again. This is the type of relationship where one person is "in love," but the other person only "loves" them back. There is a defined difference between being "in love" and having love for someone. Being "in love" has all the qualities having "love" for someone, except you are also romantically charged by that person. When you "love" someone, there is no physical chemistry present.

You need to be totally and completely "in love" with your partner. Because, eventually, this "just love" type of love will grow old and weary. You will eventually need the spark of life and love that comes through intimacy. You can be married to your best friend, but if there are no sparks in the bedroom, then I would suggest that you avoid getting yourself into this situation. I can think of nothing worse than feeling alone in a room where your spouse is sitting directly beside you.

If you date or marry someone that you are only friends with, you may have a partner for life, but the flip side of that coin is that you will never be completely happy or fulfilled either. You will be going through the motions of life. No highs. No lows. Life will be a steady and mediocre existence. Things that used to make you ecstatic, or conversely make your blood boil, will quickly no longer matter to you. There needs to be a healthy balance of some highs and lows, mixed with a stable peaceful lifestyle, with only slight fluctuations, in your day-to-day living. If you marry someone that you are not sexually compatible with, you will forever long to be loved and touched, have intimate physical contact, and feel completely loved. Do not settle for a "good person," just because they are sweet, kind, nice, and giving. You also need that primal animal attraction. So, think "Me Jane, You Tarzan," as one necessary part of your love equation.

I believe the Lord is merciful. He wants you to find tranquility in, with, and through your spouse. And if you so choose, there will be a place for you between mercy and new love. You were never created to live depressed, defeated, guilty, condemned, ashamed, or unworthy. I believe that we are each created to be loved and give love. But in your quest for love, it is better to stay single until you meet the right person who will compliment all aspects of your life.

One of the cruelest things a person can do is to awaken someone's love without the intention of truly loving them.

A Summary of My Three Relationship Attempts

My Story

I got married for all kinds of reasons, but until I married my current husband, Wade, my reasons were all misguided. So, I ended up getting divorced for all kinds of reasons too. I have learned to forgive myself and my shortcomings. I now know that there are sometimes responsibilities and situations that demand you to make such difficult decisions, including: children, personal safety, money, sex, security, convenience, companionship, fear, and the list goes on.

For example, some people get pregnant and feel that the honorable thing to do is to get married. It is something that society has dictated through the years. Some marry for financial security. They ensure that they have access to a meal or to a certain lifestyle. Or someone helps you out financially, and you feel that you "owe" them. Or your parents are putting pressure on you to marry the person, *they* feel is right for you. Or you feel that the prime time to become pregnant is passing you by. Perhaps it is as simple as you feel that you both have the same goals in life. In some cases, people seek wealth or reputation and fame in a marriage.

Sometimes when a person is not ready to settle down, they let go of the most perfect partner, because they are not yet ready for a marriage commitment. Then when they are ready, sometimes that other person has already moved on. So, they pick the first man or woman they like, and marry them. These scenarios lead to the "biggest regret is always the One that Got Away" syndrome, because one person wasn't ready or mature enough. This scenario also falls into the third type of love.

And this is all caused because sometimes people just do things without really thinking it through. Most of the time, these people have been irreparably hurt by someone else in their past, or they are running away from another bad situation. So, they don't know themselves, they don't love themselves, and they don't respect themselves. Then, they reap destruction and unfortunately, the person they marry gets dragged into it.

My Life Lesson

I have come to realize that my divorces were not caused by one of us, or the other. We were simply in relationships that did not work out. But I do believe that our relationships did not work out, in part, because of the relationship that we had with ourselves, because that sets the tone for every other relationship you have.

People have often asked me if I thought there was any chance that it could have worked out with either of my ex-husbands, or if Wade and his ex-wives could have worked it out. My answer is simple. Yes. It could have worked. But at what cost? In any of the above scenarios, we would have been simply two people, co-existing. We would be living very lonely and separate lives, just to live together and keep our respective marriages intact. We both fought for our marriages, long and hard. And I believe that God made us to be happy and to thrive. God does not want to see us suffer because we made a poor marital decision.

READ THIS NEXT SENTENCE CAREFULLY, AS THIS IS THE MOST IMPORTANT LESSON THAT I LEARNED: MISTAKES DO NOT HAVE TO BE LIFELONG SENTENCES.

But, whatever your reason, it doesn't mean that once you realize that you made a mistake you aren't allowed to correct it by moving forward. It does not have to be a life sentence. Oh, you can try to put up a façade of being happy, but that is like being arrested, tried, and sentenced to an eternal life of emptiness. There are some people that we just outgrow. These relationships may end with no real explanation as to why. There is just a shift that occurs, and I believe that it should be respected. You will begin to realize that you are not the same person that you used to be. The things that you once tolerated, have now become intolerable. Where your voice was once silenced—you are now speaking your truth. Where you once argued and battled, you are now choosing to remain calm and silent. You know the value in your thoughts, and you understand that there are some situations that no longer deserve your time, energy and focus.

Honor your partner and your own growth, even if you grow apart. Not all roots can stay planted in the same soil forever. But your time was not in vain, for I believe that we cross paths with the people in our lives for a reason. I do not think we should ever regret anyone that spends time in our lives. I do not believe that there are any mistakes in life, only lessons. And the *art of knowing* is knowing what to ignore and what to focus on. All of my negative experiences helped me grow, learn, and advance me on my self-realization journey.

When you hold your partner's hand, and the only thing you feel is that your heart beats faster and you feel giddy inside, but there is no depth to it...walk away. You want to hold the hand of a person that makes your heart beat a little faster, but who also makes you feel warm, safe, and secure. Hold onto this person. This is the person that you could share a healthy relationship with.

All, everything that I understand, I only understand because I love.

—Leo Tolstoy

CHAPTER 23

My Fourth and Final "True Love": You Have Seen My Descent, Now Read about My Rising!

Anytime you combine sets of kids, exes, two newlyweds, and the chaos of life, it is a recipe for disaster, right? Well, I think that was what Wade and I expected. We were madly in love, but we assumed we were headed for some choppy waters instead of smooth sailing. Why wouldn't we think that? That was certainly where we had come from.

However, what we found was that yes, life with all the above can be chaotic. But when you have the right partner, you have a *true* partner to help you through the tough times.

My Story

In the beginning, my current husband and I were always looking for "the other shoe to drop," in all situations. We would go on vacation, where previously there was strife and stress, but that never happened with us. We would look for arguments when we were tired, and there were still house chores to do, after our nine-to-five corporate jobs. But we happily both pitched in and had fun together, doing whatever chore it happened to be. We waited for the dreaded "money" fights to start. They never did. There just were never any expectations about how each person should be acting. We accepted one another for exactly who we were. No strings attached. It was purely unconditional love. So, there was never any pressure to become someone other than who we truly are. We were finally fully accepted. This was very foreign to us both. Usually, I had to play the "Monty Hall" mind games. Or it was like quid pro quo, or "this for that." Nothing was ever genuinely done out of love or respect for the other person. I would have to constantly bargain with most of my exes to get something that we needed, which was usually something for us, or later for my children.

My Life Lesson

It was my fourth (and final) love that I never saw coming. BAM! It is the one that causes butterflies in the pit of my stomach when I think about the other person. He set my life ablaze, and he was the one providing oxygen to my inner-fire.

This type of love is the person that you will put first, above everyone else, including yourself. You want them to be happy, and they want you to be happy. It is selfless. It is never-ending. This is the one that is right. For me, this was my third marriage. This is what confirms that all the other relationships were wrong. This love destroys your other notions that you can love and live happily with other people. I have always been the type of girl that thought someone could have a thousand different desires, but in my one desire to know Wade, everything else melted away. I only wanted, needed, and loved him and him alone.

This love destroys any lingering ideals we clung to about what love is supposed to be. This is the love that comes so easily it doesn't seem possible. It's the kind where the connection can't be explained and knocks us off our feet because we never planned for it. This is the love where we come together with someone, and it just fits.

I would always tell Wade that the beauty he sees in me is actually a reflection of himself and all of his goodness.

There is no fear in love, but perfect love drives out fear, because fear expects punishment. The person who is afraid has not been made perfect in love.

—1 John 4:18

Through wisdom a house is built, and by understanding it is established. By Knowledge the rooms are filled with all precious and pleasant riches.

—Proverbs 24:3-4

The Real "He, She, and We"

My Story

After Wade and I fell madly in love, we were finally accepted for who we are already were. And, it shook us to the core. We always felt like we had to be perfect and "on," with our previous partners. If we were not performing our daily chores, watching our children, earning enough money, looking our best, etc., we felt insignificant. We felt like we were failures. So, when we met one another, it wasn't what we envisioned love would look like, nor does it abide by the rules that we had hoped to play it safe by. But it still shattered our preconceived notions of love. And, it showed us that even though this love did not look like any of our previous relationships, this was an even better relationship-blueprint. This is the point when we both realized why it did not work out with anyone else. Those old relationship wounds that Wade and I both experienced is where true love entered our hearts and souls. Finally, all of our prior struggles made sense to us.

My husband is always telling me how he still cannot believe how much he has changed as a person after meeting me. Somewhat ashamed, he has admitted that he was never quite as attentive to his other girlfriends and wives, like he is with me. He said that everything else in his life took precedence over his relationship, like work, alumni meetings, reading books, house chores, the gym, his children, etc. He never knew that he had all this love inside of himself to give away to the right person. He rediscovered himself and what it means to truly and honestly love a woman when he met me. We both became the love that we never received in our prior relationships.

I know people who have fallen in love once, and they find that it passionately lasts until their last breath. My parents met in high school and celebrated their golden wedding anniversary a few years ago. And they are still in love. To those like our parents, we are grateful to know you, because we now know the kind of love and magic that you have shared these years. When love is right, it will leave you wondering how you survived before. It will be the truth in your heart, telling you that you never really loved before.

My fourth love will be the final time that I will ever fall in love again, because it is the first "true love" of my life. This is the one that feels like home without any rationale. This is the love that isn't like a storm, but rather the quiet peace of the night. And yes, there was something special about my first puppy-loves, and something heartbreakingly unique about my second, and something stirring and sad about my third love, but there's also something amazing about what is my fourth and final love. This is the unexpected love that I never saw coming. The love that lasts. Wade and I truly believe that we never experienced true love before we met one another. How could we? We did not even love ourselves. So, we accepted less…and we gave less too. Although this is our third marriage, it is the very first time that we have experienced the wonderful phenomena of "being in love." This love will be the one that shows us why it never worked out before, with anyone else. And it's this possibility that makes opening your heart again worthwhile because the truth is, you never know when you'll stumble into love.

My third husband found parts of me that I didn't know existed, and I found a love that I no longer believed was real.

My Life Lesson

I have found that the right love will keep knocking on our door, regardless of how long it takes us to answer. It's the love that just feels right. Maybe the reality is that we need to truly learn what love isn't, before we can grasp what it really is. Perhaps it's not about if love is ready for us but if we are ready for love.

I believe that those who find this type of love are really the lucky ones. They are the ones who are tired of having their hearts lie beating in front of them, wondering if there is just something inherently missing from them or how they love. They now understand that there is nothing wrong with them; they have just been with the wrong person.

Love depends on many different things, including: physical chemistry, timing, attitudes, discipline, self-love, morality, spirituality, give-and-take, educational backgrounds, interests, and whether your partner loves you in the same way. No matter how difficult the situation, if someone really loves you, they won't let you slip away, physically or emotionally. Just because it has never worked out before doesn't mean that it won't work out now. And it doesn't matter how many times you have failed in the past. What it really comes down to is if we are limited by how we love, or if we love without limits.

We can all choose to stay with what I described as my first love, the one that is young and immature, with nothing else to compare it to. The love that looks good but has never really undergone the many stressors of real life. Or, we can choose to stay with our second love, under the belief that if we don't have to fight for it, then it's not worth having. Or, we can remain with what I describe as my third type of love, that is a "safe love." Or, just maybe…we can wait and make the choice to believe in the fourth type of love.

It is your road, and yours alone. Others may walk it with you, but no one can walk it for you. You must decide on the quality of love you want, need, and deserve. And, you may decide to remain alone, and love yourself. And, that is okay too. Either way, you are not stuck where you are, unless you decide to be. Wade and I are so grateful that we made the tough decisions that we did, when we did. Because now, we have the love that we have been in search of our entire lives. We also appreciate each of our former spouses because not all storms come to disrupt your life. Some come to clear your path to a more harmonious relationship for all involved.

The best marriage is when the two involved know who they are as individuals. These partners are equally committed to understanding and respecting each other. Love is knowing everything about someone, yet you do not use that information against them. Love is trusting someone enough to reveal things about yourself, including the things you might be ashamed of. Love is feeling safe with that person. You each have your own strengths that help your partner with their weaknesses. Most times, each of our individual personalities, talents, and attributes play a role in the quality of the relationship, good and bad. And remember that good love conquers. It does not divide.

The best and most beautiful things in this world cannot be seen or even heard but must be felt with the heart.

—Helen Keller

Telling Your Children,
You are Separating

This chapter offers practical advice for dealing with some of the complexities of divorce. For most parents who end up separating and divorcing, their deepest angst is reserved for the impact the divorce will have on their children. It is agonizing to think, the little people we would do anything to protect, will be hurt by the dissolution of your marriage. But ultimately, a child having two happy parents—even if in separate households—will be better than a very unhappy home full of tension or downright abuse.

My Story

Your children will remember the moment that you tell them that their parents are getting divorced for the rest of their lives. To them, this moment will be as indelible on their brains, as the assassination of John F. Kennedy, the NASA space explosion, and September 11th in NYC. So, you will need to really plan exactly what you are going to say and handle it with great care. You and your spouse should both be present for this conversation.

My first ex-husband and I attempted a custody arrangement, where every few days we exchanged custody, but this was disastrous. The children said they felt like "ping-pong balls." So, we tried one week on and one week off. This did not fare much better. So, if you have joint physical custody, remember that the child must adjust and readjust, with every move from one home to the other. Under these two scenarios, my children would forget important things (for sports activities, school, or other extra-curricular activities) at one or the other's houses. So, they would be ill-prepared, embarrassed, or stressed, for the remainder of the day.

My Life Lesson

Once it has become certain that you and your spouse will be separating, you need to let your kids know. Make sure you're calm and composed when you decide to tell your children and have them sit down with you somewhere private. The children will most likely immediately have many questions and concerns about this. You will need to have some answers already prepared beforehand, and others you will have to explain to the children, as each issue arises, over time. And remember that it is best to explain the reasons why you are getting divorced in a somewhat general way. Chances are, the older children probably are already aware of the fighting and tension in the household. However, you should still be honest and explain this situation in a way that will soften the blow.

One of the first questions the children will ask you is, "Where will we live?" For me, this was easier, because my children were only ages four and a few months old, respectively, at the time. But if your children are older, you and your soon-to-be ex should have this worked out, prior to your discussion with them. You need to let the children know whether they will be moving, and where they will be living. Try your best to keep them in their same school district, so that they can lean on the familiarity of the teachers and their friends. They will also want to know exactly where each parent will be residing. It will reassure them if you provide them with a few additional specifics, like how they will spend summer vacations and holidays.

What worked best for our family was to have one "main home base," with a 70/30 split, and to be flexible with that time. Sometimes, things are going to "pop up," which will require last-minute schedule changes. Remember that if you say "no" to allowing your ex to take your child to a spur-of-the-moment basketball game, you can expect the same in return. And then, the only losers in that scenario are the children. Be flexible for the sake of your children. There is no way that you will have "other plans" every single time the other parent requests additional time with your children. And besides, your children are not possessions. You shouldn't "allow" the father or mother extra time. When you begin using phrases like, "I'll allow you to drop our children off an hour later," you imply that your children are things and not human beings. Remember, you chose to marry this person, and you chose to have children with them. So, now you must pay-the-piper. You must forget your own ill-will feelings towards your ex and help them to be the best possible co-parent that they can be. This will always require work from both you and your ex. But it is for the benefit of your children, so it is worth it.

If possible, you and your ex should agree on discipline and expectations for your children. This way you are working together on their value system. It is extra confusing for a child to have to different sets of rules at each parent's house. Negotiate this beforehand, with your ex. Think of the other parent as a business-partner. It will require some give and take, but remember that your child's well-being is at stake. Personally, I failed at this. I was never a strong disciplinarian. And sometimes I thought my co-parent was overly strict. There needs to be a happy medium.

Holidays will be extra difficult. When my children were very young, I invited my first ex-husband into my home every Christmas morning, so that I was not depriving my children of those special "Santa" moments, when they want both parents there. This may not be possible for everyone, and it certainly was not easy for either my ex or me. But we loved our children more than we disrespected one another. (And there was a lot of underlying hostility still lingering during this time.)

You should also take time to provide a little bit of money to your child, and take them shopping, so that they can pick out a special gift for Mom and Dad. You do not want the child to feel bad because they do not have a gift for both of their parents for those special occasions.

If you remember to always allow your feelings for your child to guide your decisions, and to put their best interests first, then you will be on your way to successfully navigating your co-parenting.

> *Divorce is not easy, but if you genuinely put your kids first, that dictates the civility you should show each other. What example are you otherwise?*
>
> *—Dawn French*

Do Not Spoil Your Children Because You Feel Bad

My Story

My first inclination, after my first husband and I separated was to protect (and spoil) my children. I thought that they were already dealing with enough issues, so I overcompensated by doing too much for them. Children need structure and routine, as much as possible, especially now that their worlds have been turned upside down. So, keep the same rules and discipline that were imparted by you and your spouse when you were married. My father still tells my sister and I that, "Discipline is the greatest form of love." And I now know this to be true. If you start down a path of giving for no reason, and not imparting discipline, you will lose control of your child, and this may be permanent. They must continue to respect both parents, even though you no longer possess the typical family unit. The two co-parents' communication is the key to making this work.

Obviously, going through a divorce will significantly affect your children. But the good news is that your divorce may lead to healthier relationships between everyone involved. My step-children and I have a wonderful relationship, and my children have the same strong bond with Wade. But there could be a long path to this destination, and it will require a lot of communication and work by you, the parent.

Most people do not like change. Children are no different. So, while they are getting used to their new situations and new family dynamics, there will most likely be tension and conflict between you and your children. But you can learn to help your children cope with their initial emotions and adjust to their new lives.

Remember that buying your children "stuff" to ease their pain is only temporary, and it is not a wise choice for their long-term well-being. Rather, it is your gift of being "present" that will help your children the most. Find ways to talk openly with your children. I know that my children were initially looking to have their feelings validated. They also did not fully comprehend or even understand what they were experiencing, emotionally. So, make time to discuss what they miss about their old lives, and what they may *not* miss. For me, my children seemed to share their feelings with me during car rides. So, we would discuss the whole gamut on our rides to and from their sporting events. You may find that your kids feel more comfortable talking to you in their bedroom, or during a home-cooked meal, or while eating dinner at a restaurant. There is no wrong time to talk to your children.

My Life Lesson

As parents, it is our hope to protect our children from as much pain as possible. However, when you are going through a divorce, the truth is that you cannot protect them from all their heartache. So, you must arm yourselves with essential coping skills, understanding, and time, to effectively help them handle their new normal. The real world is not easy or fair, and not everyone in their daily lives will have their best interests at heart. Be prepared to assist them through these difficulties.

> *Too much love never spoils children. Children become spoiled when we substitute "presents" for "presence."*
>
> —*Anthony Witham*

> *"Be quick to listen and slow to speak."*
>
> —*James 1:19*

Your Kids Will Grieve This Loss

My Story

There is no single way to grieve. We are all different. For my children, my daughter experienced different outward symptoms than my son, probably because of the four-year age gap. But they are also two distinct and different people. One child may seem to adjust faster than the other one, and that is okay. Or, one child may just be internalizing their pain, and consequently, they hold all their emotions inside, as if their hearts might be stolen from them if exposed.

It is also important for you to explain to your children that just because you are their parent, does not mean that you are not human. Parents are not perfect. I also explained to my children that I too was grieving the loss of what our family dynamic used to be. I was also very frank about telling my two kids that I was going to make mistakes—and I did. Divorce is one of the most traumatic and stressful times in a person's life. I was not always in a good mood, and I was open about my feelings with my children. I shared some of my distress with them and followed up by providing them with some constructive ways to handle it. This is an important balancing act. You don't want to share too much of your stress with them, or they may take on your burdens. This is not fair to the child. That said, you are not perfect. Your children are not perfect. None of us are. We are all beautifully flawed. So, forgive yourself. Forgive your children. Allow them to also forgive themselves and you. Most parents and children are doing the very best that they can, under these stressful circumstances.

My Life Lesson

No good parent sets out to intentionally harm their child during this time, or ever. But I can remember sitting in my room, crying for hours. I felt so guilty that I was not more attentive to my children during some of these days. But that was the best I could muster, during those early moments, just following my separation. Someone once told me that I was still being a great mom, because I always made sure that my children were safely supervised during this time, loved, properly dressed and fed, with a roof over their heads. If this is all you are capable of for a short period, that is okay. It does not make you a bad person. It makes you human.

But a mistake that I made was that sometimes my children would come to me with their emotional struggles, and I would say, "Yes, I understand. I am going through that too." My children just wanted me to hear them and help them. During the times when my children were crying out to me for help or attention, they did not want to hear about my problems. It took the focus off them and placed it back on me. So, while it is important to share some of your trials with your children (and how you are constructively coping with them), it is also a good idea to broach this when they are not focused on something that is bothering them.

At the forefront, you must understand, that most children still believe in fairytales, when it comes to their own parents' relationship. So, in their hearts and minds, a divorce will seem impossible at first. They may believe that this could happen to their friends, but not to their family. I tried to be cognizant of when I needed some assistance in parenting. This was difficult for me at first, because I am a highly self-sufficient woman. But, as time went by, and the children were showing some demonstrative signs and symptoms that they may need some additional support during this transition, I immediately sought help from a counselor or my extended family. It is a dangerous expectation to believe that you will be able to always handle everything on your own, all the time. It is okay to elicit the help of family, friends, mentors, and professionals.

You can't underestimate how traumatic divorce is for the children.

—*Isla Fisher*

Broken Family and Heart-Breaking News

My Story

My children were only four years old, and three months old, when it was time to tell them that Daddy and Mommy were getting divorced. Regardless of their age, I feel that the most important messages that you want to get across to your children are these: Tell your kids you love them and that this breakup is not their fault. These basic steps are of absolute importance.

Most every child will become frightened by a divorce. Remind them how much you care about them, and that you will always be their parent. Be patient and kind. I remember telling my daughter very explicitly these things, "I want you to know that this doesn't change how I feel about you at all." And, "I still love you, and I am so happy and blessed that I'm your Mom." She was still too little to really comprehend anything other than the fact that Daddy would no longer be living under the same roof with us. Simultaneously, I reassured her that this was not her or her brother's fault and that both her father and I would continue to love her and her brother. When my son became verbal and more cognizant to his surroundings, I communicated the same things to him.

If you have multiple children, especially if they are of similar ages, you should sit them down and give them the news at the same time. However, if you have children of significantly different ages, you may want to tell the older children first. If they have specific questions, you'll be able to respond to them, each in their own way.

My Life Lesson

When telling your children that you are getting a divorce, remind your children that you and your co-parent both love them, even when your ex is not present. This is extremely important for the primary custodian to do, because the children will not see your co-parent as often. Remind them that none of this is their fault. You should be certain to alleviate any lingering doubt in your children's minds, that this breakup has anything to do with them. Specifically, tell them that they did not do anything to cause the divorce. This will be worth repeating many times in the first months of their new lives. It seems simple enough; however, with your world being turned upside down, I am restating the obvious, so that these important talks with your children are not inadvertently overlooked.

Children and Divorce—
The Princess and the Pea:
Every Other Weekend

My Story

Just because I had found my Prince Charming did not mean that life would always be easy or simple, especially because we both have children. If only one of you has children, this dichotomy is a little easier to navigate. I'll share a few ways that we used to avoid some of the anger, envy, resentment, and bitterness, that is almost always intertwined with the children of blended families.

Children's perception can become their reality, especially when they see their biological parent spending time with stepchildren, and vice versa. I discuss this further, in a few pages. But either way, your children are your most precious part of each of you, so you need to handle them with care and from a well-thought plan.

If you have children, this will be the most gut-wrenching and difficult topic to accept and deal with, particularly if you have an ex-spouse that is working against you. The pieces will be like a splintered piece of wood, with many fragments that are jagged, sharp, and uneven. There will be jealousy and resentment, as a normal part of your children's daily lives. And you may have a co-parent who is adding fuel to your children's fire, just to create additional havoc in your new life. So, be compassionate to your children, as they muddle through this confusing time.

My Life Lesson

You cannot change your children's situation; however, you can change how you and your children choose to deal with it.

In any relationship, you need to keep moving forward. Life is full of ups and downs, but it is how you react to these stress-points that will either weaken you or make you stronger.

> *Family is family, and it is not determined by marriage certificates, divorce papers, or adoption documents. Families are made in the heart.*
>
> —*C. Joybell C.*

Blended Families with Children on Both Sides: Save You, Save Me, Save We

My Story

If you are like me, and you remarry someone who also has children from a prior relationship, you will have what is often referred to as a blended family. This could be very stressful at first, because the biological children may resent the stepchildren, on both sides of the fence. And all the affected children will yearn for their "yesterday," even if that was a chaotic time for them. This is very normal. However, with time and commitment to your children, your new family unit can be harmonious.

Perception is Not Always Reality

Your biological children may be subconsciously comparing what you do with and for them, versus what you do, with and for, your stepchildren. You must explain to your biological child that on your non-custodial weekends, when you would not be with them anyhow, that you will be spending time with your new partner or spouse, along with their child or children. In our case, this is because my minor child still resides with me. As a result, it is by default, not by choice that my husband, Wade, spends time with my children versus spending time with his biological children. Don't get me wrong. Wade loves my children, but if he could be with his children more, he would. Help your children all understand this.

Most of the time, when Wade's children are spending time with their other biological parent (and her new partner), it is during his *non*-custodial weekends. It is normal for your child to feel "slighted" if you are doing something fun on their *non*-custodial weekend—especially if stepchildren are involved. They are children, and they may not see the complete larger picture. They only see that you are spending time with your "stepchildren" and *not* them. They may not clearly distinguish that while you are doing that, they are spending time with their other biological parent, their new partner or spouse, and perhaps their other stepsiblings. It is very easy for children to lose sight of the fact that you would not be able to be with them during your co-parent's custodial time anyhow. Or, that you are sometimes with your step-children as a byproduct of spending time with your new significant other. Put yourself in your children's shoes. It would be extremely difficult to fully comprehend this as a child, especially if there is not a good line of communication. So, please remember this as you work through your new situation.

It is also important for both biological parents to spend quality weekend time with their children, as well as holidays. Let's face it, especially during the school year, the hectic day-to-day grind does not lend itself to much time with your child or children during the week anyhow. So, sharing *all* holidays, and the summer vacations is equally important.

But even with all the explanations, some children will get upset when they feel left out, even if it is that parent's *non*-custodial weekend, and they wouldn't be with "that parent" anyhow. This is very normal and needs to be handled with love and care. Think of how you may feel in their situation. Nobody likes to feel like an outsider, so talk to your children and explain that if you could be with them every weekend, you would be.

This is also the point when some children may try to play one parent against the other. I think that children do this for several reasons. First, they may get positive feedback from one of the parents, if they speak unkindly about their other parent. (Shame on that parent!) They may also do this to "confuse the issues," particularly to deflect any of their own wrongdoings at their non-custodial parent's home, to avoid punishment. Lastly, I believe that kids do this to get that much-sought after "attention" that every human seeks. Negative attention is still attention. But this is the wrong way to get it, and this needs to be explained to your child or children.

My Life Lesson

Children can sense who loves them. Give them time to adjust. Live one day at a time. Blend a little bit at a time. Slow and steady will win the race. All relationships take time to grow and develop. And don't forget to celebrate the smallest breakthroughs.

Wade and I view our children as little extensions of one another. And so, as we love each other—they too are loved. At our wedding, Wade and I included our four children in every aspect of the ceremony. We each wrote promises to our children and read them aloud, speaking directly to each of them. Our hope was that this would help them understand how much we love and value them. We also had a "ribbon ceremony" where a beautiful silk ribbon was woven in-between everyone's hands, symbolically tying us together as one family.

Family isn't always determined by blood or last names. Family is built and maintained through an enduring commitment to one another. Family consists of those people that love you unconditionally and would do anything to see you smile. Love, understanding, and kindness will go a long way in forging these relationships.

Neither my husband nor I view our four children as either biological or stepchildren. We view them all as *our* four children. But you must lovingly work together to form these bonds, and you will need to encourage all the children, individually, and as a family.

It is not the word that comes before parent, that defines—but rather the love and dedication in the parent's heart.

Three things in human life are important: the first is to be kind; the second is to be kind; and the third is to be kind.

— Henry James

Cope: Co-Parenting Pitfalls

My Life Lesson

One of the biggest hurdles that you may experience with your children will undoubtedly exist if your co-parent is faithfully working against you. Parents should always strive to work together, in the best interests of the children. Everything children see or hear, by nature, is usually based on their perception. So, be careful what you are promulgating. Because, without knowing all sides of the story, children are left to their own devices, when trying to interpret the situation. And, their presumptions are usually not based on all the facts. The truth lies somewhere in the middle. Or, the truth has been intentionally distorted to some degree, to make their co-parent look bad.

If you are the non-custodial parent, it is extremely important to see your child when you are supposed to, unless there is an unforeseen conflict that cannot be avoided or postponed. There is nothing that breaks my heart more than hearing about children standing for hours, looking out the window, waiting for a parent who isn't coming. If a parent can, but chooses not to ever see their children, it is a conscious decision. It is my belief that even if you feel, or your co-parent feels, that your child is better off "without you in their lives," it seldom ever is. Instead, get you and your children into family counseling to heal the wounds that sometimes fester during and after a bitter divorce.

If your ex has primary physical custody, the time that you do have with your child or children is crucial. So, on your custodial weekends, ensure that you show up, on time.

My Story

One example of a common co-parent pitfall happened after one of my prior step-children had finished a basketball tournament. As it was not my then-husband's custodial evening, her mother graciously allowed us to take her for a little time after the event was over. We offered to take his daughter to eat dinner, as it was around seven p.m., because the final game took approximately three hours. We asked if she had eaten at her mother's beforehand. She said that she did not because it would have upset her stomach during her game. Knowing she was probably hungry, we suggested a very nice seafood restaurant that she had eaten at before and liked. She dismissed this, saying, "I do not like the food there." So, we suggested a steakhouse, near the mall that she previously asked to go to. She politely said that she did not like that either. So, the next logical step was to ask her where she wanted to dine. We said that she could choose any place she wanted, within reason. She did not respond, but she was also preoccupied on her cell phone. We asked several more times, to no avail. So, we chose the steakhouse that was inside of the mall. She did not order anything to eat, and we knew she liked many of the appetizers and food choices. After we were done eating, we walked around the mall. My husband and I asked her three more times if she wanted anything to eat at any of the little eateries that we passed. She said, "No thank you, I am not hungry. I always eat dinner around nine p.m., after a game." We replied that seemed unusually late to eat dinner. But we *finally* realized that she simply wasn't hungry, and that was okay too.

Later that evening, my then-husband received a text from his co-parent, asking why we "never fed their daughter," implying that he was somehow inattentive in his duties. So, even after all the attempts that were made to get her a nice meal, my husband was still questioned about not feeding his daughter. As a fellow mother, I would have questioned this as well. Therefore, *simple communication* is vitally important between co-parents. It eliminates the assumptions that could made, on both sides, because the other parent was not present. This was not his co-parent's fault; however, this could have been alleviated had she called her ex-husband to confirm the story with him (the adult), before making an incorrect supposition. This is easier said than done. I know, because my children would sometimes come home with tall-tales or exaggerated stories. It was easy for me to get sucked into the emotional charge of the situation, because let's face it...we want our children properly cared for. A second option existed that night too. My partner could have proactively let his co-parent know that their daughter wasn't hungry (and did not eat) during the time that he spent with her that evening. This situation can be alleviated with proper, clear, and concise communication between the *adult* co-parents.

My Life Lesson

Perhaps you may have a co-parent who is committed to continually only believing their minor child and never gets the other parent's version of events. If this is the case, co-parenting will be much more difficult. Many times, you may not only have the child attempting to manipulate you, but you also have an ex attempting to manipulate your words and/or actions to suit their perceptions and needs. As parents, we have feelings and emotions, just like our children. We cry behind closed doors too. So, it is easy to fall into the trap of being manipulated by our precious ones (children), especially in a weakened state.

Get both sides of the story before jumping to any conclusions. Listen to the child's version of events, but then follow-up by getting your co-parent's side of the story. It will be extremely important for you to remember that no matter how you feel about your ex, *some* children will manipulate, lie, and try to pit you and your ex against one another. Sometimes it could be done very innocently, and sometimes it could be done out of spite or anger. This is very common, so many of you should expect this behavior. Because of the way things ended with your ex, you may be tempted to only get your child's version of an incident. But remember, your children are hurting, and they are yearning for the days when you were together as a "family."

So, if your child comes home with dreadful stories of what occurred at your co-parent's home, just breathe for a minute. Stop everything. Call your ex-spouse to get their version of the events. Sometimes it may be a simple misunderstanding because your child is not yet an adult. Sometimes it can be the truth, and you will need to take appropriate steps to ensure the safety and welfare of your children. And other times, it can be just out-and-out lying going on by your child, to get Dad mad at Mom, and Mom mad at Dad. If they get the two of you fighting, the focus is removed from them, and any possible disciplinary action from the weekend may be delayed or avoided altogether.

The second piece of advice I would like to give is that you should meet in person with your ex, whenever possible. If your ex is remarried, please invite their spouse to join the meeting as well, because they play a very important role in your child's life now, whether you like it or not. Prepare an agenda, even if it is rudimentary. This will help keep you focused and on track.

There are inevitably going to be misunderstandings over text and e-mail. There are no inflections, tones, or connotation when you only communicate in writing. So, do yourselves a favor, and meet in person over major issues. This will also let the children know that Mom and Dad are in sync with one another, and on the same page regarding child-rearing boundaries. This has worked wonderfully for Wade and his co-parent, and he is very thankful that she is willing to openly participate in these exchanges.

> *We all make basic assumptions about things in life, but sometimes those assumptions are wrong. We must never trust in what we assume, only in what we know.*
>
> —*Darren Shan*

Twisted Words and False Accusations

My Story

People rarely get "the" truth. They get "a" truth, especially in the scenario when a primary custodian is attempting to alienate their co-parent, from his or her children.

I have been accused, on several occasions, of "leaving out or excluding" my stepchildren. I had stepchildren with both my second and third marriages. Specifically, I have been told that I was "not being nice" to them. This is certainly not true. I have a plethora of texts and e-mails that would bode otherwise. Truth be told, I have always been nicer to all my past and current stepchildren (in both of my marriages) than I am to my own biological children. This is because I am a "people-pleaser" at heart, so I went overboard trying to ensure that they always felt welcome and part of the family. I also know inherently that I have the unconditional love of my biological children.

Conversely, I also did not/do not actively discipline my stepchildren either. So, the perception of my biological children is that I "treat my stepchildren better" or "it's not fair." But I do not view overt discipline as a stepparent's place (just my opinion). However, I will exert my authority with them if one of them is in immediate danger. And I will tell Wade in private if they have done something that I feel may warrant discipline. But that is up to my husband and his children's biological mother to decide how to deal with the punishment, if at all.

To ensure peace, another suggestion would be to ensure that all children know that they are all treated equally, especially with your finances. As of this writing, we have one child in the military, that is also balancing college classes; one child working full-time as an EMT, while attending school to become a Paramedic; and two children in high school. My husband and I keep a spreadsheet of all monies given to each child, even those that are now older than eighteen (i.e., the two that we are not "legally required" to pay for). We want to help all our children to the best of our ability. But—we do have four kids to think about. So, if we purchase a cellphone for one child, the older child may need new tires for their car, or gas money. At the holidays, I use an iPhone application called, "Christmas." This app is amazing. I put all the children's names in, and it tracks what I have purchased with the cost details. This is my way of ensuring the same money is spent on each child, whether they are my biological child or stepchild.

We all have heard the saying, "Life is not fair." But, when trying to blend a family, with children on both sides, there needs to be some equality. If the biological children and stepchildren all understand that you are two parents, working together, for each of their individual best interests, it will make things run smoother.

My Life Lesson

Children are like butterflies in the wind. Some may fly higher than others, but each one flies the best it can. Each one is uniquely different, special, and beautiful. Treat them equally, and do not compare them against one another.

When dealing with your children, honesty is always the best policy, on all topics. But you can only control yourself. You cannot control what is said or done in the other household, and I would explain this (gently) to my children when they wanted me to "fix" my co-parent.

Parents want the love of their children too. But, giving into them when they are wrong will not get this for you. If you love your children, do not allow this. Ever. This is something that I still struggle with—which is why my wise father always reminds me that, "discipline is the greatest form of love", and it will earn you their respect (hopefully, at least when they are older).

And step-parents must find a balance between supporting and defending, without overstepping visible and invisible boundaries. In time if you are a steady and good influence for your stepchildren, I believe that most biological parents will accept and respect you for your role in their children's lives. Even if they don't...you keep loving the children. They did not ask for this situation.

Wade's children are little extensions of him, and therefore loved as he is loved. And my children are little extensions of me, and therefore loved as I am loved. For all children of blended families, the main thing is to effectively communicate, love, and support each of them. We explain to our four children, that one day, we will not be around on this earth to help them. But they will have one another to lean on.

We remind them that although they did not choose one another, they will always be family. And we point out that they have two sets of loving parents now, and they can never have too much love. Sometimes blood is not what binds people together, but rather it is love that does.

The sign of great parenting is not the child's behavior. The sign of truly great parenting is the parent's behavior.

—Andy Smithson

The Kids and Their "New Normal": Try Not to Steal Their Childhood

My Story

When I look back at what my children went through after my divorces, I felt that my daughter was forced to grow up entirely too fast. She was extremely mature for her age, and her teachers would tell me this too. My daughter was in no way mature enough to help rear her younger sibling at such a young age. Nor should he have been her responsibility. However, sometimes when she was at her father's house, there seemed to be an expectation that she would be the little mother. She told me that she changed his diapers, even though she was just six years old at the time. She fed him his bottle, and she cleaned up after him. I did not feel that was right. Although it was teaching her how to be responsible, my daughter misinterpreted these chores to mean that she was fully responsible for her little brother, and this was stressful for her.

My son's sense of stability was also affected by this. He has said that many times he felt as if he was a burden to his older sister, and as a result, he has a harder time coping with social situations now.

I did not understand why my ex-husband parented so differently from me. He sometimes disciplined in ways that I found frightening and that upset my children. I felt like I could not protect them, because there was a whole second house they were growing up in, that I had no control over. And I think my ex-husband felt the same way about how I was parenting. He felt that I did not impart enough discipline, which by my own admission was true.

My Life Lesson

This is the most difficult part of a divorce. It is your job to help ensure that your children get adjusted to this new living situation. Always remind them that you are not divorcing them. The kindest thing that you can do for your children is to not blame things on your ex or bad-mouth them to the children. This will seem insurmountable at times, especially if your ex is not happy themselves, because they may want to place blame at your feet for their unhappiness. When I have disagreed with my co-parent on his actions, I tell my children that their father is doing the best that he can, and I am doing the best that I can. I remind them that nobody is perfect, and that he still loves them, and I still love them. I also delicately tell them when I think their father is wrong or could have handled the situation differently, and I hope he has reciprocated this for me. Remember that your children's innocence goes by very fast, and before you know it—it is in the past. The kids have enough to deal with, without feeling that one of their parents dislikes them. And it is not fair to the other co-parent either. After all, you are both "equal-amount" parents to your children.

The innocence of children is what makes them stand out as a shining example to the rest of Mankind.

—Kurt Chambers

It Takes Two to Tango: Everything Is Not All One Parent's Fault, and Being a Good Parent Isn't Always Easy

My Story

Hard as this is to say, your current life is partially the fruit of your own doing, so don't get caught in the parental "blame game." Everything is not always one parent's fault. So, don't get caught in only seeing the faults of your co-parent, while being blind to your own faults. For actively good parents: If your children feel that one parent is always wrong, then you should have a "sit down" with your co-parent. I believe that this situation generally stems from one parent alienating the other parent, from the child or children. They may be doing this consciously or subconsciously. It is probably the parent that is not involving the children, that is doing the least amount of harm to them. A parent that is continually "finger-pointing" at their co-parent, to their children, needs to understand that this is extremely detrimental to their children's emotional well-being.

What I always try to remember is I love my children more than I dislike my ex-husband, so I will encourage and assist in their relationship, as much as possible. Your children have a right to love their other parent, even if you don't anymore.

When I went through the mandatory C.O.P.E. or co-parenting program through our courthouse, I remember one thing vividly that we were taught. Children view themselves as half their mother and half their father. So, if the two parents continually badmouth one another, to their children, what happens is twofold. First, you are unfairly skewing a child's mind, regarding an essential parental bond and relationship. Second, when a child is not helped to rid themselves of resentment and hate for one of their biological parents, they are really being taught to hate half of themselves. This outcome is never good.

Co-parenting is not a competition between two homes. It's a col-laboration of parents doing what is best for the kids.

—Heather Hetchler

My Life Lesson

Co-parenting may be very difficult for most of you. I know that it is still very difficult for me to successfully co-parent with my ex, and it has been almost fifteen years since we were divorced. But I continue to try and pave a way (with my ex) for the benefit of my kids. I believe that it is important for my children's well-being to form whatever relationship they can with their father, so long as they want to, and so long as it is healthy.

As I write this, my daughter is finally strong enough not to put up with any mistreatment, from anybody. At almost twenty-one years old, she now sees her father on her terms, which I think is a giant step in the right direction, for them both. I believe that my daughter and her father finally have a good and respectable relationship, although she tells me that she sometimes still feels like an outsider to him. I hope in time, this will change too. But I can see that her own self-esteem has improved because of the positive steps taken in their relationship, and for that I am grateful.

My son is still not completely embracing his renewed relationship with his biological father. However, he now goes with his father every other weekend, which is a good sign that they too are developing and fostering this important relationship. I am certain that old, sad memories weigh heavy in the recesses of my son's mind.

As I said earlier, I suggest trying to work with your ex, as if he or she were a business associate. It helped me to remain calm and neutral in front of the children. I had to (and still must) train myself to walk away from an argument with my ex, because ultimately, I just want peace for myself and my children. Always keep it on a business level, rather than a personal level. You are now in the "business" of raising your children with a person who no longer lives in your home. Keep an open dialogue and regular communication and remember that consistency is important. This is something that I still struggle with.

Unfortunately, I think all children of divorce have additional "battles" to overcome, and we should try our best to remain impartial and help guide them as they try to restore themselves.

The Judgment of Solomon

My Story

Co-parenting, after a divorce or break-up, will more than likely be one of the most difficult endeavors of your life. I hope that is not the case for you, but I wish someone had better prepared me. Remember that you are going through a divorce or breakup, most likely because you could not get along with your partner. So, once you are broken-up and living separate lives, things will not magically become easier.

There are areas of conflict, between me and Anthony, which should be limited to the proverbial "spousal arena," as opposed subjecting our children to it. And, this is true, even for our daughter, who is over the age of eighteen now. A good parent will support their child's relationship with the other parent.

My Life Lesson

I liken co-parenting to the Judgment of Solomon. This is a story from the Hebrew Bible, in which King Solomon of Israel ruled between two women. The story says that two mothers were both living in the same house, and each was claiming to be the mother of the same infant son. The two mothers came to Solomon. One of the women had an infant who had died, and now each mother declared that the remaining boy was hers. Calling for a sword, Solomon declared his judgment: the baby would be cut in two, and each woman shall receive half. One mother thought the ruling fair, but the other begged Solomon, "Give the baby to her, just don't kill him!" The king declared the second woman the true mother. A true and loving mother would give up her own baby, if it was necessary to save his or her life. This judgment became known throughout all of Israel, and it was considered an example of profound wisdom. I retell this story, because I think that this is an example of unconditional love. A parent's love should never be intentionally hurtful or deceitful, so don't mix this pure love with retribution against your co-parent. Put your children first. Learn to love yourself and your children, more than you dislike your ex.

> *It is vital that when educating our children's brains that we do not neglect to educate their hearts.*
>
> *—Dalai Lama*

You Are Not Alone: Difficult Co-parenting

My Story

At times, co-parenting with my ex has made me feel like yanking my hair out, by the roots, hour by hour. After a conversation with Anthony, I have felt like I was spiraling out of control, and nothing I do is right or good enough. I felt like I was left holding a bouquet of condescension. Even when my current husband, Wade, and I have done exactly what our ex-spouses requested, it was still sometimes construed as wrong. I believe that this is mostly because of a lack of proper communication and a lot of misinterpretation, sometimes based on assumptions (from both sides).

Another issue that frequently comes up is control. I know of a couple of divorces that had crazy wording put into the divorce documents regarding dating, schedules, and quarrels over things as trivial as school supplies. Do people really need to fight over loose-leaf paper? I know Wade and I have experienced situations with our exes that feel like battles over control. They may likely feel the same way about us.

My best advice is don't be a vengeful or controlling co-parent. Do not road-block your ex, just to spite them. This only places the child in the middle, and it isn't helping anyone. It doesn't matter if being a good parent inadvertently helps your ex. Make decisions that are right, fair, moral, and just. If you cannot do it for your ex, then do it for your child or children.

My Life Lesson

Try to understand that good people, on both sides of the fence, sometimes have poor methods of communicating or make mistakes. It only takes one person to change the face of the co-parenting relationship. If need be, set the example, and let the other parent catch up to you.

> *The best security blanket a child can have is parents who respect each other.*
>
> —*Jane Blaustone*

Turning of the Tides: Custody Issues

My Story

Approximately six years after Anthony left me, he challenged me for custody. The details don't matter beyond two huge things. One, a ridiculous amount of money was expended by both sides for a battle that simply should not have occurred. And two, the period of this battle, which went on for years, was psychologically and emotionally stressful for me, my co-parent, and the children. They were all I cared about. Quite frankly, I would have signed over the deed to my house and all my bank accounts, in order to have my children safe and in my custody full-time.

In the end, the custody arrangement was to my detriment financially. But I ended up with significantly more custodial time. All that mattered, in my mind, was my children would have stability.

My Life Lesson

People were created to be loved and cherished. Things were created to be used. When things are being loved and people are being used, love is not present. From my perspective, having some extra spare cash would not have made me, or my children, much happier, than having very little disposable cash. My parents have always instilled in me that money doesn't buy you happiness, and part of the reason for that, is that money itself distracts us from what we really enjoy. Oddly enough, my parents have money, but they choose to live frugally, but happily.

Through these court battles, my lawyer taught me this important lesson: You need to learn to minimize your reactions to your ex. Set firm boundaries for yourself. Assert yourself against demands that feel unjust and unreasonable. Know what you are fighting for. I was very clear on one thing. I was fighting for my children—not financial gain.

My lawyer would get so angry with me when I would call him saying that my ex threatened "this or that" legally. He would tell me not to discuss the legal issues with my ex, ever. I finally overcame this by establishing a planned mental escape route for myself. For example, you can say, "I am happy to continue this conversation with you, when you can speak to me in a respectful and civil manner." Vent to, and buffer yourself with, your family and close friends. They will reassure you when someone is making you feel unworthy or wrong. They will keep you balanced and grounded.

During this long year and a half, I also became very aware that anything you or your ex puts in writing is admissible in court. So be careful when writing e-mails to your co-parent. You do not want your own angry written words to be used against you, by your ex. Worse, you do not want your words to come between you and what is in the best interest of your children.

No matter how much ranting, raving, and screaming the toxic individual does, remember that you never need to explain your position, immediately. And never broadcast your next move. You should remember to respond intelligently, even to the most unintelligent treatment. If you can look yourself in the mirror every night, knowing that you did right by yourself and your children, then you owe no answers. Any attempts to change your ex, will only leave you more frustrated than before, especially if they attempt to spin the situation, in order to blame you. A toxic person by nature and definition is a person who refuses to hear your perspective.

The sad part is that there are no real winners or losers in child custody battles. It is always best to try to work custody out, between the parents, outside of court. First, it is extremely expensive. And it is a long, drawn-out process that involves the children. Most importantly, you are knowingly asking someone who knows nothing about you, your children, or your co-parent, to decide where the kids will live.

When you choose to use your children as a weapon, just remember that one day you may end up without any ammunition.

How to Deal with a Difficult Co-Parent: Not Everything is About You!

Peace does not mean an absence of conflicts; differences will always be there. Peace means solving these differences through peaceful means; through dialogue, education, knowledge; and through humane ways.

—*Dalai Lama*

My Story

I am still a "work in progress" on this subject. And the below tips are what I am still utilizing to help guide me. Every day I find a bit more clarity on this subject, and I have learned *not* to allow my past experiences, to dictate or affect, any of my current happiness. But I still find myself overreacting, when someone is being accusatory, especially regarding a subject that they do not have all the facts on.

It was hard for me to grasp the concept that some people are truly great manipulators. They can lie, cheat, and treat you badly, and they do so very convincingly. And somehow, they also manage to make it all seem like it's your fault. Don't fall for it. That is just what they do.

And sometimes, people will make assumptions about you that are not true. I learned that time not only heals, time reveals too. Sometimes, in due time, the truth flutters to the surface, all on its own. Trying to "out-parent" or undermine your ex is a form of competition. These tactics belong on a sports field, not in your child's life. Remember that while you are busy trying to punish your ex, you are actually harming your child instead.

If you are like me, you may need to enlist the help of a trained professional if you are co-parenting with a difficult individual. The best way to shield yourself from bad behavior is to severely limit your interaction (or cut it off completely—if possible) with these types of people.

A wise counselor once told me that, "Silence can be a person's loudest answer." Sometimes, silence can be a great source of strength. It took me a long time to realize that my silence did not mean that I was agreeing with, or consenting to, what my exes were saying. I would always immediately and vehemently stand up for myself or my children. I would stand up for the truth. I would raise my voice, and my blood pressure in the process. Now I am realizing that my silence does not make me weak. My silence is a sign of inner-strength, self-control, and virtue.

I am now armed with a new thought process. Think of it this way: Never waste your time or energy trying to explain yourself to someone who is committed to misunderstanding you. As my husband, Wade, often tells me, "Don't ever wrestle with a pig. You'll both get dirty, but the pig will enjoy it." This is easier said than done, but it is very good advice. My husband is very adept at doing this. I used to think that he was too good at keeping quiet in an argument. I worried that some people viewed his silence as "giving in" or admitting he was wrong, or they were right. He looks at it differently. He always tells me that he refuses to put good energy into bad things. And he doesn't. He never has. He realizes that he cannot and will not change some people or how they think, so he doesn't waste time on this futile endeavor. Also, he believes that yelling and demeaning someone else, even exes or people you do not get along with, is wrong. So, even if it is being done to him, he literally "turns the other cheek."

My Life Lesson

DISENGAGE!

If you have a strained relationship with your co-parent or ex, the very best advice that I can give you is to DISENGAGE! DISENGAGE! YES. DISENGAGE! Do whatever you need to emotionally remove yourself from attacks, manipulations, and lies that your co-parent may throw at you. These types of people will not change. They believe they are 100 percent correct, and you are 100 percent wrong. Unfortunately, many parents seem blind to the fact that they are only hurting their children when they attempt to put up road-blocks for their ex. Put your child's well-being above your revenge agenda.

Some people think they know and understand your reasons and motives behind your actions, when they are completely and utterly off-base. And, most people do not listen with the intent to understand. Most people listen with the intent to reply. Never respond to an angry person with a fiery comeback...even if he or she deserves it. Do not allow their anger to become your anger.

Establish boundaries for yourself and learn to end the conversation when it no longer becomes effective.

Calmness is a human superpower. It is the ability not to overreact or take things personally. Doing this will keep your mind clear and your heart at peace. Do not surrender your dignity to someone else, by stooping to their level, by yelling back. No matter how tempting, do not respond to emotional talk, insults, or attacks made by the high-conflict co-parent. Reply only to the facts. Talk (or email) only about the children. Put up boundaries so that you lessen any arguments, misunderstandings, and circular conversations that lead you round-and-round, leading only to frustration.

When you get angry, your heart rate, arterial tension, and testosterone production increases, and your cortisol (your stress hormone) decreases. As soon as you get "hot under the collar", your body begins to prepare for a "fight." Your muscles get tense, certain brain centers are triggered, which alter your brain chemistry, and your digestive processes stop. Chronic anger can also weaken your immune system. A weakened immune system can lead to a variety of other health problems such as: headaches, problems with digestion, insomnia, increased anxiety, depression, high blood pressure, skin problems such as eczema, heart attack and stroke.

It helps me to believe that I was the lucky one chosen to be Gabi and Savino's mother. If I think this, then it also means that I was meant or "chosen" to co-parent with Anthony. Because of this belief, I try to search for meaning in my co-parenting struggles versus acting like a victim of my own circumstances. This thought process allows me to seek better ways to help my children. I believe that none of us are victims of our circumstances. Rather, we are a product of our own decisions.

These manipulative people know you very well. You were married to them or dated them, and for some of you, for a long time. So, they understand your "triggers" better than most. My solution to this is simple. The best defense is often a good offense. Make a list of the things that you know he or she will say, write, text, or email to you, so that you are cognizant of these things. Now, you must steer clear, when he or she tries to engage you in this negative talk. In certain very important circumstances, you should only communicate by email. I say via email, because this is a form of communication that you can keep and print, should you need it in a court of law.

Train your mind. You show more strength by not responding to someone who has unjustly criticized you again and again. These people may have even openly told others that you are a terrible parent. Again, the only people that need to know if you are a good parent—are you and your children. These naysayers are only out to "win," especially in the public arena. They feel better when others think poorly of you. So, should you defend yourself in public? You can try to respectfully set the facts straight, but do not get into a pissing match over it. Leave calmly, if they begin to get loud. You will look like the mature adult, not them.

One of the biggest parenting "no-no's" is when one parent, or both, show (or worse, copy), their children on e-mails or text messages between the two of you. If this is done to you, step away from the computer for a while. Do not ever seek reprisal, by doing the same to them. If you are only trying to "make your point" or think you will ever change your co-parent's mind, you are fooling yourself. This will rarely, if ever, happen. You have better things to do with your time, than to play ping-pong email games with your ex. Wade has taught me *not* to put good and valuable time into bad and negative things. So, immunize yourself, and avoid these aggressive people, and the drama queens/kings.

To involve children, at any age, in adult conversations and decisions is wrong on many levels, but people still do it. There will be many adult issues that arise, but this is not your child's place or burden to endure. Your child is not your or your ex's referee. Sometimes parents get so wrapped up in "being right," or they get their pride involved in the senseless tug-of-war, that they totally lose sight of one major fact. Their behavior adversely affects their children. Their jealousy and hatred towards their ex overpowers the love that they should have for their kids. I live by the motto that I love my children more than I dislike their father.

However, I believe that you have a right to defend your good name, and your position on important topics, if your co-parent copied the kids on an email from you or lied to your children about you. But, do this verbally, in person with your child. It will bring clarity to the children, on where you stand morally, ethically, and principally. Do *not* take this opportunity to bash your co-parent. Explain your thought process to your children. Allow them to hear your reasons for your decision or action. Reiterate to your children that they should not ever be placed in the middle of adult situations. And give them permission to respectfully bring it to your attention, if they ever feel that *you* are doing this to them. They may have questions. Do your best to answer them, without discussing your co-parent, or their position on the topic, whatsoever. This is not about your co-parent, and you should not be speaking for him or her anyhow. It is about you clarifying your position with your children. Sometimes, I would not even bring up the emails or text messages in my conversations with Gabi and Savino. I would just generally provide them with my feelings on that subject matter. That is the goal anyhow.

Be prepared that if do you attempt to defend yourself, you could be opening yourself up to your ex's wrath. When you engage in this level of distress, you are losing control and reacting emotionally, thereby giving the high-conflict person the weapon they need to continue hurting you. So, don't do this either. End the email chain altogether. I found it best to let the situation calm down, and a few days later, briefly verbally discuss your version of the story, with your children (not your ex). Do not prolong this conversation. Keep it short and simple.

Wade has rarely explained "his side" of things with his children. He did this because he never wanted to involve or upset them on adult issues. But sadly, as a result, his perspective and his rationale have rarely been revealed to them. The consequence of this is that his children only have one side of the story, to draw their conclusions about him and his family. Another result is that the children will not understand his position, until they are much older, probably with children of their own.

If you have a negative co-parent, the only version that the children have (of you) *may* be negatively skewed. But, in time and because children are extremely perceptive, I think they will understand that all arguments are not "black and white." I have confidence that children will see that there were always two sides to every story, and that *both* parents had their best interests in their hearts. After all, it is not about being right. It is about doing what it best for the children. In Wade's case, he is a very loving parent, and his co-parent is also a very loving parent. So, it's a win-win situation for their daughters.

> *A gentle answer turns away wrath, but a harsh word stirs up anger.*
>
> **—Proverbs 15:1**

> *Non-violence means dialogue, using our language, the human language. Dialogue means compromise; respecting each other's rights; in the spirit of reconciliation there is a real solution to conflict and disagreement. There is no hundred percent winner, no hundred percent loser—not that way but half-and-half. That is the practical way, the only way.*
>
> **—Dalai Lama**

Some tips on how to deal with a high-conflict co-parent:

- **Minimize contact and keep it brief.** High-conflict people love to engage in psychological battle. The hidden agenda is to keep you entrenched in the relationship, even years after the ink has dried on the divorce decree. In my opinion, there are few things more toxic than exposing a child to constant below-the-belt blows and mental combat. They don't need to hear this garbage. Keep your conversations with your co-parent brief. Discuss only the pertinent issues about your child or children.

- **Keep your children out of the middle.** Establish firm boundaries. Never use your children as pawns. And never ask your children for "updates" on your ex. Ensure that there is structure in your child's life. This includes all settings, like your home, school, extra-curricular activities, friend's houses, etc. No matter the setting, you should provide your children with a safe, predictable, and secure buffer from sinister psychological damage. This emotional roller coaster can become more detrimental to a child's healthy ego-development than overt abuse. Don't punish your children for your mistakes.

- **Avoid feeling sorry for your child.** Do not overcompensate for your co-parent. Nobody deserves to grow up with a selfish, self-absorbed adult, but there are worse plights. Showing pity for your children, when disciplinary action is in order, will only perpetuate a victim mentality with them. Your child runs the risk of becoming self-centered, spoiled, and reckless. They may not be able to move forward and have healthy relationships of their own.

- **Limit the amount of telephone or texting your child has with your ex while in your custody, and vice versa.** When Anthony had his custodial time with my children, barring any emergencies, I found the best-case scenario was for my children to have limited contact with me. Although this was very difficult for me, I think it allowed the transition to their father to flow a little more smoothly. However, I would call my children, once a day, to tell them good-night and that I loved them. It will inevitably take your children some time to decompress as they shuffle between homes. Unless you suspect that your ex is not adequately caring for your child, it's best to allow them the privacy of their allotted time with your children. I did this, to keep my children out of all adult conversations and situations. Allowing your child to contact you about mundane things that your ex is doing, or not doing, is to invite triangulation. Obviously and importantly, if your children feel that they are in danger, they should be told to contact you, (or the authorities) immediately, regardless of who has custody at that time.

- **Vow to be calm, pleasant, and non-emotional.** This is a Herculean task if ever there was one, but if your ex is gaining emotional intensity and threatening to take you along for the ride, someone's got to consider the impact on the kids. I found that my yoga deep breathing, meditation, and mindfulness, along with my support groups did wonders for my physical and mental well-being.

- **Nurture your child's unique qualities and independence.** I read that somewhere between infancy and adolescence, a narcissistic parent loses focus (if they ever had it) and stops seeing the child as a distinct individual, with feelings and needs. The child becomes, instead, an extension of that parent. Researchers found that in these cases, for the child to get his or her parental approval, he or she must meet a spoken or unspoken need of that parent, and their approval is contingent on the child meeting *that parent's* needs. Allow your child to seek their own path and encourage them to find their own place in this world. Help guide them in this pursuit. Encourage them to express their individuality and explain to them that sometimes it is our differences that makes us stronger. Put your child's needs above your own selfish ones.

There is a well-known quote that says, "A lion never loses sleep over the opinions of sheep." Remember this, and post it somewhere prominent in your home, if you want. It doesn't really matter what your ex thinks about you, so long as you can co-parent for the welfare of your children. The quote is a wonderful reminder to put your children first, over becoming argumentative with your ex. Be the bigger parent. Be the lion. Don't raise your voice, improve your argument. You have nothing to prove to your ex.

The same lesson goes for wanting or desiring to "be right." Keep it simple. Whatever is in the best interest of your children—do that. If you are dealing with a self-absorbed co-parent, you will never get the apology, appreciation, credibility, or recognition that you are searching for. They may not have it to give. Some people are incapable of giving that acknowledgement to you, so stop looking for it. Do not enable your ex to suck the happiness, spirit, and the life out of you. If you do, they have won. And Wade taught me that just because you don't "call your co-parent out" on something, doesn't mean that you don't know the morality of the situation. If it is not adversely affecting your children—move on.

And remember, most of the time, your silence speaks volumes. I have also learned that you never look good trying to make someone else look bad. As your children grow older, they will eventually figure out who had their best interests at heart. My father always tells my sister and I that, "Cream always rises to the top." If you can look yourself in the mirror every night and know that you did the best you could for your children, then you had a successful parenting day. Choose your battles wisely. And, know what battles are not worth your time. If it is only to "prove your point" to your ex…fuhgeddaboudit. (Sorry I digressed. I am Italian, so say that with your best *Godfather* accent.)

Do not allow your pride to steal your joy. The older I get, the quieter I become. Life has humbled me, and I do not care to waste any more of my precious life on nonsense. And, apologizing or remaining quiet, does not always mean that you are wrong, and the other person is right. It means that you value yourself and your children more than you value your ego. Some people have said, "Silence is the language of God, and all else is poor translation."

My final thought on this is that a lie remains a lie, no matter how convincingly it is told. And, the truth remains the truth, no matter how effectively the liar covers it up. Eventually your children will sort through the deceit brought on by you or your co-parent. Children are extremely perceptive, and in time—the good done by you, will prevail.

The tongue that brings healing is a tree of life, but a deceitful tongue crushes the spirit.

—Proverbs 15:4

Not responding is a response.

—Jonathan Carroll

25

Out of the Ashes, to True Relationship Happiness

For every minute you are angry, you lose sixty seconds of happiness.

—Ralph Waldo Emerson

"I don't believe in magic," the young boy said. The old man smiled and replied, "You will, when you see her."

My Story

I hurt. I burned. I bloomed...just when a caterpillar thinks their life is over, it becomes a beautiful butterfly. I believe that everything happens for a reason and when the timing is right.

Everything that I have never done, I want to do with Wade. I choose to believe that real love stories never have endings. I tell everyone that I picked my first two husbands blindly, but the fully self-realized Francine chose my third husband. My eyes were wide open. I also believe that my faith in a Higher Power played a role in finding Wade. From the very beginning, Wade's love roared louder than my many demons. But this is not to say that I didn't have to "kiss a lot of frogs" before my Prince Charming arrived. Because I did.

Who is the very first love of your life? You are. You cannot let good love in without self-love. In simple terms, Wade helps reveal and bring out the best version of me, and I do the same for him. We finally are comfortable in our own skin, and we love who are as individuals, and as a loving couple. Wade made me forget all the bad, and he made me believe in myself, happiness, and love again.

My current husband and I both revel in the fact that he was forty-eight years old, and I was forty-three years old, when we both experienced our first adult relationship "high." We felt joy in our hearts, for an adult relationship, for the very first time. My husband and I both agree that there were some days that we were good in our past relationships. But that was mostly because of our children, and not our spouse. We would smile for the obligatory photographs, snapped with our respective spouses dutifully by our sides, but they were mostly for the camera. We felt numb deep inside of our hearts. We felt that there was something missing from our lives. And our spouses probably felt the same way about us.

My Life Lesson

I truly believe that we are each on our own journey of destiny. I believe that there is an invisible thread that connects us to those we are destined to meet, despite time, place, or circumstance. But I also believe that it is up to us, what to do with these encounters. Your life will not get better by chance. It gets better by change. Some people are meant to only pass through our lives to teach us life lessons, while others are meant to be in our lives forever. It is up to you to decide who is right for you.

The difference between happy people and unhappy people is in their level of gratitude, attitude, and whether they have learned from their prior mistakes. Failure provides us with the opportunity to try again, more wisely. And Wade and I are so terribly grateful for one another and each of our past relationships, because we grew and learned from each prior relationship. Because of this, we ensure that we show gratitude to each other, every day, in small gestures of love.

And when you are dating or married to someone, you must be a "match." I do not buy into the saying, "opposites attract." They might attract, but I do not think there is staying power there. You must have common backgrounds, common interests, common parental views, common financial habits, common eating and exercise regimes, etc. This does not mean that your partner must be the mirror-image of you, but there needs to be a lot of commonalities. There are many good and great individuals out there, but when paired with you, it may be disastrous. It does not mean that either person is bad or wrong, it just means that you are not right for one another. I now believe that lovers do not finally meet somewhere. But they are in each other all along. You must be patient and wait for that special person.

Love changes some people. It changes some for the better and some for the worse. So, you want to find someone who brings out the best in you. Too many relationships bring out the worst in one another. You cannot be with someone that feels that you owe them something, just because they put so much of themselves on the line and opened themselves up to you. Be observant. You can see good relationships and bad ones, all around you.

My husband Wade and I love to "people-watch," especially other couples in love. We love to watch couples, walking together, or dancing like nobody else is watching them. And it is so refreshing to watch couples and families talking in restaurants versus fidgeting with their cell phones (which we see way too frequently). We used to be the people with our heads in our one-dimensional phones. But now, we always cherish our meals together. We eat slowly, and we mindfully talk and catch up on one another's day-to-day events. That is now the highlight of our day. We no longer need to "invent" a highlight reel to post on Facebook. We are living the life that we always dreamed about.

The final key to happiness is knowing that you have the power to choose what to accept, and what to let go. Everyone puts great trust

in their relationships, but this does not give someone the right to lash out with horrendous fervor, when things don't go their way. Fears, rage, and self-doubt are a few of the ignitions that you want to avoid. You need to be with someone that can lift you up in times of trial. And, you should want to reciprocate this gift, back to them.
You will be exactly as happy as you decide to be.

True Love Brings Out the Best in One Another

My Story

Wade often tells me that he was "not a fun-loving or happy-go-lucky" guy before meeting me. Rather, he was always the business-driven, serious guy, with a rigid schedule of work tasks. He said that he discovered a side to him that he did not even know existed. He still revels in the small things that he does for me, because he says that these sweet gestures never crossed his mind in prior relationships. (Wade was never cruel or mean, and he has always been extremely respectful and giving in all his prior relationships. But he admits that the things he does for me never even crossed his mind to do before.) For example, Wade is a man that now faithfully puts toothpaste on my toothbrush for me, every morning and every night. And he did this on his own, and he continues to do this without prompting.

Wade admitted that he never really laughed with any of his exes, yet we belly-laugh, many times, every single day. We have been laughing so hard on three occasions, that we had to pull our car over to the side of the road to regain our composure, to drive safely. These are the moments that we treasure the most because neither one of us had it before.

When I met Wade, I felt as though I had been given a new lease on life. The entire weight of the world was lifted off me—by his love, affection, attention, and care. Before Wade, I was always made to feel childish and immature when I would act silly and loud. Instead of criticizing me, Wade joins in on the fun.

Everything seems better and brighter because of him. We often joke that even food tastes better when we eat together. It was as though our hearing got better too, because now we listen with our entire body and soul, versus with just our ears, when we talk to one another. Our sense of touch is heightened, so even the simple gesture of holding hands felt better. My husband is a very tactile person. He says that when you are with the right person, even their skin will feel "right." He said that the texture and softness of my skin does not feel like anyone else's ever has. We both also believe that when you smell the person that you are supposed to be with, that their natural smell (no cologne or perfume) will radiate around you, and you will feel like you are "home." This will be true, even after a long day at the gym. I believe that is because we are the perfect fit for one another.

We can still vividly remember every date and time, in the history of our love—because they were all that special. And, today, they still are. The magnitude of our love is not diminishing; it is getting stronger. Just when we think we cannot love one another any more than we already do, we feel it even more powerfully the next day.

I had two co-workers (very close friends) who knew every side of me, and I knew every side of them. Almost every day, we would ask one another, "On a scale from one-to-ten, how good are you feeling about life and yourself?" The scale was measured at "zero" being the worst day ever, and "ten" being the perfect day. Every day, Kelley and I would rate our day between a "three and four." And, that was on a good day. But our other friend, Rachelle, always ranked her day between an "eight and ten." She had this response, even if it appeared to us like she was having a relatively bad day. Much later, I analyzed this. All three of us had successful careers. All three of us had at least average humor, health, intelligence, looks, style, personality, and morality. We all came from very good families, whose parents have all been married close to fifty years, each. The two major differences between us was that only Rachelle had a good, loving, and steadfast relationship. And only Rachelle was self-assured, self-confident, and loved herself. When I say that Rachelle "loved herself," I do not mean that in an arrogant or egotistical way. She was grounded, and she knew who she was. Hopefully now you can compute for yourselves why my friend, Rachelle, who had a healthy amount of self-esteem and a happy marriage, always scored much higher than us. I am very pleased to say that since then, Kelley and I have both worked on ourselves...a lot. And now, we are both extremely happy and at peace with ourselves. Kelley is now in a healthy marriage, and I am also happily married. We went from "zero-to-hero", by focusing on loving ourselves first and by realizing that we were worthy of love.

My Life Lesson

Wade and I tell one another that we are the exclamation point, in the happiest sentence that we could ever possibly write. It should not be difficult to love someone and be loved back. Someone can appear to be perfect on "paper" when you write down all their redeeming qualities, but it is really the interaction of the two of you that matters. So, stop rowing upstream and fighting the current. If you are working that hard, every single day, at either loving yourself, or loving someone else, then you may want to reconsider the path you are on.

This is not to say that relationships are not hard work. They certainly are. But they should not be excruciatingly hard, every day of your life. Wade and I have disagreements with each other, and he is the love-of-my-life. The big difference is that these arguments do not last long, and do not occur often. And, we would rather disagree with one another, than make love to anyone else. We love one another just as deeply when we do not agree. There are never any deep-seated feelings of animosity or disrespect.

I liken a true love story to an automobile tire. You can overinflate the tire, or underinflate the tire, and it will wobble out of control. However, if you take your time and put the exact amount of recommended air pressure in a tire, it runs smoothly and perfectly. Do not settle for an uncomfortable ride that could be very bumpy, at best—and could be downright dangerous and life-threatening, at worst.

Wade and I kept breaking our hearts until we found each other. It was only then that our hearts truly opened. Wade loved me, even at my darkest. Wade loved me exactly as I was, and this caused me to transform into the greatest and truest version of myself. I felt "seen" and appreciated in my own essence. As I began to trust our love, I became empowered to let him see my authentic self. When someone sees you for who you really are and loves you anyhow...that is powerful. That is life-changing.

> *Love is happy when it can give something. The ego is happy when it can take something.*
>
> *—Osho*

Your BFF is Important but Should Not be Mutually Exclusive

My Story

First and foremost, you must become your own best friend. That is the only way to experience the joy of someone else's friendship and love.

Once I loved myself, Wade became the best friend that I have ever had. We are as close as my sister and I are, and she is only one year older than I, and we have been extremely close since 1969, the year I was born.

Best friends have no pretenses and no limitations. Wade once drove two hours, on a chance that I might be available for an impromptu dinner with me. This occurred before we began dating. We had been friends for the prior twenty-five years. He was driving from New York, back to Maryland, where he lived. This was after his divorce, and he tells me that his heart was steering his car that day. He is not the type of person to ever deviate from his "plan." But he did on this day. He stopped by Pennsylvania, not even knowing if I could meet him. We had been emailing one another for a few months, here and there. He did not call beforehand. He called only when he was near my house. I had just come out of the dentist office from having a tooth extracted, and my mouth was swollen and numb. I was mumbling from the anesthesia, and I was having difficulty even put together a cohesive sentence. I remember him telling me that he did not care what I looked like. He just wanted to see me. I was mortified at my swollen jaw and the fact that I was wearing an oversized pair of sweatpants for my oral surgery. I cancelled on him, because I was afraid that he would take one look at me and run. (He never told me that he had driven two hours out of his way, until recently.) We laugh about it now because I know with complete certainty that he would have seen "me" and not my black and blue mouth and sweatpants. He loves me with makeup and a beautiful outfit, but he loves me just as much in a pair of ripped blue jeans, ponytail, and no makeup. Actually, he prefers the latter. For the first time, I can literally wipe away all other facades, except the real me.

My Life Lesson

Men and women seem to forget that when they become a married couple that they are friends too. Yes, there may always be small and real fundamental differences between the two of you, as people. But, at the core of any good relationship, there must be mutual respect, honesty, vulnerability, companionship, trust, admiration, and friendship. Friendship also implies a certain outlaying of time and energy, because it will require your effort.

I seldom had the emotional support and understanding from my past relationships, that I do with Wade. And my guess is that I was not providing that to them either. I was so emotionally broken, that I had nothing to give back.

Never lose sight of your extended family and other friends because they should always play an important role in your life and your relationship. It is not healthy to put all your focus and energy into your one "special friend." Both men and women sometimes need the company of their family and friends, without their respective life-partners or love-interest present. It is not uncommon to expect one's significant other to be his or her "everything." However, I believe that it is unrealistic to expect one person to meet all your emotional needs. Just because you are out with your relatives or friends, does not mean that you value your primary relationship any less. Conversely, it illustrates that you value your relationship enough, not to suffocate it. You cannot show your love and devotion to your life-partner, by being entirely emotionally exclusive to them. The idea of giving one's self entirely to the other person is what most people are taught going into marriage. But closing off your other support systems, is how you could isolate yourself as a couple. The unintended consequence of doing this is that you will feel guilty because you cannot give everything to your partner, and they will feel resentful and angry *because* you are not giving them everything. This is a no-win situation for both of you.

It is easy to lose the fire of friendship that once defined your relationship. Everyday responsibilities can take over, like keeping up with schedules, work, finances, church activities, and taking care of your children and your home. Being that busy, it is not uncommon for couples to go a week or more without having a mere fifteen-minute conversation about anything. Therefore, Wade and I instituted "date night," twice a week, and every other weekend. We take this time to unwind and catch up on our important issues, funny things that happened to us, and the pesky mundane day-to-day stuff that everyone deals with during the work week.

Aside: You should also set up a date-night for yourself too. This is a night (or day) that is all about you. If you cannot take an entire evening for yourself, then you can delegate a few hours of alone-time. Try to set it for the same night, and same timeframe, each week. That will help everyone in your house to respect this time as yours. You will learn that this night is essential to your wellbeing and mental health. You can treat yourself to that fancy Starbucks, get a massage, take a walk and photograph nature, get a manicure and pedicure, drink some beers while catching up on sports, read a magazine, etc. But you must turn your phone completely off during this essential "you" time.

And if you must "dress to impress," chase someone, bend over backwards to accommodate their schedule, change your plans, or worse, your persona, to fit into their life...you are not their friend, and you are not a significant part of their life. But when your love is not skin-deep, when your love transcends all worldly things, you will know you have stumbled across something great. That is a good place to begin your new friendship. Someday, when the pages of our lives are over, Wade and I know that we will be the most beautiful chapters of each other's lives.

Friendship in marriage is the spark that lights an everlasting flame.

—*Fawn Weaver*

Comparison is the Thief of Joy

My Story

Social media is a wonderful mechanism to stay in touch with people. However, if you have just undergone a breakup, it can be the sword that cuts both ways. Today, where we sometimes check our phones every hour, the last thing that you want to see in your Facebook or Instagram news feed is your ex's name, or worse, photographs of him or her out having fun without you. And, communication capabilities are now instantaneous, with the technology of texting. Try your best to avoid texting your ex, and if you break down and text them, do not text them again, to find out if they received your first text. They did.

You are only making yourself appear to be weak, and this is doing the opposite of what you intended. In other words, your unintended consequences are making yourself appear to be needy and desperate to your ex. Do not give them that satisfaction. And believe me…they are getting a cheap sense of happiness from your misery.

I used to compare and criticize myself, when thinking about anyone else in Wade's past. But I have learned that the only person that you should try to be better than, is yourself—and who you were yesterday. This is something that I learned from Wade, because this is the first healthy adult relationship that I have been in with a man. I used to always compare myself to other people, and their lifestyles, or even his prior relationships. But what I have learned is that comparison is the thief of joy. You should only be focused on your own relationship. Do not compare it, or yourself, to anyone else. First, you may be comparing your beginning to someone else's middle or end. For example, a beginner student in the art of tae kwon do should not compare themselves to someone who has studied the art for five years and has earned their black belt degree. Focus and look to your own orchard. Ensure that you water it and nourish it daily.

I changed the way I feel about jealousy and comparison because Wade is always so reassuring. My jealousy was never directed at my love interest, but rather whomever was trying to consort with them. I was always chasing love, and consequently, I was always afraid that the love of my significant other would go away or be lost. I was not self-assured, and my partners never made me feel secure either.

It was when I met Wade, that I realized that real men don't go out of their way to make their women jealous. If someone needs to try and make you jealous, they are not worth getting jealous over. Both Wade and I realize how rare our love is, and we appreciate and value that. We won't do anything that would ever risk jeopardizing the trust we have for one another. Wade tells me that, "It is a man's job to give all other women a reason to be jealous of the person that they love, and vice versa."

My Life Lesson

Social media has created jealous behavior in many people, many times over illusions. Sadly, some are envious of things, relationships, and lifestyles that do not even exist. Now my goal is not to be better than anyone else. And, I never compare myself to anyone else. My goal is to only be better than I used to be. The only time that I look back now is to see how far I have come.

I have learned *not* to compare my life to others' "highlight reel"! In the social media world that we live in today, I like to say that people post their "highlight reel." There is a very real and dangerous downside to the way that everyone's "best life" is currently on display for all to see. You cannot be happy all the time, and neither can anyone else. So, it may seem impossible to escape comparing your life to others. But most people only share the perfect parts of their lives, and they leave out the bad parts. We can quickly forget that "perception is not reality." It is easy to become overwhelmed by all the "perfect" relationships out there and forget that everyone has problems.

Marriages are not always perfect...mine certainly isn't. But you are aiming for as close-to-perfect as possible. So, avoid your urge to "look backwards in time" to your spouse's prior relationships. Those relationships did not work out for a reason. And don't "project forward," based upon anyone else's reality, except your own.

No one can make you feel inferior without your consent. Confidence has no room for jealousy or envy. When you truly know who you are, you will have no reason for hate or dreaded comparison.

A flower does not think of competing to the flower next to it. It just blooms.

—Zen Shin

Regret is a Horrendous Waste of Energy: Regret is a Form of Punishment Itself

My Story

One thing that Wade beats himself up over is that he did not date me when our paths crossed, twenty-five years ago. Neither of us were married yet. He is always telling me, "I wish I could go back to the day I met you again. I would do things completely different. I would have asked you out on a proper date, and never looked back again."

The quote, "hindsight is 20/20," comes to mind. Distance gives a clearer view. Wade has realized that he cannot see the façade of a building, while he is standing inside of it. He now understands that time has a wonderful way of showing us what really matters. And in the end, we found one another, and we ended up together.

Now, Wade and I both realize that there is a season for everything. There is a time to embrace love, and a time to refrain from embracing love. Wade and his second ex-wife have two beautiful daughters from their marriage. And Anthony and I have a beautiful daughter and a beautiful son, from our first marriage. And these four children are our greatest blessings. If life would have "zigged" and not "zagged" those many years ago, we would not have these four amazing young adults, who are the source of our pride and joy. So yes, we regret some of the time that we spent with the wrong people, but we don't regret our past—many good things came from it. You cannot rewind your life. There are no "do-overs." But there are second (and in our case third) chances to start a new and improved life. And you can learn from your past unpleasant experiences so that you never have to regret anything, as much as you do right now, during your breakup or divorce.

Lastly, Wade and I have realized that we can no longer be prisoners of our past. Our real future is now, with one another and our four children, in the present. And we do everything possible to nourish these relationships. One way we do this is by traveling together. We make everyday excursions that are close to home a special adventure. We pre-plan our weekends, so that we can look forward to our time together with one another, and with our family.

Now, the happiness is nestled inside of the little things in life, that Wade and I share together. We also walk together almost every single day. We change our scenery, by changing walking-paths. We seem to find renewed beauty all around us, and between us. During these shared moments, we have seen shooting stars, amazing double rainbows, flocks of geese winging their way back south, kids frolicking in water fountains, famous people tucking into small eateries, snow-covered trees with bending bows, vivid colors of purple, orange, and red lighting up the night sky, and snowmen made with love. Together, we have intertwined lives that are full of peace, compassion, forgiveness, and love. We are breathing in the "here and now," and we don't ever look back.

My Life Lesson

The bittersweet reality of wanting or exacting justice for your pain… is that you will be controlled by your ex, forever. If you keep an iron-grip on being "right" or justified in your ex's role in your breakup, you will also limit your access to all your positive emotions. It does not matter one iota if your ex feels that you were wrong, or you caused the breakup, or vice versa. And, if you are waiting for them to admit that they were cruel and wrong, don't waste your time. That conversation isn't coming. At least not anytime soon.

We are all a sum-total of our experiences. We are certainly made up of our genetics, the way our parents raised us, the books we read, the music we listen to, the movies that we watch, the dreams we have, the jobs we hold, the people that we meet and interact with, etc., but we are probably most affected by the one person that we chose to build a life, a home, and a family with. I believe that each of us takes something positive away from every long-term relationship or marriage.

Even if your relationship ends with divorce, if you think long enough, there will be silver linings that you got from that experience. So, choose to let those good and positive colors run through your psyche. Wade and I believe that if we had not weathered through our respective divorces, we would not be together today. So, we choose to be thankful for our ex-spouses. We also choose to be thankful for our trials, because we would not trade one another for anyone or anything. Becoming "awakened" in our current marriage, involved seeing our past relationships more clearly and learning from them. Life is a delicate balance between holding on and letting go.

Make this a rule of your life: Never regret, and never look back. Regret is an appalling waste of your time and energy. You cannot build on it, and it does nothing constructive to help you. Its only purpose is to keep you stuck in the past. You will not be able to start the next chapter of your life, if you keep re-reading the last one. I thank God for protecting me from what I thought I wanted—and blessing me with what I didn't know I needed.

We all make mistakes. We all have struggles and regrets in our past. But to dwell on these trials will not solve anything or serve you in any positive way. Focus on your life, here and now. You have the power to shape your day, today, and all the rest of your days here on earth. I know that I said this earlier, but it is worth repeating. My father has always told my sister and I that, "Life is an attitude, so you should get a good one." And he is correct. One of our personal greatest discoveries was that we can alter our lives by simply altering our attitude. And, you can begin this today. It costs nothing, and it will make an immediate impact on your level of happiness. One of the only frailties in life, is a negative attitude. So, look forward with confidence, not backwards with remorse and regret. Think like the person you want to become.

Don't live your life regretting yesterday. Live your life so tomorrow you won't regret today.

—Catherine Pulsifer

Same Journey, Different Road: My Path May Be Different, but My Purpose is the Same

My Story

Sometimes it's the journey that teaches you a lot about your destination. In this chapter, I hope to present you with some examples of my *current* marriage. I will speak to the things that my husband does for me, and how I reciprocate. I truly believe that I am blessed beyond measure with this wonderful man, who has taught me the true meaning of love. He has left an indelible mark on my heart and soul.

When I attempted to set my pen to this page, to properly describe the love that my (third and final) husband and I share, it was nearly impossible. I will begin by telling you what it is not. You cannot have a healthy relationship with people who wear a mask. You must each be your authentic self, and this person must bring out the best in you, and vice versa.

I can say that my love with Wade is a faithful love that is so deep, intimate, and profound, that it cannot be reduced to a simple definition. It is a strong and powerful force, with an endless emotional attachment. Our love has a myriad of different qualities. It embodies shared beliefs, along with an emotional, sexual, psychological, intellectual, and philosophical connectivity. This love is mindful, spiritual, active, forgiving, cognitive, sensitive, caring, and tender. I think that love can only occur when you are at peace with yourself, and your desire is to do what is best for your partner.

I believe that to have a lasting relationship, you must invest your love and time into your partner. For us, we found a similar intellectual dimension in one another. We also hold the same ideas, belief system, morality, and spiritual values. This allows us to better understand ourselves, one another, and the world around us. We grow together. We share our hopes and dreams, and we work towards them, together. We also know the most intimate details of one another's lives. We are best friends that care deeply about one another. We know each other's worst fears, weaknesses, and sorrow. We do not use this against one another, but rather, our life's storms strengthen our anchor.

We also share in each other's greatest joys. It is best summed up by a Jerry Maguire quote, when he said, "You complete me." Where one of us ends, the other begins. When love is real, it allows your partner to appear in the best light possible, and it triumphs at the other's victories. It is a continuous circle that never ends.

Our marriage now is our crowning achievement. Wade and I finally got this most important decision right. They say that the third time is the charm! And it was for us. We finally married the exact perfect person, for us. And, we hope that our children see a marriage worth imitating, when they look at our marriage.

I believe that true love between two people includes two separate desires. You must desire to love your partner, and you must also desire to be loved by your partner. Fate had entered our lives twenty-five years earlier, but we missed the signs. But destiny is persistent. And our paths crossed once again about six years ago, as of the publishing date of this book. We finally listened to God's meaning, because now we were healthy enough to truly listen and accept this love that was placed at our feet.

Now we are strong because we understand our weaknesses. We can look in the mirror and feel beautiful because we accept our own flaws, and we accept one another's flaws as well. Neither of us are perfect, but we are wiser, because we have learned from our past mistakes. We laugh a lot because we have known unfathomable sadness. Most importantly, we can now love because we have felt the pain of rejection.

I think love is the greatest gift that God ever gave to mankind. I finally understand the entire premise of true love. I know that my life would have no meaning, without Wade. I absolutely care more about Wade's happiness than I care about my own, even when my choices may cause me temporary pain. When I am not with him, I feel slightly off-kilter and sad. But this is not an unhealthy co-dependent love. This is a caring love that will last through eternity. This is the love that I know will never leave me, no matter what. We both long to include each other, as a part of ourselves. We were never willing to open ourselves up to this inclusion before.

Wade has made me understand that I have always had the power to believe in myself—and to love myself. I just needed a little space and time to absorb this foreign concept. Wade's undying and unyielding love for me has helped me learn to love myself. I never really understood how important it is to love yourself, even though my parents continually preached this to my sister and me. Even if you are not quite at the point of accepting this, begin to embrace the glorious mess that you are. Then, continue to fall in love with your mind, body, and spirit.

My Life Lesson

Admittedly, I am not yet at my own "self-love" destination. I think it is good to always learn and always evolve. To truly be free, you must become less concerned with another person's approval of you—and more concerned with your approval of yourself. And anyhow, you cannot please all of the people, all of the time; you can only please some of the people, some of the time. Ultimately, what you think of yourself is much more important than what other people think of you. So, demonstrate love by giving it, unconditionally to yourself.

Emily Dickinson wrote the poem, "That I did always love," and I feel that it aptly describes a perfect love.

> That I did always love,
> I bring thee Proof:
> That till I loved,
> I never lived—Enough—

That I shall love alway—
I argue thee
That love is life—
And life hath immortality—

This—dost thou doubt—sweet—
Then have I
Nothing to show
But Calvary—

In the poem, I believe that Ms. Dickinson is suggesting that without love, no one can truly live. Love is life, and life is love. I also believe that she is saying that when love is right, it never ends; it is everlasting.

Because Ms. Dickinson was never married, I also believe that she wrote this poem perhaps about her love for God or a Higher Power, which I think is beautiful.

Love does not necessitate that you are in a romantic relationship. You can love yourself. You can love God. You can love your family and friends. You can love your pet. Each of these different types of love can lead to a happy and fulfilled life. It is up to each of us to determine what type of love we want to encompass our lives. But remember, if you don't love yourself first, you will always be chasing after that elusive dream of how you define "love." You are love. You are beautiful. You are wonderfully made, and you have purpose. Work on being in love with the person in the mirror. You have been through a great ordeal; however, you are still standing. So, be proud of yourself. Love yourself and give love a chance—because love wants to find you.

She remembered who she was, and the game changed.

—Lalah Delia

Stop trying to 'fix' yourself; you are not broken! You are perfectly imperfect and powerful beyond measure.

—Dr. Steve Maraboli

26

How Do I Love Thee?
Let Me Count the Ways

So, when you finally have deep and abiding love with your soul mate, you will explore all the different facets of love. I think of love like a diamond—its many facets are what make it sparkle. If you have ever attended a wedding, when it was clearly a love match, you can *see* the sparkle and the glow. And the vows reflect that kind of love. This is why marriage vows talk about "in sickness and in health" and why they talk about being there for someone through all the ups and downs of life. When you love deeply, there will be a never-ending well of reasons why you love your soul mate. And there will be an endless number of ways that you and your partner try to show and "count" the ways...that they love you, and you love them.

My Story

In my experience, I have seen love expressed in many ways, depending on the couple's age, personality, and even cultural backgrounds. There is no "one way" to properly love someone.

What Wade and I have learned from our past mistakes is that love is nothing without action. Trust is nothing without proof. And sorrow is nothing without change. We finally discovered love, trust, and happiness with one another.

A soul mate usually comes only once in your lifetime to show you true love. Part of this love is standing up to you in ways that no one else ever has. They adore you—yet challenge you to your fullest potential. I believe that a true soul mate is like a mirror. The other person will show you everything that is holding you back from your own happiness, goals and dreams. Your soul mate will bring these things to your attention so that you can change your life for the better.

Love is reverence, glory, and worship. It is not a bandage for dirty wounds. Those who speak of love most wantonly are often the ones that have never truly experienced or felt it. I have found that I could not make some sort of feeble stew out of emptiness and contempt, or worse, general indifference, and call it love. But once you have felt what it truly means to love another, you will be incapable of anything short of total all-in commitment to one another.

> *Browning asked; "How do I love thee—let me count the ways?"*
> *For me there is no way to count.*

> **—Ronald Reagan, love letter to Nancy Reagan**

Physical

Even though times have changed, please do not give yourself away, physically, too quickly. If you move too fast, and it doesn't work out, the pain and recovery time will increase greatly. And this is true, regardless of your age. For those women reading this, we are emotional beings. Chances are that if you get physical with someone, you will become emotionally attached. And this will occur, whether your partner is emotionally invested…or not.

Although the rules of attraction might drive our initial decision to date, you will need more than an attraction to someone's looks and smell, to make a relationship last. But at first, there must be a physical attraction. In time, when you have allowed all of yourself to be completely transparent to your partner, you will find the true meaning of love. This is done by disclosing those traits that you do not like about yourself or maybe didn't even know existed inside of you. These are the traits that you wouldn't have thought to be beautiful. But the right person will love you unconditionally, even with your unattractive frailties.

Wade is beautiful to me, on the inside and on the outside. If I had to choose anyone in the world to love, and to love me in return, I would always choose Wade. We have an emotional connection that surpasses anything that I have ever experienced before. I melt every time I look at him, because I think he is the most gorgeous and sexy man alive. And he feels the same about me. He is always telling me that my beauty "stops him in his tracks" and makes "his heart skip a beat," even on those days where my hair is in a messy bun and I don't have any makeup on.

They say you only truly fall in love once, but that cannot be true. For, every time I look at you, I fall in love all over again.

My Life Lesson

I believe that the physical must encompass someone's body, brain, and heart. You must have chemistry in all three of these areas, to have a lasting charmed connection.

Physical Attractiveness

This is the degree to which a person's physical traits are considered aesthetically pleasing or beautiful. The term often implies sexual attractiveness or desirability, but it doesn't have to be. There are many factors that influence one person's attraction to another, with physical aspects being one of them.

From a pure evolutionary standpoint, if a person has good symmetry, it shows that an individual has the genetic goods to survive development, is healthy, and is a good and fertile choice for mating.

I believe that physical attractiveness is a necessary ingredient in any successful romantic relationship. In the beginning stages of a relationship, someone's physical appearance may serve as a gate-keeper, that simply directs us to certain partners to date, who are healthy, age-appropriate, etc. Let's face it. In real-life dating, physical appearance dominates. We choose to pursue and begin relationships with those who are attractive to us and vice versa.

But we cannot forget about the other extremely important char-acteristics that are also considered desirable in a partner or spouse, including things like a sense of humor, intelligence, kindness, understanding, empathy, work ethic, and family interactions and bonds. Oddly enough, research consistently shows that we rank most of these non-physical traits as more important than good looks.

I have always believed that most people fall in the middle of the graph, as far as outward physical attractiveness is concerned. But I also believe that someone's personality can take someone who is "average looking" and make them either ugly or beautiful.

Sex: Let's Get Physical

My Story

This is a difficult section to write, because I will have to make some admissions that are very difficult.

Prior to meeting one-another, neither Wade nor I had much sex in many of our previous relationships. The reason for this is twofold. One is that the magnetic attraction dissipated very early on, for both of us, and we believe that our ex-partners felt the same way about us. In at least one of our respective marriages, the attraction was never even there to begin with. So, it went from bad to worse, and quickly. And, after children came along, our sex lives were basically non-existent. We believe that you need an active, passionate, and loving sex life to sustain a happy marriage. This is probably why the first question that most marriage counselors ask is, "How is your sex life?"

Sadly, before we met one another, sex was just an act, or an obligatory marital requirement, where we simply went through the motions. We would always hear other married couples joke about how if someone put a penny into a jar, for every time they had sex in the first year of marriage, and then they took one penny out, every time they had sex *after* the first year of marriage—that when they die…there will still be plenty of pennies left in the jar. But we both knew, despite that penny tale, that we were probably having sex a lot less than most of our married friends. Our guess was that others shared intimacy at least once per week or once every two weeks. It is not exactly the type of question that you ask your friends. But we were having sex maybe once a month, and that dwindled down to maybe once a year. For the last five years of two of our respective marriages, the sex stopped altogether. During this time, when a lot of time had elapsed between sexual interludes, it felt awkward for me to initiate it, mostly because I felt undesired. I am not sure how my partners felt, but I certainly wasn't doing my part to make them feel sexy or loved.

So why am I telling you all of this? I am revealing some of my most personal details with you, so that you understand how important intimacy is in a relationship. If a man feels physically rejected, he will begin to withdrawal (or remove altogether) his desire for his partner. And when a woman feels rejected, she is probably more inclined to lose that softer side—that affectionate nurturing side. And so, over time, this is a recipe for disaster. Soon, you will have zero physical contact with your partner, leaving you both feeling secluded, unloved, undesired, and alone.

Because Wade and I both know what it feels like to be isolated from our partners in the bedroom, we make a concerted effort to passionately love one another, and we do this with devoted frequency. For us, one of the most compelling ways that Wade says he can *feel* my love for him, is when we make love. And I share his sentiment, so I reciprocate this love back to him. We both know the feeling of being rejected by previous partners—being zapped of any and all energy or motivation to try to physically love them. Suffice it to say, we have learned from our past mistakes in the bedroom.

As most of you know, sex is based on more than a physical act. There are strong emotions tied to it, and when you are angry, sad, hurt, tired, and/or lonely all the time, the last thing that you want from (or to give) your partner is sex. But *this is precisely when* it is most important.

Wade and I have an active and healthy sex life. I am not saying this to share our most intimate and personal details with you, but I wanted you to understand the stark differences in the bedroom, between the right marriage and the wrong one. You should be able to (and want to) kiss your partner for hours and especially during sex. If you have sex without kissing, you may want to rethink your intimacy. Making love to your partner should reaffirm how deeply you need one another in your lives.

Every single time my husband touches me, and I touch him, we are electrified all over again. We never tire of one another. When we make love, we are connecting on all levels: physical, emotional, and even spiritual. We are firing on all pistons, as the saying goes. We can "feel" the love being shared between us. I often tell my husband that my cup "runs over" with how much he loves me. This is because I feel completely loved, satiated, and completely safe with him. I have stripped down all my fears and emotional guards for the first time in my life. I know he will never hurt me. And, he knows that I would never hurt him. And, we hold one another all night long. When we are in one another's arms, it is our "safe place" and where we feel the least vulnerable. Generally, the desire and infatuation with our past partners lessened over time. Well, our desire for one another gets stronger with time. This is all new to us.

I also know that I sleep better at night when my husband holds me. But, let's face it, we all "twist and turn" throughout the night, and his arm sometimes falls asleep. So, we will sometimes just reassure one another, by placing one of our hands somewhere on the other's body. Just knowing that his hand is on my arm, or on my neck, makes me feel so safe and loved that I sleep better now than I ever have. Wade could never sleep through the night before he met me either. This was due to pain from old football and Army parachute jumping injuries, and he now realizes that it was also because he was not sleeping with the right person. It is truly amazing how manageable and fun life can be, with only one blanket and the right two arms.

My Life Lesson

I have lived in a sexless and emotionless marriage, and if you are not having regular sex, there will probably be a disconnect between you and your partner. I believe that men and women need sexual affirmation. Many times, for men, this area of his masculinity (sex) is an inseparable part of who he is, as a "man." While a woman's picture of romance tends to revolve around her emotional needs and thirst for a "connection" in the relationship. But trust me, I have lived years without the connectivity of sex, and I felt completely detached from my then-spouses. I felt like I was simply a "roommate" with my spouse, when we were not having sex. I believe couples need this deep close sexual intimacy to thrive, even if that only means long, intimate hugging and kissing.

I always say that coffee and love taste better when hot!

> *Let the husband render to his wife the affection due her, and likewise also the wife to her husband.*
>
> *—1 Corinthians 7:2-5*

No More Running Away: Emotional Love and Peace at Last

My Story

My husband, Wade, and I made a solemn vow to one another the day we got married. We could not fix all each other's problems, but we could pledge that we would never again have to face them alone. We finally realized that running away from our problems is a race we will never win.

When I first reconnected with Wade, I was no longer a hard girl to love, although I still had many emotional scars that we are still working through. My life is no longer full of the dramatic "ups and downs" that plagued my former life. When the sun shines brightly now, I can experience the "highs" of life.

I have a heart that holds a lot, maybe too much. My head holds too much too. And to be frank, sometimes my heart and my head still rebel against one another, probably out of fear. But now, you will never see me clinging to that rope, that is so frail and worn that it is ready to break at any time. And you won't ever see me let go of Wade. I have conquered most of my internal demons, and I will not allow them back into my life. And let's face it, for most of us, our inner-demons don't always play by the rules. But I know myself now. The walls that I had built around me no longer shield my love from shining brightly. I have learned that getting stronger, emotionally and physically, was one of the best cures for most of my problems.

Wade is now, as of this writing, fifty-four years old, and he is finally able to spend some quiet time at home and be content. In his prior life, there was always so much discontent surrounding his home life, that he would literally "run away." He would take his children to anything and everything under the sun. Part of this was to help educate them by seeing the world around them. But part of it was him trying to avoid being at home. (To me, it seems that Wade and his children have been to every museum, park, and tourist attraction in our tri-state area.) This seems especially true to me, because I was the exact opposite of Wade. I was a homebody who did not want to face anyone or any type of change. Worse, I did not want any of the outside world to bear witness to my unhappy home life. But we all have our own ways of dealing with heartache and pain.

Wade gives "high-energy" a new name. Wade wakes up at 4:45 a.m. every morning. He immediately goes to the gym for his first workout session. When he arrives back home, he wakes me up, and we go back to the gym or we walk, together, as his second form of daily exercise. Once home, he immediately showers and begins his work day. He is literally doing, going, moving, or working, from sunrise to sunset. He confided in me that part of this ritual of "constant movement" was to avoid his stagnant home life that was bleeding him dry of vitality. He wanted to avoid conflict at any cost. So, he would go. He would do. He would work. He would sightsee. Literally, he would do anything to mask his sadness, loneliness, guilt, and feelings of failure. He did not want to subject his children to this, nor himself. And he is certain that his ex-wife wasn't happy in this situation either. And so, to an extent, he did it for her peace too.

It has taken Wade a long time to realize that he can be happy at home by simply reading a book. He has peace at home now, and so do his exes. Wade can now be happy in his silent, calm home. Granted, old habits die hard, but Wade is trying to create a good balance of vacations and "staycations." And both are equally as appealing to him, now.

Alice only got to Wonderland by plunging far down, into a deep hole. We both know what it feels like to be suffocating in a deep hole, so we will not take our current love for granted. Ever. We will never ignore one another, because we share love, caring, and a deep-rooted commitment to our union. We do not ever want to wake up and realize that we lost our moon because we were too preoccupied counting the stars.

My Life Lesson

There must be an emotional bond, for any long-term relationship to last. First and foremost, do you feel safe with your partner? Do they support your ideas and goals? Do they love you unconditionally? If you answered yes to those questions, then you are well on your way to experiencing a deep love that will survive the test of time.

I believe the emotional connection that a couple must possess, to sustain a healthy and long-term relationship, is quite simple. The emotional bond must entail real love. And real love is knowing someone's weaknesses and not taking advantage of them, and it is knowing their flaws and accepting them as they are. You should run "to" your partner, not away from them, when you have good news or bad.

I remember telling my pain to, "Stay right there, and be quiet!" while I did other things during the day. Once I had spent time with my pain—grieving and reflecting, I learned how to put my heart back together again...but better and stronger, this time around. Emotionally, you possess more strength than you think. I have learned that strength does not come from physical capacity. Rather, it comes from an indomitable will.

A good life is when you smile often, dream big, belly laugh a lot, and realize how blessed you are for what you have. Emotionally, allow love to guide you. Savor the little things in life, because one day you will realize that they are the big things. These everyday small miracles are the very things that will satiate you and make an indelible mark on your emotional psyche.

Happiness, success, peace, and love are experienced when we live accordingly. They are not something you have, they are something you do.

—Steve Maraboli

Spiritual Health and Morality in Marriage: Master Thy Self

Just as a candle cannot burn without a fire, we cannot live without a spiritual life.

—Buddha

My Story

Before I married Wade, I experienced very little morality in many of my past relationships. Coming to that realization...well...sucked. When I discovered indiscretions or falsehoods, it did more than just twist me up inside, emotionally. I experienced physical pain as one of my symptoms. I have read that emotionally-charged events can activate the parts of our brains that react to physical discomfort. I also felt as if I had just quit a strong addiction, cold turkey. All my feel-good chemicals ceased immediately and without warning. So, it was as-if my "fix" was taken away. I then began to ruminate about these indiscretions, repetitively replaying the various women and scenarios in my head. I guess I did this because I felt so bad. And I began to feel good about feeling bad. It was my new comfort zone. Ultimately, this did not lead me down a garden-path of roses. I began doing and saying things, that I am now ashamed of, in my futile attempt to mask my pain.

Wade is the total opposite, living in truth. He and I now attend church together. He was raised as a Protestant, and I was raised as a Catholic. But we believe in one God, and we believe that worship and prayer helped lead us to an inner-peace that we could not achieve on our own. We have an overwhelming sense of joy when we hold hands and pray together, sing gospel hymns together, and seek answers that only come from our faith. We read from my mother's Catholic Missal. It is a book that outlines the instructions and prayers necessary for the celebration of the Catholic Mass, throughout the year. We discuss what the liturgy means to each of us, and then listen to the stories during the sermon, and we compare it to what the priest teaches us.

When you meet the right person, you will drop everything for them. You will lose interest in anyone else. Your feelings will be so strong that you will have no choice but to be with that person. We don't take each other for granted—but we also, neither of us, fear the other one cheating. We're simply too connected.

My Life Lesson

I believe that your moral compass guides you. I also believe it is one of the foundations of who we are as individuals. And truth is the substance of all morality. So, this concept goes together with a healthy marriage. People who have a sense of moral commitment to themselves and one another, typically place a strong emphasis on marriage as a covenant versus a contract. The focal point of the union is their promise or pledge to each other. They believe that righteousness and integrity dictate that marriage vows be honored and never violated. I did not always feel that way, but I do now.

Personally, Wade and I also believe that without a strong faith, many good people can come unglued, especially in today's electronic society that is chock full of easy-access to many temptations. It is all too easy to slip-up or stray away from morality. Frankly though, neither of us has ever felt the need to ever look outside of this marriage, because we are finally and wholly loved unconditionally, and we don't take one second together for granted.

Morality may consist solely in the courage of making a choice.

—Leon Blum

Action is a Form of Love: The Mirror of a Person's Heart is His Actions...Look Closely

My Story

My husband does things for me that I could never even contemplate a husband doing for his wife. And my husband will tell me that he never did any of these niceties for any of his previous wives or girlfriends. He tells me that he would never have thought to do these things for them. As I said earlier, he was certainly never cruel or mean to anyone in his past, but he explains to me that he did not know this kind of love was inside of him, until he met me.

My husband was a former football player and powerlifter. In 1987, Wade placed fourth in the country, in the 220-pound weight class for power-lifting, while a cadet at the United States Military Academy. He still works out twice a day and has completed the Spartan races (difficult obstacle races) for the past three years with his oldest daughter. So, when he told me that he would like to dye my hair for me, I thought he was joking. He wasn't. He said that he loves to spoil me and spend time with me. So now, dying my hair is another way that we bond. And it is one less thing that I must worry about with my full agenda. He knows my hair color better than me, and it is always stocked in our house. He bought a special cape, so that I do not get the permanent hair dye on my clothing. My very own in-house stylist also has his professional brushes, for the dye application. His work does not end here. He also removes the dye from my long hair, in the shower. He follows this up by massaging the special conditioner throughout my locks, before combing it through and rinsing it out. It is another small way that he pampers me.

He also has every single piece of MAC make-up that I use, all carefully cataloged in his phone. He knows when I am running low on a product, and out of the blue, he will surprise me with a new replacement. He does this with my shampoo and conditioner, my favorite bath soaps, and prescription drug refills too.

A few years ago, when I was still commuting to work, before working from my home office, my drive was approximately 1.5 hours, one-way. My office was approximately sixty miles from my house, but congested rush-hour traffic made things even worse. He knew how mentally exhausting my corporate management job was for me, only to come home to my second "labor of love," my two teenage children. So, we would get up each morning at approximately 4:45 a.m. and head to our local Planet Fitness gym. We would then go home, shower, and prepare for our workday. Then my husband would have my breakfast and a to-go coffee ready for me, and he would drive me to and from work, every day that he could. He was already able to telecommute with his job. So, once or twice a week, I would get the great privilege of being his passenger, over the long stretch of highways. Sometimes I would catch up on my sleep. But, most of the time, we would talk, laugh, and generally enjoy one another's company. This was our only "quiet" time together during the day, and we both treasured it.

My husband gives me at least a thirty-minute full-body massage every single night. This is not an exaggeration, and most nights it is an hour long. It began as another special thing that he did for me, but about a year ago, I began experiencing severe pain in my neck, back, shoulder-blade area, down my left arm, and into my pinkie finger. We had an MRI done, and the physician's assistant discovered a mild disc herniation was most likely the culprit, causing muscle spasms in the areas of my left shoulder and back. So, Wade attended every physical therapy appointment with me. He watched how they massaged my neck and where the isolation points were. He also asked how "traction" was performed on my neck, and he now does this every night. (This is a gentle way to stretch your neck.) He brings me ice-cold water every night, with a straw, to dispense my evening medications. He also applies the heating pad to my affected areas, most nights, before his massaging commences. His hands are extremely strong. I have gone to many massage therapists before, and I would choose my husband over any of them. This act of kindness is not only physical, but it is emotional for me as well. His generosity still astounds me.

Now that you have read about my nightly massages, it will be no surprise to you that my husband attends every single doctor's appointment with me. At first, this was very embarrassing. There I would go, with my husband in tow. He would ask all kinds of questions and take copious notes throughout the appointment. The doctors that he has been to with me include my family doctor, dentist, ophthalmologist, foot doctor, OB-GYN, counseling/therapy, and to get my MRI and mammogram scans. He is there to help me stay healthy, so that we can continue to enjoy many more years together. Now, I realize that he is there because he genuinely cares about me, and he loves me.

Another undiagnosed problem that I have is that my feet are numb, but they also hurt. I know that this does not make much sense, but it is the only way to describe it. Sometimes, I cannot tell when my feet are on the ground, so my husband always holds my arm, when I am descending stairs, or there is snow and ice on the ground. He also puts on my shoes, every single morning, and he removes them too. He even gets my socks out for me. I tell him that this is not necessary, but he tells me that he enjoys pampering me. He also knows that it is difficult to put on some shoes, because my feet have a numbing, yet stabbing pain. Most of the time, we exercise early in the morning, and then go to work. So, it is no less than two shoe-changes per day. He is always more than happy to do this for me.

One day, Wade noticed that I was only wearing two different bras. One was black. One was white. The essentials, right? Well, he wanted to ensure that I had a few extras, so he went to the store with me to go "bra shopping." It was hysterical. He walked right up to the sales lady, looked at me, and he said, "Babe, tell the sales lady what kind of brassiere you need." Then, he went to work. He found approximately ten various bras, of all colors and makes. I told him that I would only need two or three more, and I began to sort through the ones that he chose. He said, "You must try them on, to ensure the proper fit." I quickly advised him that I never try on bras at the store. Well, this night would be different…very different indeed. He followed me into the dressing room and proceeded to assist me in trying on each of the assorted bras. When I found the ones that fit me the best, he went to the checkout cashier and proudly purchased them for me. He told me, "Now, you have the right 'tools' for the job." Hilarious. This trip really made me see the depth of his care and concern for me. He wants me to be happy, whole, and yes, a little spoiled.

Like most of you, we both work long hours, so many weekends we go out to dinner. But, during the week, we try to cook and eat healthy. We both go to the grocery store together. This is a novel concept for me. In all my prior relationships, I would do most of the grocery shopping and schlep all the bags into the house to unload them, alone. Wade and I either cook together, he cooks, or occasionally he will let me cook. It is not because he is a control freak, but because he loves to take care of me. And I love to make him special dinners to spoil him. He sets the table, including drinks (with a straw), napkins, and the meal itself. I must "beat him to the punch" or he would do the dishes every night too.

My Life Lesson

I shared some of my personal and joyful stories, to illustrate the stark difference between my relationship with Wade and my relationship with most of my exes. Wade and I attribute our overwhelming martial happiness to finally being equipped, on what to look for, when choosing the best partner.

In the beginning stages of my relationship with Wade, I would watch the way he interacted with his mother, his aunts, and his two daughters. (If your significant other has a sister, watch this interaction as well.) Generally, the way a man treats the important women in his life is the way that he will treat you. This is also true about the way women treat their father, brothers, uncles and sons. So, pay attention.

We took our time. Because it is only *over time* that you can properly determine if someone is a good "match" for you. And remember, someone's past behavior is a good predictor of their future behavior. Therefore, the length of time you are with your partner is important, before ever making the decision to marry. Wade and I spent over two years together, prior to tying the knot. Wade and I saw one another at our best...and at our worst, *prior* to getting married. This is just another of the many reasons for our success story. There is no magic number of years that you should date, prior to getting engaged or married. However, I would strongly urge you to date long enough to see your partner in *every* situation, from happy to sad, in good times and in bad, and under long-term chronic stressful conditions. Life is great. But life is also difficult, and you want to ensure that your relationship is strong enough to withstand life's setbacks and pressures. Ultimately, only you know when the time is right to take that next step in your relationship. Just remember that anyone can be agreeable and get along, during the good times. Sometimes people's armor doesn't crack until there has been an accumulation of (or reoccurring) stress over time. And if you see these stress fractures in your relationship, you need to act. You need to either resolve your issues or determine that you are no longer going to proceed in the unhealthy relationship.

When you choose the "right" partner, there is no better feeling in the world. At times, we have agreed that we both feel "guilty" at the amount of love and attention that we give one another. But this is the way it should be. It is a "give-give" that will make a winning relationship. You should never feel guilty for being loved or loving another. It is what we all deserve.

Wade and I truly do unto one another, as we would want things done unto us. More importantly, both Wade and I get a feeling of satisfaction and appreciation from the genuine gratitude that we receive from one another. You add value to your significant other when you value them. From the beginning, we worked on fulfilling one another, and the more we did that, the more we could rely on that support. So, even when one of us inadvertently lets the other one down, we understand that the other did the best that they could.

Wade always wants me to shine brightly, while he takes a back-seat to the limelight. And, I want him to shine, just as brightly. Wade and I were very clear to one another, from the very beginning, on what we wanted in a life partner. We respected this candor, and with each other, we were never afraid of commitment, as we had been in the past. We both realized that all of our previous relationships were preparing us for one another. I hope that every person that reads this book has this type of "big love" in their lifetime.

The bottom line is this…life is hard; and this world can sometimes be a shitty place, and sometimes people can be mean. But I am a firm believer that when you put positivity and goodness out there into the Universe, YOU yourself *will* become a happier person. It will reflect from the outside, in. Random acts of kindness for your significant other (or anyone), will change your life—and maybe someone else's life too.

> *But love, I've come to understand, is more than three words mumbled before bedtime. Love is sustained by action, a pattern of devotion in the things we do for each other every day.*
>
> *—Nicholas Sparks*

> *Give your hands to serve and your hearts to love.*
>
> *—Mother Teresa*

Not Everyone that You Lose is a Loss: Care Versus Being Taken Advantage Of

My Story

If you characterize people by their actions, you will never be fooled by their words. Wade says that he is finally happy to be with someone who wants him for him and not his house, or to take care of them financially, etc. I am extremely cognizant of this fact. I own my own house, and I pay all my own bills. I tell my husband that he does not have to "pamper" me as much as he does, and that I would love him just the same, without all his dutiful attention to me.

Wade has explained to me that in some of his prior relationships, the women were using him. One ex-girlfriend would email him with online links to very expensive diamond and gold jewelry, from stores like Tiffany's and Nordstrom. She would then proceed to basically demand that he buy these various items for her if he wanted any sexual relations to continue. I was appalled when I read some of their email exchanges. She felt "entitled" to whatever he had. What was hers was hers. And what was his was hers. And what he didn't give her, she took. For example, she racked up over $10,000 in credit card debt, on Wade's credit card, after only dating Wade for three months and quitting her job. The worst part was that Wade was completely unaware of these charges, until after he received the monthly statement. I asked him why he didn't end their superficial relationship then and there? His reply was, "I did not want to be rebuffed. My psyche could not take another rejection at that point in my life. I already felt like a complete failure. And, I was also scared of being alone for the rest of my life, so in my distorted mind, someone was better than no one."

Wade and I have discussed the difference between caring for someone versus being taken for granted or using someone, at length. Where do you draw the line? We have both experienced being taken for granted. This is when someone underestimates the value of another person. In other words, they expect someone to be always available, and serve them, without giving recognition, thanks, or ever returning the favor. In our cases, many of our counterparts would ring the proverbial bell, and expect us to hop to their latest demands. Wade and I were always the reliable dogs. The problem is that the dog gets tired of getting whipped. There are limitations to every human being.

My husband has explained to me that I appreciate him. He describes appreciation as, "the act of giving something or someone their proper value." And everybody has value. Value in a relationship is important because it lets a person know where they stand, and what they mean to you. Your appreciation is your special way of letting that person know how you feel.

When someone is dedicated to a relationship, and they don't know how valuable they are to that partnership, it changes how they function, and how they operate in that union. When a person believes that you don't value them, they tend to devalue the relationship they're in. This is what happened to both Wade and me, on multiple occasions, because of our generosity. Therefore, I am extra careful to always acknowledge everything that he does for me, and vice versa. It is easy, because I have never been treated this lovingly either, so I am truly grateful. My husband never looks for reciprocity for his many acts of kindness, because he loves his family and friends. But I am always very cognizant of the way he was mistreated in the past, by some of his partners. So, simply telling him how much I appreciate his efforts makes him very happy. It's usually the small things in life that mean the most, and a thankful receiver bears an abundant harvest. Sometimes the smallest gestures, of understanding, recognition, and compassion, are the only things that can reach some wounds.

My Life Lesson

True love will never take advantage of another person, especially when that person is in a susceptible and vulnerable state.

If you are like my husband and me, we enjoy doing things for other people, and we derive happiness from being generous and giving. It's when we never get a simple thank you, or an acknowledgement, that we become unhappy.

A true test of someone's character, including your own, isn't measured on how you act on your best days, or when things are going according to your plan. Character is tested by how you act and react on your worst days. Imagine this: You just spent the entire day preparing a special dinner for your significant other. It turned out exactly as you wanted it to, and you have already taste-tested everything. You absolutely love it, and you are excited to share it with your partner. You set the table with your fancy dinnerware, and you light candles to create a perfect ambiance. But when they come home, they are in a bad mood. You did not cause their bad mood. But they come through the door, mad all the same. Like a hornet ready to sting, they begin their attack, by pointing out all the flaws with your well-planned meal. "You know that I like asparagus more than I like broccoli." Or, "Why would you make steak for dinner, when you know we are on a budget?" Think about how these remarks would make you feel. It is often the small things in life that mean the most—and conversely can hurt the most. Be careful with your actions and your words.

Wade and I both freely admit that we are not perfect—far from it. But, when someone has tried to make your life a little more special, or a little easier, then there should be some sort of readiness on your part, to show your appreciation for this, and to perhaps even return the kindness in your own way. It is a common courtesy among all people, to give thanks and appreciation. Gratitude in our various relationships was severely lacking. And once you feel that every, and anything, that you do is an "indebtedness" or obligation, then you may begin to reciprocate this poor behavior. Your appreciation for your partner's good deeds may also begin to diminish. This is how the deep-rooted resentment reared its ugly head, in some of our past relationships.

You are responsible for how you act, no matter how you feel. Remember this simple rule: Show simple graces, like virtue, kindness, thanks, and appreciation. Don't waste your time focusing on the way some people may have taken advantage of that. Rather, focus on the fact that you were able to give love, and that means that it lives inside of you. That is what makes you who you are. That is what makes you a beautiful person.

Do you want to be happy? Push forward with your decision to change your life for the better. Those series of decisions may be difficult, but it will be worth it in the end. Don't sacrifice the rest of your life's happiness because you are afraid of change. I think of FEAR as an acronym: (Face Everything And Rise). Let go of what's gone and be grateful for what remains. Always give kindness and compassion wings. But most importantly, look forward to what great things are coming to you.

It only stands to reason that where there's sacrifice, there's someone collecting the sacrificial offerings. Where there is service, there is someone being served. The man who speaks to you of sacrifice is speaking of slaves and masters and intends to be the master.

—Ayn Rand

If you want others to be happy, practice compassion. If you want to be happy, practice compassion.

—Dalai Lama

People rise out of the ashes because they are invested in the possibility of triumph over seemingly impossible odds.

—Robert Downey, Jr.

27

The Soul of My Soul: Broken Hearts Can Become Brand New

...and when one of them meets the other half, the actual half of himself...the pair are lost in an amazement of love and friendship and intimacy and one will not be out of the other's sight ... even for a moment.

—Plato

My Story

I can finally tell my story, without lamenting over my perceived injustices. This is how I know that I am healed. I also now believe that fairytales are true; not because they remind us that dragons exist, but because they illustrate that dragons can be slayed, even the demons that lurk inside of yourself. Just because you are struggling does not mean that you are failing. Sometimes you must lose—to win.

Love—I have waited for you. And Love—I was hurt by you. But, "love" finally came and took me by the hand. Love found me. After failing at loving my other partners properly, I have, for the first time, found someone that I can truly love. I found Wade. He is my better self. I am bound to him with an indescribable attachment. He is good, gifted, kind, gentle, trustworthy, and supportive. A solemn passion was conceived for him on our very first date. I now wrap my existence around him, but I am always aware that I am strong enough to stand on my own too. We are fused together in love, as one.

Simply put, for the first time, I have found someone that I hate leaving. You will attract what you are ready for. I finally loved myself, so, I was finally ready. I have found someone that will never satiate me, because I can never get enough of him. I found someone that accepts me for who I am and doesn't tell me that I need to change.

He is the soul of my soul. In time, our bodies will wear out, but I know that Wade and I will still be holding hands and laughing in the retirement home. I know that people will marvel that we are still "that" in love with one another. My husband and I have left the storms behind us. We can finally enjoy the sunlight. We accentuate one another's positives, and we still our voices of insults. We more generously complement one another and those around us, because we are truly happy. We endorse virtue and the effort that each of us puts into our marriage. We respect each other, and we are one another's biggest fans. We connect in every way and on every level, which brings us both a sense of peace, calm, and happiness.

My husband and I have discussed our life's achievements. We agreed that when we reach the end of our days here on earth, and we are asked what our greatest achievement is; our answer will be the same. We loved.

My Life Lesson

They say a person needs just three things to be truly happy in this world: someone to love, something to do, and something to hope for.

—*Tom Bodett*

I will end my book, where it began. I was a self-doubting and scared woman, who thought I was so broken, shattered, and used, that nobody would or could ever love me again. I was wrong, and if you think that about yourself, you are wrong too. Though no one can go back and make a brand-new start, *anyone* can start from now and make a brand-new ending. The sky is not the limit for you. Your own belief system and attitude are the only things holding you back from the life you deserve. Forgive yourself for not knowing what you didn't know, before you learned it.

It's funny how we outgrow, what we once thought we could not live without. And how we can fall in love with what we didn't even know existed. Life keeps leading us on journeys that we would never go on, if it were up to us. Don't be afraid. Have faith. Find the lessons. I believe that it is God's will that we imitate how he lived his life. To put it simply, God wants us all to live a life of love. The tough part is to decipher how to best achieve that goal. As you learned through my experiences, you must start by loving yourself. I love *love*, and I love me. And I hope you do too…enough to shatter the personal barriers that are keeping you from the love that wants to find you. And then, you must not settle on just any love, but a love that is good, fair, healthy, magnetic, and just.

God has given each of us a mind and free will, to choose romantic partners for ourselves. So, choose wisely my friends, and do not ever settle. Your special someone is worth waiting for, and you are worth the wait. Remember that how he or she treats you is how they feel about you. Think of God telling you, "I'm turning your pain into power, your fear into focus, and your difficulties into determination. What the enemy intended for evil, I intended for good. Put your trust in me. I have a great plan for your life."

The road to happiness will not always be easy. Stop breaking your heart by trying to make a relationship work that clearly isn't meant to be. You cannot force someone to care about you. You cannot force someone to love you. You cannot force someone to be loyal. You cannot force someone to be the person you need them to be. And sometimes the person that you love the most is the very person that you are best without. Some people are meant to come into your life, but they are not meant to stay there. Don't lose yourself trying to "fix" someone else. You cannot get the relationship you deserve, from someone that is not ready or willing to give it to you. You may not understand everything right now. But I promise you—your future will always bring insight and understanding as to why things did not work out. There is a difference between giving up and letting go.

You must remove yourself from people who treat you as if your time doesn't matter, your feelings are worthless, and you are replaceable. When someone treats you like you are just one of many options, help them narrow their choice. Remove yourself from the equation. Know your value and what you have to offer. Then, do not settle for anything less than what you deserve.

I sit back now and think about every person in my life, whether we talk every day or not. I know who lifts me higher and who motivates me to be a better person. Surround yourself with these people. You should continue to rely upon those family members and close friends that have helped you along your winding path to happiness. I am also cognizant to show my gratitude to these treasured few in my inner circle. I needed my family and friends then, and you may also continue to need them. It's up to you to let them know how special and important they are to you. Let them know how much you appreciate them. I had a "Gratitude and Thank You Party" for my family and friends, to let them each know that I would not have come through these ordeals, without their help, concern, and love. Even my family-law lawyer and his lovely wife were in attendance, because they became a stronghold for me, at my lowest point.

Some people say that love is blind. I disagree. Infatuation is blind. Infatuation is fragile and will shatter when life is not perfect. Love is all-seeing, all-knowing, and accepting. Love is seeing the flaws but accepting them. Love is recognizing that we all have fears and personal insecurities, yet we are willing to be patient and comfort our partners through their difficulties. Love is working through all the painful and challenging times, together. Love is strong, and it strengthens over time, because it is real. And when love is real, it doesn't lie, pretend, cheat, or make you feel unwanted or unloved. Love will not abandon you. True love is tenacious. True love lasts.

And, if your partner doesn't knock you over, wow you, and if he or she doesn't make you wake up in the morning, a little better person, then you are on the wrong path. Remember that happiness is not determined by what's happening around you, but rather what's happening inside of you. I go to bed every night with Wade as my last thought. And, I wake up every morning with Wade as my first thought of the day. I can do this now, because I learned this valuable lesson: Every time I learned to love myself more, I also learned to love others a little better too.

> *A bird doesn't sing because he has an answer. He sings because he has a song.*
>
> *—Joan Anglund*

Do you have a song to sing? You may think you have found all the answers in another person, but do *you* have a special song? And I am not referring to the musical song, but the song of internal joy and peace. Nobody sets out to be unhappy. But if we fail to make the choice to be happy, then unhappiness can move in without invitation. And unhappiness is bound to swarm all around you, like an unrelenting angry horde of bees. Believe me—being stung repeatedly will perpetuate your pain. You may have to struggle through some bad days to earn the best days of your life. Keep going. I salute every single one of you, who has found themselves in a dark place, but are trying to rise above the pain. You are standing tall, even with all your broken pieces. You may not be where you to want to right now, but you will get there. Stay strong.

It all begins and ends in your mind. What you give power to, will have power over you. New beginnings are often disguised as painful endings. Get rid of negative thoughts and focus on the fact that your happiness and ability to love, and be loved, truly does dwell inside of you. Never settle when it comes to these three things: the love you have for yourself, your heart, and your choice in a romantic partner.

When wading through troubled waters, you may not see changes inside of yourself, day to day. But, when you look back, everything is different. I hope it is better. The sun was always my daily reminder that we too can rise again, from the darkness. We too can shine our own light.

My desire for you is that you have many years of singing beautiful songs, both alone and, if you so desire, with a special someone. Remember to make yourself a priority. Love is what you want it to be. It is this self-empowerment that will lead you to happiness, both alone and possibly with a significant other.

Love is unique to everyone, much like a fingerprint. Some of you will have a hard time letting love in, while some of you are built for love. And some people are searching for someone to love them in a way that they deserve. Whatever your current situation, begin by making peace with your past and keep moving forward. Everyone comes into our lives for a reason. It is our job to figure out what we are supposed to learn from them. If any of my exes or my husband's exes read this book, I hope that they will discover that we had no interest in portraying them in a bad light, for we certainly had our own issues that ultimately assisted in the downfall of our past relationships. It takes two people to make a relationship work, and it takes two people to make a relationship end. This book is not about judging or hurting anyone—or pointing fingers. It is about my self-realization and learning from my past mistakes. Just because one person is right—does not mean that the other person is wrong. Both people have different perspectives because they have not seen life from the other's vantage point. And by all appearances, most of our exes are living happy and fulfilled lives, with their respective significant others. Just by knowing each of our exes, Wade and I have become better people.

The point of my book is to illustrate how much better our lives are now, both alone, and with one another. I have found that the best way to love someone is not to change them, but instead, help them reveal the greatest version of themselves. Love is that condition in which the happiness of another person is essential to your own. With every day, our lives become even better and more enriched, due to our shared love. And by all accounts, our exes seem to be happy and at peace with their lives now too, and we are happy for them. Divorce doesn't have to be a tragedy. I believe that staying in the wrong marriage, living, and teaching your children the wrong example of love, is the real tragedy.

In my life, I have lived, and I have lost. I have been loved, and I have been hurt. I have trusted, and I have made mistakes. I have been my own worst enemy. But, most of all...I have learned, and I have loved. Now I am my own best friend. Your story is still waiting to be written. Begin writing the best chapters of your life, now. If you can love the wrong person, imagine how much you can love the right one.

I believe that Wade and my hearts were meant to be together, no matter how long it took, how far we traveled apart, or how tough it seemed. In the end, we found one another, and we will share our profound love forever.

I am now married to my Prince Charming. The truth is, the more intimately you know someone, the more you will see their flaws. But Wade still tells me every day how much he values and loves me. Wade cherishes me just the way I am. He often whispers to me, "I was born to love *all* of you." In other words, Wade loves me *despite* my flaws and shortcomings. And I love him in that same unconditional way. I would like one of your takeaways from my book to be that you understand that there is no such thing as "perfect." You certainly do not have to be perfect in order to love or be loved. Your faults are seamless for the heart that is *meant* to love you. I no longer doubt myself. So now, when my husband asks me, "Who are you going to believe, Francine... the mirror, other people, social media, or the heart and the eyes of a man who thinks you are the most beautiful woman, inside and out, on earth?" I will forever always respond, "I will believe the man that I love—and who loves me. And, I will always believe in myself."

Wade and I love each other more than we have ever found a way to say it.

Only love gives us the taste of eternity. And, it is my sincere hope that you make yourself a priority and realize that—*love wants to find you* too.

> *Love is patient and kind; love does not envy or boast; it is not arrogant or rude. It does not insist on its own way; it is not irritable or resentful; it does not rejoice at wrongdoing—but rejoices with the truth.*
>
> **—1 Corinthians 13:4**

> *Your task is not to seek for love, but merely to find all the barriers within yourself that you have built against it.*
>
> **—Rumi**

Francine's Wedding
Vows to Wade

People usually say that opposites attract, but I think that is wrong because I have never met anyone that is identical to me in every way, until I met you. Where I end is where you begin. And where you end is where I begin. I didn't know what love was until you filled my heart with pieces of yourself.

You fill an emotional void that I have had my entire life. I wanted to explain to you and our guests why this wedding ceremony was so important to me. We all know that this is our third marriage. But the reason we are having a wedding is because this is the first time that I have truly understood real love. And I know that this is the first time that I have truly loved a man and been truly loved in return. You taught me what love is. I used to watch movies and think it was all fairytales and stardust. But now I know that it can be a reality. We share a love that I would hope everyone would experience.

You made me see, feel, and believe in love. You made me believe in myself. We met twenty-five years ago and kept in touch as friends over the years. I believe that it was serendipitous that we met in 2013 again, and then fell in love in 2014. You and I were destined to be together, from the very start. Although our paths took us in different directions for some years, my heart knew it was meant for you, and you alone.

In my book, you are my Prince Charming. In my movie, you are my hero. In my body, you are my heart. In my life, you and our four children are my immediate family. You love me in ways that I have never been loved before, and for reasons that I cannot comprehend to this day. And I know for certain that I will love you, with more love than I ever knew existed inside of me.

I can finally be proud of my marriage. You are the best part of me. I am not complete without you. I now feel that I can set a good example for all four children.

Before I met you, I was a victim of my own poor choices. I prayed to God for my mercy and my healing, mostly for my children's sake. You see I never really found myself until I met you. I never really knew love until I met you. I now know why things did not work with anyone else. I was always supposed to be yours.

I'm grateful for the wrong paths, for they are what keep me humble and kind. I am thankful most of all that through God's intervention that we met and fell in love. I now know how to express love in a healthy way because it is the right love. It is a forever love.

I now live in moments that I would give my life for. I will stand beside and with you, forever and always. You took my breath away the first time I laid eyes on you, and you still take my breath away. I have the kind of love that I never knew existed, and it is the kind of love that I know with complete certainty, will never end.

You are my purple crayon, the one that I never have enough of, and the one that I use to color my world.

And every time that I say, "I love you more," I am reminding you that you are the best thing that has ever happened to me. My heart would stop without you, because when my heart felt yours, I knew I was finally home.

Wade's Wedding Vows to Francine

My Dearest Princess,

I've already professed my vows to you, and I want to tell you, and those gathered here today, a few reasons for our wedding today.

A wedding is a public proclamation to the world that we're committed to each other, to only each other, to none other and to forsake all others. We've talked about this many times and why this day is important to both of us.

I've made choices that took me along a very long path to this place today. I offer my apologies for the time it took to get here, but I promise to always cherish every day we have together, now that we are here.

You are my favorite person in this whole world. You are my Princess, as I'm your Prince Charming, and I choose you to be my partner in life and to keep all the commitments I've just vowed to keep.

I both love you and am in love with you. You are the most beautiful person in this world, both on the outside and the inside.

You are the one person I can spend all my time with and never wish for a moment alone or to be with others.

You are also my purple crayon; the one I never have enough of, and the one I use to color my world.

I've seen your kindness and your strength.

I've seen you patient and frayed.

I love your passion, determination, and perseverance in everything you do.

I will always encourage you to be a better person, to reach your goals and to live your life in a way that will make us proud.

You make my skin tingle when you hold my hand, and you take my breath away, every day.

You make my side hurt from laughing with you, even though many times we can't remember what we were laughing about.

I will laugh with you in good times and comfort you when you are downhearted and hug you when you cry.

I will come to mutual decisions with you.

I will help you when you need help and turn to you when I need help.

I will always remind you that I love you, even if we disagree, because you should always know how much I love you and what you mean to me.

I will always hold your hand because when you hold mine, my nerves calm, I sleep better, and though not all may be right with the world, all is right with us.

I will choose you, every day, over and over, in good times and bad.

I will always be your partner in life and always be there for you, whether you need someone to help you get through tough times, someone to support you as you work towards your goals in life, or just someone to put on your shoes.

I will never take you for granted and strive to always be thankful and grateful for all that you are and all the love you give to me. You are the best thing to that ever happened to me. You complete me.

Above and beyond all this, I will always love and cherish and honor you through this life and into the next.

And... I love you "more."

Faithfully Yours,

Wade

About the Author

Francine Putkowski was born and raised in Indiana, Pennsylvania. She was a cheerleader, ran hurdles, and threw discus in track and field, and she was a gymnast for a private gymnastics school in Washington, Pennsylvania. As a Gym-Dandy gymnast, she was part of a State Championship team. She was accepted into the prestigious United States Naval Academy (USNA) in 1987, where she spent a little over two years. She competed in collegiate gymnastics at USNA. Ultimately, she graduated from Penn State University, at the top of her class in 1991, with a major in Labor Industrial Relations. She has spent the last twenty-five years as a successful corporate director of risk management and continues in this capacity. She now resides in Allentown, Pennsylvania, with her two cherished children and her husband, the loves of her life. Francine and her husband also spend a lot of time near Annapolis, Maryland, where they own a second home. Her two beautiful stepdaughters live in the Severna Park, Greater Washington D.C. area, and she loves visiting them. She is extremely family oriented, and both of her parents, sister, nephews, and in-laws live nearby. In her free time, you can find her taking photographs, playing tennis, traveling, reading, hiking the many outdoor trails where she resides, or donating her time to local charities. Although, her greatest accomplishment, blessing, and joy is being a mother to her twenty-one-year-old daughter, her seventeen-year-old son, her twenty-one-year-old stepdaughter, her sixteen-year-old stepdaughter, and being a wife to her soul mate.

To learn more about the author, visit:

Website: https://www.lovewantstofindyou.com
Facebook: https://www.facebook.com/lovewantstofindyou
Instagram: https://www.instagram.com/lovewantstofindyou
or email her at: francine@lovewantstofindyou.com

CPSIA information can be obtained
at www.ICGtesting.com
Printed in the USA
BVHW041836051119
562988BV00014B/437/P